T0386779

ELIMINATING POVERTY IN BRITAIN

ELIMINATING POVERTY IN BRITAIN

HELEN ROWE

FL◊NT

First published 2023

FLINT is an imprint of The History Press
97 St George's Place, Cheltenham,
Gloucestershire, GL50 3QB
www.flintbooks.co.uk

British Library Cataloguing in Publication Data.
A catalogue record for this book is available from the British Library.

ISBN 978 1 80399 247 1

Typesetting and origination by The History Press
Printed and bound in Great Britain by TJ Books Limited, Padstow, Cornwall.

MIX
Paper from
responsible sources
FSC® C013056
FSC
www.fsc.org

Trees for LYfe

For my beloved daughter and all the little ones.
You are too good for this world, so the world is going to have to change.

CONTENTS

PROLOGUE

Springtime in London is glorious.

A morning stroll through one of its city farms can be a transporting experience. The further you walk, the more enveloped you become in a landscape of lush new growth glazed in morning dew. A clear blue sky and crisp air shivers your senses awake and your skin gratefully receives the slowly warming sun.

At our local farm, there is a spot by the paddock where, if you look in the right direction, everything you can see is either green leaves or sky. It is easy to imagine yourself in the depths of the British countryside. The horses take no notice of passing humans and the birdsong carries across the fields. They were in full voice on the particular morning I was there.

I leant my elbows against the paddock gate and circled around to take in the view. My eyes lingered on the only part that wasn't green, a large white sack of fertiliser sat among the wild flowers in the distance. I thought it was a strange place to leave one, but as a city-lover I could hardly pass judgement on the running of a farm, so I turned back to watch the horses.

I began to hanker for coffee and so set off on the short stroll to the farm café. The closer I walked to the sack, the more confused I became. Its colour changed and the texture was softer than expected, until I stopped on the wet grass in a cold silence. It was not a sack at all. It was a duvet that hung across a bench and dangled down to the floor. The only sign of the person beneath was a thick, grey sock poking out of one end.

My stomach hollowed. In amongst this tiny Garden of Eden was the hard reality of poverty and loss. This was not a London issue; it was a countrywide issue caused by decades of spiralling change. A small flock of birds flew over our heads and settled themselves in a nearby tree – a reminder that nature and the world beyond would carry on regardless of a person's circumstances. The beauty of the morning dimmed and the cold air nipped at my fingers. *The person underneath must be freezing*, I thought. I couldn't bear the idea that they might not be alive at all. I trudged past quietly, not wanting to wake them.

Wrapped in the warmth of the café, I pondered the future.

It's a new decade, I thought. *What will it contain and for whom?*

INTRODUCTION

The idea for this book came to me after a surreal conversation with my colleagues in 2013. We were working at a housing association and in the midst of new austerity measures, which were coming from central government thick and fast. We were grappling with the implications of the bedroom tax, which required residents in social homes that were too large for their needs to pay extra rent, move to a smaller property, or rent out the spare room. The sudden rise in housing costs had caused many people financial harm and we had a duty of care to those involved not to make their situations worse.

The question was this: should we allocate a pregnant woman a two-bedroom property, as we would normally do to ensure her a permanent home with the space for her child, and accept the risk that, if she had a miscarriage, it would not just involve the heart-break of losing a baby, but she would also have to pay the bedroom tax as well? Or, should we offer her a one-bedroom home, which would mean the inevitable disruption of moving to a larger property with a small child later on and be costly and difficult?

Which would you choose?

The fact is that, if there had been enough social homes built over the decades, this kind of debate would never have been needed. However, when it comes to social mobility, Britain's past and present do not look different enough. On the face of it, the years 1986 and 2016 seem to have little in common. Advances in technology and medicine have recreated our economy, education and world view. If you had said to an adult in the 1980s that, one day, they would be doing their weekly shop on their mobile phone, you would have received a hearty laugh and roll of the eyes, and yet, here we are. However, take a more detailed look at our social advancement and the gap closes rapidly. A snippet of a childhood memory is as clear to me as a camera reel:

Under a grey London sky, my father held my hand tightly as we walked down the wet, slippery steps of King's Cross station and into the underpass. The corridors were busy, but for a moment there was a pause in the passing commuters and I looked down an adjoining subway to see a cardboard city continue into the distance. The air was dank and the yellow tiled walls were dirty below the cold strobe lights.

The memory returned to me as I sat on the top deck of a bus driving through Brighton city centre in 2016. Every empty shop doorway (and there were many) had people sleeping rough. The same dank feeling hung in the air as the homeless sat on their sleeping bags in entrances to once-affluent shops. Afterwards, I wandered along the sea front in need of some fresh air, but people were sleeping in the shelters there too. As far as Hove, I found tents pitched on rough land and even outside the swimming pool, on a spot which provided only marginal protection from the wind. It was disorienting. I thought, *Aren't we meant to have sorted these problems out by now?* As a mother, I wondered, *Is this it? Is this the society I have brought my child into?*

Life in the twenty-first century for many millions of people is not what was expected and social stagnation was never part of the vision. Yet, while the technology and new products are as shiny and innovative as had been hoped, no one had mentioned the huge underbelly of people who would still be struggling to get by. It is now clear that waiting for busy politicians to solve enormous issues like poverty is not practical. They are humans like the rest of us and they need new ideas to act upon. I am not prepared to live in perpetual hope of change, and so I write.

This book has taken five years of discussion, interviews, research and thought. Authors who have previously written about ending inequality have generally done so from a global perspective, but I prefer to write about Britain and what I know. In my lifetime here,

I have lived alongside some of the wealthiest people in our country and I have worked alongside some of the poorest. I have dined at the most prestigious private clubs in London and spent my evenings filling dishwashers on minimum wage. I have stood at a cash point exhausted from endless hours of work only to see a bank balance that wouldn't make ends meet. From those I have loved who have known poverty, I have seen how its shadow lingered throughout their lives; it never entirely went away. Through all this, I have learned that extreme wealth brings choice, but not automatic happiness, and that poverty can make people savvy and cynical, but when they are released from its grip, the joy is a shining light in their eyes.

From all these experiences and from listening to those who have gone before, it is clear that the structure of our society is severely wanting. The churn of government policies made on the fly and without full consideration of the consequences has done serious harm. It is not just the lack of political vision that hinders us, but the lack of realistic thinking, and it is not necessary.

I have delved deeply into the subject of poverty in Britain and believe that the way to deal with poverty globally is to create a tailored plan for each country based on the problems and needs of the population, while having regard for their political systems and environmental constraints. The way deprivation affects British society is staggering. Each research paper published on its social or medical effects adds to the growing tide of understanding of just how much poverty affects every person in our country, irrespective of individual income.

This is a book for realists in whichever section of society they may be, whether the upper echelons of political life, people living in hope for a better future, or students starting out on their studies. I am not working to create a utopian society, just one in which our wealth and prosperity reflect our humanity towards one another.

This book is split into three parts: Our Society, Our Money and Our Future. The first part relates to the pressure that poverty puts on our social structures, including the education system, the economy and policing, and how it impacts our biology, from our mental and physical health down to our DNA. The second part focuses on where the money could come from to fund a poverty elimination agenda and how it would need to complement the green agenda, as the two issues are inextricably linked. Here there are a lot of descriptions around how much projects will cost in terms of millions and billions of pounds. For me, these figures can often blur into unimaginable amounts, so here is a way to understand the difference: 1 million seconds equates to eleven and a half days, whereas 1 billion seconds is thirty-one and a half years.

The final section, Our Future, considers the practicalities of removing inequality from Britain and how it could be achieved using three key concepts: compassion, focus and a plan. The plan begins on the first day of a new prime minister's government and talks through the options and policies that need to be considered. After the plan come the consequences – some will be expected and some less so, including how other countries may respond to a Britain without poverty.

This book draws on medical journals, social research, writing from investigative journalists and authors, and lived experiences to create novel ideas and ways of working. New concepts are rarely perfect, but they don't need to be. The core ideas are there to be remoulded and worked upon and a full list is provided in the final chapter. What I hope to offer in this book is a foundation on which we can build and go on to consider and question how we create a society of the future that is so exceptional that it is fit for every generation that lives in it.

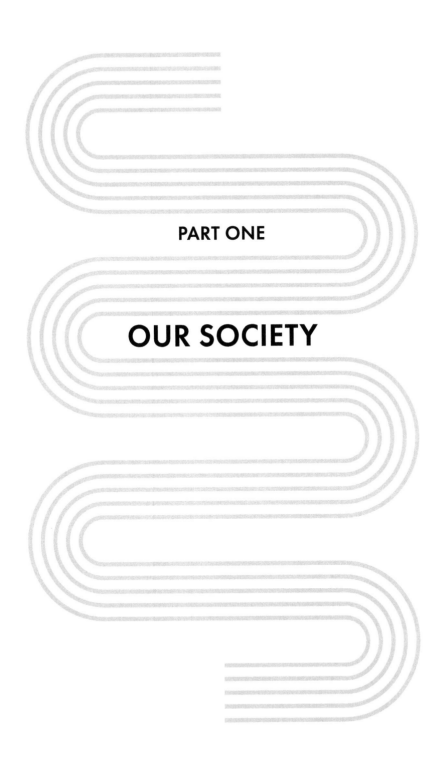

PART ONE

OUR SOCIETY

1

POVERTY AND THE PANDEMIC

Before the coronavirus pandemic, it seemed a far-fetched dream that the whole of government could have a single focus during peace-time, but then Covid-19 came along and changed everything. On 19 April 2020, Britain was into the fourth week of its first lockdown. During the daily press briefing, the then education minister, Gavin Williamson, commented, 'This is a whole government effort. We are doing everything that is required, everything that is needed.'

His words reverberated; so, it was possible after all. Many journalists and politicians compared the situation to a war. Undoubtedly it was a frightening and uncertain time. It was a life-or-death situation with huge economic and social implications, but it also showed how collegiate working could be done during peacetime and that systems could change rapidly when given the right impetus.

To prevent the spread of the disease and aid the struggling tourism sector, the government gave over 37,000 homeless and rough sleepers temporary accommodation in private hotel rooms, meals and a laundry service under the government's Everyone In scheme. Lord John Bird, who created the *Big Issue* magazine for the homeless, highlighted the irony that government attitudes towards the homeless had gone from utter neglect to sudden focus because of the fear of spreading the disease.[1]

The move became a huge opportunity to get proper support to people with complex needs and had the potential to reduce homelessness significantly in the longer term. Sadly, it was clear that it would not have happened without the virus.

The homeless charity Shelter estimated that, by February 2021, thousands could have returned to the streets and thousands more continued to live in emergency accommodation with no long-term plan for the future.[2] Records from the Dying Homeless Project suggest around 1,000 homeless people died during the pandemic, despite government efforts to bring all rough sleepers inside.[3] In Scotland, those deaths were mainly caused by drugs and suicide, with none directly related to the virus itself.[4] The councils' response to the virus show how important it is to have specialist support available to deal with street homelessness and have more to offer than simply giving people temporary accommodation for a few months.[5] (For further discussion, see Chapter 4.)

By trying to create a nostalgic, wartime spirit during the pandemic, the government sought to suggest that we were *all in it together*. It was a view that sounded sensible until properly analysed. As the prime minister, Boris Johnson, lay in intensive care with the virus, BBC *Newsnight* journalist Emily Maitlis put it clearly:

> They tell us coronavirus is a great leveller. It's not. It's much, much harder if you're poor. How do we stop it making social inequality even greater? ... The language around Covid-19 has sometimes felt trite and misleading. You do not survive the illness through fortitude and strength of character, whatever the prime minister's colleagues will tell us. And the disease is not a great leveller, the consequences of which everyone, rich or poor, suffers the same. This is a myth which needs debunking.
>
> Those serving on the front line right now, bus drivers and shelf stackers, nurses, care home workers, hospital staff and shopkeepers are disproportionately the lower-paid members of our workforce. They are more likely to catch the disease because they are more exposed. Those who live in tower blocks and small flats will find the lockdown tougher. Those in manual jobs will be unable to work from home.
>
> This is a health issue with huge ramifications for social welfare, and it's a welfare issue with huge ramifications for public health.

Tonight ... we ask: what kind of social settlement might need to be put in place to stop the inequality becoming even more stark?[6]

The American Nobel Prize-winning economist Joseph Stiglitz offered Maitlis some answers. He suggested the disease had highlighted the fragility of the US market economy and the inadequate social support system, which meant that front-line workers could be so poorly paid. He believed there was a need to rethink the US economy once the pandemic was over.[7]

In Britain, one of the hardest things to hear, along with the death rate, was the food banks' alarm that they were running out of supplies because the public was stockpiling food.[8] None of this suggests that this is a country that has completely solid social foundations. It would be easy to claim that any country under that kind of excep-tional pressure would react in the same way, and yet international leaders behaved very differently from each other. The USA's leader-ship was slow to react compared with New Zealand's, which locked down quickly after the first few cases emerged.[9] The attitude of a leader is paramount when dealing with a crisis or period of great change. To create a country free from deprivation, our prime minister would need to be empathetic, well informed and practically minded. Humanity does itself a disservice by forgetting the extraordi-nary things it is capable of achieving. The density of vying voices, fake news, fake democracies and some charismatic but low-skilled politicians have meant that compassionate policies do not tend to dominate the agenda, unless they make politicians look good. To succeed, a government would need a detailed and holistic plan that can sit above the competing territories of political life. The response to Covid-19 has shown what can be achieved. A focus on eliminating poverty is not impossible.

The implications of the pandemic are slowly becoming clear and will create immense difficulty and hardship over the coming decade. The UK's national debt, which was already sizeable before corona-virus, will have to be repaid at some point, and that would suggest further years of austerity to come, unless there is somehow a sig-nificant boost to the economy. The damage that the cuts inflicted on the lowest-paid people after the 2008 global financial crisis have been obvious for years. However, it is important to remember that austerity was a choice; other options were available, although all had their flaws.

Covid-19 may be an opportunity to press the 'reset' button on British society, as we question whether we want to return to an economic model that was so imbalanced. Over the years, it has created and maintained poverty, inflicted harm on the environment and enabled wealth gaps to increase, not just between the richest and poorest, but also between women and men, between communities and between children. Thoughtful innovation and a focus on the needs of the whole population could engender lasting change while reducing pressure on the National Health Service, social services, police and the education system. These organisations consistently place a sticking plaster over the social problems caused by inequality.

With over 227,000 deaths in Britain from the disease, the impact is now clear and continues to be felt. The lack of widespread education in science combined with misinformation on vaccines has increased health inequalities by making many groups hesitant to accept their Covid-19 vaccine. I have met numerous men in our diverse area of London who speak with pride about how they haven't had a vaccine because they are 'strong' and don't need one. They appear to have ignored or not known the fact that they may be spreading the virus without having any symptoms. Figures from the Health Foundation show that, a year after the pandemic had ended, people living in the most deprived areas, some ethnic minority groups (including 40 per cent of African Caribbean adults) and people without English as their first language are least likely to be fully vaccinated.[10]

Inequality lies at the heart of so many issues related to the virus that it is now possible to ask the question: if there had been no poverty in Britain when the pandemic began, how much lower would the death toll have been? We now know it would have been significantly lower, as people who lived in the most deprived areas of England and Wales were around twice as likely to die after contracting the virus.[11]

Yet, in light of this, the elimination of poverty, rather than the alleviation of it, remains on the outskirts of public policy, awaiting its day. When the next pandemic comes, it will be poverty-related issues that will determine how the disease controls our society and economy, so dealing with deprivation now is key to Britain's future stability.

Protecting the NHS from becoming overwhelmed with patients was at the heart of the government's strategy against Covid-19, but even without the pandemic, our beloved system has been struggling to deal with the impact of deprivation on the health of the nation, and the costs have been immense.

The NHS spends around £16 billion a year on medicines (excluding pandemic-related costs)[12] and the British Medical Association (BMA) has stated that poverty costs the UK health-care system around £29 billion per year. The knock-on effects are serious and include significant changes in life expectancy: for example, in affluent areas of Wales, women can expect to live seven years longer, and men can expect an extra nine years compared to less affluent areas. Children who live in cold homes are more than twice as likely to suffer from a range of respiratory problems as those living in warm homes. And many people cannot afford the cost of their treatment, such as pre-scription charges, resulting in their condition worsening over time.

It is not surprising, then, that the virus had such a disproportion-ate effect on the least well-off, as it exacerbated people's underlying health conditions and increased their chances of death. The BMA highlights that doctors within the NHS can play a role in reducing the impacts of deprivation on their patients by spending more time on prevention, advocating for their patients by writing to local poli-ticians, becoming involved with other organisations, community projects or school boards, or by focusing on health literacy.[13]

However, this simply highlights the additional workload asso-ciated with patients in poverty that doctors have to deal with in addition to their normal clinical duties. If there were no poverty for the NHS to address, staff would have significantly more time to devote to clinical research and further study, or have shorter work-ing hours and be less exhausted.

Research by the Health Foundation and Nuffield Trust in 2020 found that people living in the most deprived areas of England expe-rience a worse quality of NHS care and poorer health outcomes than people living in the least deprived areas. This includes spending longer in Accident and Emergency and having a worse experience of making an appointment with their general practitioner. Yet, many of the causes of these issues are beyond the NHS's control, such as poor housing.[14]

For as long as poverty continues to be accepted, the NHS will have to deal with its consequences, while being unable to change the underlying causes. It is an expensive and unhealthy situation for our country. Ending deprivation would be a highly effective way of reducing the costs of the NHS while protecting the public from further pandemics. Covid-19 showed the way that governments can focus on a single issue for years. Dealing with poverty for five years straight would be significantly more productive than ministers continuing to instigate cost-cutting efficiency drives that put further pressure on to an already exhausted medical profession.

2

POVERTY AND PHYSICAL HEALTH

Sleep is a non-negotiable biological necessity ... Mother Nature, throughout the course of evolution, has never had to face the challenge of this thing called sleep deprivation, so she's never developed a safety net and that's why when you under-sleep, things just sort of implode so quickly, both within the brain and the body.

Professor Matthew Walker, neuroscientist and sleep expert[1]

Of all the great wonders of nature, the most laborious and perplexing is parenthood. Should you be lucky enough to survive childbirth – as so many in the world tragically don't – then parenthood brings its own variety of breathtaking highs and mind-bending lows, so great is the entwinement of love. One of the hardest parts is the intensity of sleep loss, which can make your bones ache and your eyes sting, where you feel every breath in your ribcage and sometimes crawling on all fours seems like the only sensible way to get around. You have entered survival mode, and if you are lucky, it will only last a few months; if not, it can last for years.

Anyone who has been through it will understand why sleep deprivation has been used as a form of torture. Those who are full-time parents or trying to work while looking after a little one will be well aware of the impact on performance and emotional stability. For any government that wants a more productive workforce, it is important to understand the deeper impacts of exhaustion. Professor Matthew

Walker, Director of Sleep and Neuroimaging at the University of California, explains:

> There is simply no aspect of your wellness that can retreat at the sign of sleep deprivation and get away unscathed ... sleep loss will leak down into every nook and cranny of your physiology. The decimation of sleep throughout industrialized nations is having a catastrophic impact on our health.[2]

Walker highlights that every major disease in the developed world has a strong link to sleep deprivation, including Alzheimer's, cancer, obesity and diabetes. However, he also offers hope, as researchers at the University of California have shown that improving sleep quantity, quality and regularity can heal a variety of serious conditions, including depression, bipolar disorder and anxiety. It can even prevent suicide.[3] So, how do we build a society that enables everyone to have a good night's rest? It is an important question that is rarely asked, and yet it needs to be answered if we are to create a stronger economy and generally lead more contented lives. How can a person raise themselves or their family out of poverty if their body has no respite or time to heal? While some vocal newspapers and politicians condemn those who need government benefits and support, it should be recognised that people can't work at their best when exhausted and also face greater mental and physical health problems, alongside a rising cost of living. Stress and poverty are directly linked and unsurprisingly affect a person's ability to sleep, particularly if the obstacles include the lack of a proper bed. Everyone needs a bed and it is not an unreasonable expectation in the twenty-first century.

Getting enough sleep (between seven and eight hours each night) is a basic human need and yet there are many people for whom it is not possible. This includes rough sleepers and those who are sofa surfing or living in cars or noisy temporary accommodation. Children are particularly at risk from sleep loss. Sleep is needed for their growing brains and yet it is difficult to obtain for those who have to share a bed with their siblings, sleep in cold homes, go to bed hungry or who are trying to sleep in cots that are too small because their parents cannot afford a larger one.

The lack of a bed has been a constant issue over the years. In 2021–22, the charity Buttle UK provided over £360,000 in grants to furnish the bedrooms of deprived children. The charity described the impact of their work: 'Having their own fully furnished bedroom is repeatedly seen as helping to reduce anxiety and stress. Simply having a safe space of their own is so important ... particularly for those who are recovering from fleeing domestic abuse.'[4]

While charities provide excellent and much-needed support, a key concern is the piecemeal provision of the help available, as there is no countrywide system. Access to support depends heavily on where you live and this further exacerbates existing inequalities within the population.

Shift Work

The relationship between poverty and sleep also affects the wider functioning of the economy. For shift workers, including members of the emergency services who work unpredictable hours, a disrupted circadian rhythm (body clock) can have a serious effect on the individual's ability to function mentally and physically. For front-line workers, these decisions could mean the difference between life and death, or failing in their duties and being charged with misconduct.

Researchers at the Brigham and Women's Hospital in Massachusetts, USA, examined the effect of shift work on 270,000 people. They found that shift workers were significantly more likely to develop type-2 diabetes regardless of their genetic risk, compared to those who had never worked a night shift. The cause was partly due to weight gain from eating at irregular hours. The pancreas does not work as well at night and so cannot produce enough insulin to break down fats that are consumed when the body should be fasting.[5]

It is also worth noting that permanent night shift workers exhibit some healthier lifestyle characteristics, including lower levels of alcohol intake and higher levels of physical activity, than other groups ... Intervention on body weight and work schedules might be useful in improving metabolic health in all individuals, independent of their genetic(s).[6]

A recent pilot study on employment patterns found that removing night shifts for people with early morning body clocks, and changing morning shifts for those who prefer evenings, improved the quality of sleep and reduced the chances of contracting chronic illnesses.[7] Diabetes costs the NHS around £14 billion each year and can be a debilitating condition. Much of this money is spent on complications caused by the condition, such as amputation, blindness, kidney failure and strokes.[8] Governments and businesses have a duty of care to individuals and the health service to reduce the levels of shift work where possible, to ensure that shift timetables are matched to people's individual sleep cycles, and to ensure that those who do undertake shift work understand how it affects the human body and are compensated accordingly.

A key government priority must be the creation of a society in which sleep is viewed in a positive light. Economic performance cannot continue to revolve around sleep-deprived people at all levels of the wage scale, especially with the rise of home working enabling employees to work longer into the night. It would be interesting to know how many exhausted people were involved in making the high-risk decisions that led to the 2008 global financial crash, or the austerity policies that went on to disproportionately affect the poorest in society.

The relationship between poverty, stress, sleep loss and poor physical health is a nexus that needs to be highlighted and actively dealt with by doing more than simply urging people to get more sleep (as I saw on a billboard once). The NHS will continue to pick up the tab when it comes to the physical effects of poverty, but as funding continues to be tight, some areas of the NHS are becoming less and less 'free' for those adults who are not in receipt of benefits. This is unacceptable and NHS dentistry is at the forefront of a health sector that is only accessible to those who can afford to pay.

Dental Health

'Seventy-five pounds,' the receptionist said nonchalantly, while punching the numbers into the card reader. It was 2006 and I gulped weakly, feeling sure that there must have been some mistake. I knew private dentists were expensive, but I'd only been in the chair for two minutes – the length of time needed for polite introductions and to ask for a prescription to heal an inflamed wisdom tooth. I wondered if I should have tried harder to organise an NHS dentist, but the trial to find one, travel there, get registered, organise an appointment and wait days or weeks to be seen had felt like an insurmountable challenge. The blinding pain in my mouth had pushed me into saying 'yes' to the cost of any local, private dentist with a short waiting time. Perhaps I should have bought some pills online, but there would have been no guarantee of what was inside them, so I walked glumly downstairs to pay more money for my prescription.

When politicians speak with pride of the free health-care system we have in Britain, they never seem to mention dentists. The number of practitioners prepared to do NHS work has been falling steadily over the years until now, in the 2020s, the system is in crisis. It seems farcical to suggest that dental care is free when the provision of it is so low. It is also ironic that many health conditions that the rest of the NHS will deal with for free can be pre-determined through gum disease. Strokes, arthritis, heart disease and diabetes have all been linked to infection in the gums, caused by the build-up of bacteria from plaque. This creates too much inflammation in the body, affecting the bloodstream and slowly damaging blood vessels in the heart and brain over a long period.[9] Inhaling bacteria can also infect the lungs and cause pneumonia.[10]

Ill-health breeds inequality, and the scarcity of NHS dentists can be identified as a governmental system that creates and maintains inequality. It would need to be a key area of change in any poverty elimination programme. Many people don't have savings, especially since the pandemic, so the costs of an infected tooth could push struggling households into debt. When it comes to dental care, the quiet move towards 'health if you can afford it' feels an unpleasant reality from the dark ages before the welfare state.

In his autobiography about growing up during the Great Depression, Harry Leslie Smith described a time when health was based on wealth, and how it echoed into the streets as he played with his childhood friends:

> At times, as we traipsed across our patch in the dead of night, our merriment was stopped in its tracks by inhuman noises ... they were cries of pain and of torment... The cries that came from open windows sounded like howls from a circle of hell that even my parish priest would have been reluctant to admit existed. They were not the growls of the damned, just the screams from people who were too poor to pay for morphine to ease their pain from cancer and make their passage to the next world gentle rather than grotesque.[11]

Smith's experiences led to a life-long love of the welfare state and he acknowledged that, had it not been for the Beveridge Report that promised its creation in 1942, he and many other working-class people would have questioned the benefits of fighting for a country that had so actively maintained their poverty. He was not enamoured with Hitler, but he was aware that his own society had done little to help his family and had directly contributed to the deaths of his sister and father, who were buried in paupers' graves.

Today, having a healthy body or set of teeth should not depend on how much money a person has or where they live. The system of dentistry in the UK needs to be updated quickly and the government cannot rely on the hope that more people will train as NHS dentists, considering the tuition fees cost a minimum of £35,000. This may be a situation where artificial intelligence (AI) could provide a new, cheaper service for patients.

If an automated scanner could be developed to offer routine check-ups and email the dentist a preliminary report, this could reduce waiting times and free up dentists to focus on more complex work, in the same way that local doctors have passed vaccinations and other medical work on to nurses. The use of AI in dentistry is being studied and early indications suggest it could be helpful.[12] A scanner could also be manufactured domestically, creating new jobs, and be offered abroad as part of the international aid package. The Covid-19 Test and Trace system cost £37 billion to set up; an automated dentistry service would surely require a fraction of this and make the system fully accessible again for everyone and especially those on low incomes.

Epigenetics, Inflammation and Poverty

When I studied biology in the early 2000s, university lecturers confidently taught that evolution was caused by random changes in our body's code: our DNA. (A section of DNA is called a gene and these produce proteins and other chemicals that build our bodies. Genes decide what hair colour we have, how our bodies grow and develop and, sometimes, what we die from.) It was believed that if an unexpected change (mutation) was helpful to an animal or plant – such as improving camouflage – then it would be more likely to survive and pass the new gene on to its children. For harmful changes, the organism was less likely to breed and so the gene died out with it.

However, since then, new epigenetic research has completely transformed this view and has shown how the environment in which we live can directly change the way our genes work. Epigenetics is the system that turns genes on and off. This process works by attaching chemical tags, known as epigenetic markers, to DNA. These tell the cell either to use or ignore a particular gene. The underlying DNA code is not changed, but the manner in which the genes are turned on or off is affected.[13] In bees, the queen, workers and drones all have very different bodies and yet they have identical DNA, showing that when genes are expressed (turned on or off) differently, they can create a different animal.[14]

In humans, an example of epigenetics can be found in post-traumatic stress disorder (PTSD). A traumatic event or series of them can leave an individual in a constant state of stress as the body fails to properly regulate cortisol, the stress hormone. The cortisol gene is wrongly left in the 'on' position, causing the body to be in a perpetual state of fight-or-flight. Stress levels in the body are significantly higher than they would normally be, causing a variety of mental and physical health problems for the sufferer, including panic attacks, anxiety and chronic pain. Researchers have found that some of these changes can be passed down from generation to generation, although research is continuing.[15]

The neuroscience of poverty is a field of research that focuses on the links between brain development and the environment a person is living in. Studies in children point to a disturbing conclusion, that poverty and the conditions that often accompany it – violence, excessive noise, chaos at home, pollution, malnutrition and abuse – affect how the young brain develops. The brain is made up of two substances: grey matter (brain cells) and white matter (nerves – these send signals around your body and help you feel sensations and move your muscles).

Researchers have found that deprivation creates less grey matter, which is used for processing information and controlling behaviour, particularly in the hippocampus (memory), the frontal lobe (decision making, problem solving, impulse control, judgement, and social and emotional behaviour) and the temporal lobe (language, sight and sound processing, and self-awareness). Together these brain areas are crucial for learning, following instructions and maintaining attention.[16] It is therefore hardly surprising that children growing up in poor backgrounds often struggle in school.

Researchers at University College London have found that inflammation in the brain may be the cause of the reduction in grey matter/brain cells. Normal levels of inflammation help the body to repair tissues after an infection or injury, and in removing and replacing cells that show signs of stress or malfunction.[17]

Studies have also shown that people on lower incomes have more brain activity caused by stress and this is linked to greater inflammation in the body. Chronic inflammation is thought to play a role in developing many health conditions, such as heart disease, stroke, diabetes and cancer. People with higher levels of stress have increased activity in the amygdala (the brain's core system for processing fearful and threatening situations) and this has been associated with greater inflammation in bone marrow and arteries. This type of inflammation may account for almost a third of the increased risk of heart disease in people on low incomes.[18]

American neuroscientist Professor Mary Helen Immordino-Yang has conducted a lot of research into the impact of poverty on the growing body. She has found that growing up in turmoil, even when it is not at home, but on the streets where you live, has an impact on how the brain functions.[19] Her work has also highlighted that schools must educate the whole child and not just focus on academia. British schools often try to support vulnerable children, but cuts to special educational needs budgets have made this increasingly difficult. Immordino-Yang's research suggests that, if Britain did eliminate poverty, it would change the shape and function of children's brains and even alter when they begin puberty. The brains of children who experience ongoing adversity react by enhancing the sections that promote aggression and anxiety, at the expense of the areas involved in reasoning and memory. Her work has found that, while the brain can change at any time of life, it is particularly sensitive during pregnancy and childhood, in adolescence, on becoming a parent, and in old age.[20] In essence, if we want children to have enough self-control to learn and behave well, then our country needs to support their emotional and economic well-being, rather than simply piling on the exam pressure.

In their book, *The Neuroscience of Socioeconomic Inequality*, Noble and Giebler highlight some essential areas of future scientific research, such as working out the mechanisms that cause changes in the brain, identifying the times in life when the brain is most sensitive to change and providing information on effective cures.[21] A focus on eliminating inequality by the British government may not solely involve lifting people out of poverty, but could also provide funding for this type of research. The knowledge gained could be used not just in the education system, but also in the criminal justice system to provide the most appropriate rehabilitation for teenagers and adults.

A child born into poverty will have a significant uphill struggle not just in socioeconomic terms, but also from a genetic and neurological standpoint. These struggles begin in the first year of life and continue through adolescence and into adulthood. By this analysis, dealing with deprivation could create a significant shift in the genetic health of the country, not just now but also in the future. If it is found that DNA markers can be inherited, then dealing with deprivation now could make the coming generations less susceptible to suffering as well.

For the NHS, the impact of poverty on its services are broad. Chronic inflammation is a common factor in diseases such as diabetes, heart disease, depression and anxiety disorders. Antidepressants have been found to deal successfully with inflammation and chronic pain, but they come at a cost.

A proper bed, jobs that enables a good night's sleep, and truly free NHS dental care are all ways to create a healthier society and stronger economy. However, it is the neurological and epigenetic research that has shown how poverty traps people and that it cannot be simply blamed on a personality defect (as discussed later). Continuing to alleviate deprivation will provide little more than an expensive sticking plaster over problems that cannot be solved by tweaking government policy. Scientists have shown that much more ambitious change is required.

3

POVERTY AND MENTAL HEALTH

Whether an illness affects your heart, your leg or your brain, it's still an illness, and there should be no distinction, because we know that mental health is just as important to our overall well-being as our physical health.

Michelle Obama, former First Lady of the USA, and author[1]

My early 30s were rough. The combination of a traumatic childbirth, sleep loss with a baby, and a succession of family deaths led to me being diagnosed with PTSD. To have this condition is to live in a state of permanent hyper-vigilance and stress. Every moment of the day and night is spent in an ultra-sensitive state, where all your senses are looking out for the next danger or threat, even if you are just pottering about at home.

I was prescribed anti-depressants and they were wonderful; it was like taking a holiday from my mind. Within two days of the first pill, the incessant internal dialogue stopped and the pleasure of silence returned, along with the space to breathe once more. The psychiatrist who prescribed the pills referred me to a psychotherapist for eye movement desensitisation and reprocessing (EMDR) therapy, which is a common treatment for PTSD.

'OK, so what's EMDR?' I asked the psychiatrist.

'Well, I'm not exactly sure, but that's what you need,' came the slightly perturbing answer.

Within the mental health field, clinicians are not always aware of how to treat PTSD, but there is information online that can help. It can take weeks, months or years to be cured, depending on circumstances. If life has been particularly difficult, then complex PTSD, which is caused by an ongoing series of traumas, may be diagnosed and then the treatment takes longer.

EMDR is a type of mindfulness technique that is conducted with a therapist and helps to turn traumatic memories into normal ones by stimulating both sides of the brain. A normal memory has emotional distance from a past event, where something awful could have happened, but you can laugh about it afterwards. With traumatic memories, there is no distance. If you see or hear something that reminds you of the trauma, then it triggers the memory and your body reacts as if you are back in the moment. Your heart rate increases, breath shortens, palms sweat. You can be having a quiet picnic in the park and yet, if triggered, you can suddenly feel utterly overwhelmed and in extreme distress. Often you may not know what your triggers are until you are in the midst of an episode. At that point, a hug from a loved one, controlled breathing and a change of scene can all help you to calm down.

The therapy works on one memory at a time and changes details within it, which allows you to create distance and stop the triggers. The stimulation can be created in different ways, by using hand-held buzzers or tapping your body intermittently. (To see how the process works, there is a documentary of Prince Harry having EMDR therapy – *The Me You Can't See*.)

The relief is palpable when you discover that it has worked for the first time. It is a difficult journey of recovery, but having a positive relationship with your therapist can make it much easier. If you feel that you are in safe hands, then you only have to focus on making the EMDR work. Before each session, I would steel myself to face my fears and that normally involved eating biscuits or handfuls of chocolate to boost my energy levels before going in.

The first question was usually the hardest – 'How are you?'

Don't ask me that! I used to think, never quite sure where to start.

Between sessions I would put all my stress and worries into a mental box and close the lid so that I could get through the week behaving reasonably, but during the session the box was opened and I had to face it. When my therapist finally told me that I was cured,

I walked away from the session and saw the world afresh again. The leaves were greener than before, and nature's beauty leapt out with a vibrant energy.

EMDR therapy should be considered for broader use than just PTSD. It is available in prisons, but could be used more widely to reduce the rate of reoffending and increase the chances of successful rehabilitation. The problem, of course, is that while it is effective, it is also highly resource-intensive and British prisons are regularly underfunded and overcrowded.

Experts in the field share the desire for EMDR to be used more broadly. The EMDR Institute states:

> Given the worldwide recognition as an effective treatment of trauma, you can easily see how EMDR therapy would be effective in treating the 'everyday' memories that are the reason people have low self-esteem, feelings of powerlessness, and all the myriad problems that bring them in for therapy ... unlike talking therapy, the insights clients gain in EMDR therapy result not so much from clinician interpretation, but from the client's own accelerated intellectual and emotional processes. The net effect is that clients conclude EMDR therapy feeling empowered by the very experiences that once debased them. Their wounds have not just closed, they have transformed.[2]

The therapy also works faster if the trauma, such as a car crash or experience of domestic violence, happened recently. This would involve the need for significantly more trained psychotherapists and a broader understanding of the benefits of EMDR within government, so that medical professionals and the public know the options for treatment and can access them quickly. Recovering from each session can require around two days of rest and sleep to let the mind rewire itself. For anyone taking the therapy, it is essential that their employers, family or the prison service are aware of the importance of this rest time, as it prevents the mind from reacting badly to the treatment.

There have been over thirty studies showing the positive outcomes of using EMDR as a treatment for PTSD. Depending on the levels of trauma and the number of sessions taken, the recovery rate can be between 80 and 100 per cent. EMDR has also been used by Norwich University Hospital to treat tinnitus caused by PTSD.[3]

Poverty is a form of trauma and significantly affects the workings of the brain. Children and adults who are struggling should be offered EMDR as a way of recovering from the mental health implications of poverty and an insecure life. The therapy often works faster than talking therapies and enables the individual to move forward safe in the knowledge that they will never again have to carry the emotional baggage they have been dealing with. As someone who has recovered, I would say that it can be a tough process to go through, but it is unquestionably worth it.

Francine Shapiro, PhD, who first developed the EMDR practice, highlighted that adverse childhood experiences (ACEs) can increase the likelihood of heart disease, cancer, lung disease, bone fractures and liver disease, but stated that more research was needed to understand if the therapy could prevent these conditions from occurring.[4] The ACE questionnaire asks ten questions to measure the level of childhood trauma a person has experienced and each positive answer gives a point. If an individual has four points or more, then they are significantly more likely to have depression and attempt suicide. In 2018, the government created a new minister for suicide prevention to focus on reducing suicide rates and addressing barriers to seeking help. Statistics show that, in Scotland, people living in the most deprived areas are three times more likely to die by suicide than those in the most affluent areas.[5] The minister's role is directly linked to poverty rates and each incumbent politician should understand this as the government seeks to end deprivation. If the minister could work themselves out of the role entirely, then it would be a sure sign of success.

At present, there is a cap on the number of therapy sessions an individual can receive on the NHS, and some people are choosing to spend their money on therapy, rather than heating their homes.[6] As someone who now knows the benefits of a quiet mind, I would have taken the same decision too, but it would be far better if the choice was not needed at all.

The cap is a false economy that perpetuates health inequalities, as those who have the money to continue their therapy privately can gain stronger mental health in the long term and benefit in ways that are not possible for those with more limited finances. Furthermore, if a person has taken the brave and thoughtful step to begin therapy, whichever sort it may be, then they should be able to continue until they feel fully healed. Stopping the process halfway through can make a person reluctant to seek help again. The mental and physical health support that is offered by the NHS needs to have a better financial balance. Mental health cannot continue to be seen as second rate when it has a direct impact on the physical health of an individual, which the NHS may then have to deal with further down the line.

From the late twentieth century, research into the impact of poverty on mental health has increased and the effect on society and the economy is now clear.[7] Statistics from the Mental Health Foundation show that people living in households with an income that is in the lowest 20 per cent are two to three times more likely to develop mental health problems than those in the top income bracket,[8] and this could be costing the UK economy over £100 billion per year – equivalent to the entire cost of the NHS for around nine months.[9]

In spring 2016, the Money and Mental Health Policy Institute opened its doors and began conducting research on the subject. It discovered that 46 per cent of people in problem debt also had a mental health problem, and 72 per cent said that their mental health problems had made their financial situation worse.[10] The cycle is understandable and yet its impact on the individual and on broader society is significant as mental health problems make it harder to earn and manage money, and to ask for help. Financial difficulties then cause stress and anxiety, which is made worse by going without essentials, which leads to further mental health problems.

This is an increasingly serious issue. In 2018, 74 per cent of UK adults were so stressed at some point in the previous year that they felt overwhelmed or unable to cope, and 32 per cent experienced suicidal feelings as a result of anxiety.[11] The charity Christians Against Poverty found in 2022 that over half of the people they helped with debt stated that their illness – either physical or mental – was directly caused by their spiralling financial problems.[12] Stress is the connector between deprivation, human biology and human behaviour, and it can manifest itself in different ways, including drug addiction and overeating. Ending privation in Britain would unquestionably create a more emotionally stable population, ease the burden on our support services and make the country easier to live in and cheaper to run.

Poverty and Addiction

The desire to ease the impact of stress can often lead to addiction. Canadian specialist Dr Gabor Maté spoke of his research on the topic:

> One of my patients said, 'I'm not afraid of dying, I'm more afraid of living' … why are people afraid of life? If you want to understand addiction, you can't look at what's wrong with the addiction, you have to look at what's right about it … relief from pain … a sense of peace, a sense of control.
>
> Why are these qualities missing from their lives? … Look at drugs like heroin, morphine, cocaine … alcohol, these are all painkillers. One way or another they all soothe pain and the real question is not, why the addiction, but why the pain?[13]

After recovering from a childhood steeped in deprivation, neglect and addiction, Darren McGarvey wrote his autobiography *Poverty Safari*:

> The first time I took ecstasy was the first time in my life I had ever been free of fear. As the drug washed over me, cleansing me of resentment, anxiety and self-concern … I had never felt so emotionally free.
>
> One of the reasons people become hooked on drugs so quickly is because coming off them is such a soul-destroying experience. And that's before you even become addicted.[14]

Some politicians have used dependency as a way of negating their responsibility to deal with deprivation at a national level, by arguing that it is caused by bad personal decisions. The key question is: how much responsibility should the state have for helping its population and how much is it each adult's own responsibility? In reality, it is both. An individual cannot get out of poverty if there are insurmountable barriers in their way, but they must also be prepared to ask for help when they need it. Deprivation makes people fragile, and while it can create resilience in some people who manage to climb out of it, little consideration is given to the effect on their long-term mental and physical health.

When doing the rounds with various media, McGarvey found his views on responsibility were often disliked by politicians and those in the poverty sector, who preferred to pity destitute people, instead of listening to their views. He found he was often used in the media to highlight the ills of privation, but was disregarded when he suggested that the responsibility for getting out of poverty belonged equally to the individual and the state:

> Taking responsibility is a hard thing to do. Especially when you believe it's someone else's job to pick up the slack. All my life I was told that the system was to blame for the problems in my family's life and that my family were to blame for the problems in mine. This belief that it was always someone else's fault was reinforced by the poverty industry and politicians who stood to gain from my willingness to defer to them.[15]

Stories of beating the odds and overcoming social barriers make great Hollywood films, but in reality, they should not be necessary. There should be no barriers in place if the state is doing its job properly, and personal responsibility would then become easier. The government should view its role as a facilitator to support those in need, instead of acting as a judge. While people cannot be forced to take counselling for their mental health, the government can fund services properly, so that when people do have the courage to ask for help, access to it is fast and reliable.

In Wales, reports suggest that hundreds of people have to wait over a year to receive specialist mental health support.[16] The Scottish government aims to treat 90 per cent of its children and young people within eighteen weeks of a referral, but between 2017 and 2021 this target was never reached.[17] In Northern Ireland, over 17,000 children and young people waited over a year for their first out-patient consultation for any physical or mental health condition, the worst in the UK.[18]

There are a variety of reasons why young people need more mental health support than in previous generations. Partly, it is because mental health is championed more than at any other time in British history, so children are more aware of it and able to ask for help. Other reasons include the rise of social media and the impact of the pandemic on isolation and feelings of helplessness. Marsha Powell, the CEO of BelEve, a mentoring charity for deprived 8- to 22-year-old girls and women, spoke to me of how the role of materialistic wealth and its links to social status have had a harmful effect on the emotional resilience of young people:

> For 16- to 24-year-olds, social media is a menace. It's a 'microwave world' for them. Influencers make out like earning money is easy because they don't show the journey of what it's taken to get there. Everything appears to happen instantly and when it doesn't happen in reality, it's disorientating for young people and this explains their mental health issues. They have no emotional resilience or bandwidth for patience. Their expectations are extreme.
>
> Once reality hits, social media then becomes an escape. The Covid lockdowns were a huge social experiment. It showed many teenagers quite how much poverty they were living in. They couldn't just go to the fridge ten times a day like lots of us did, because there was nothing in it. It was a time of realisation.

If there had been no poverty during the pandemic, not only would the death rate from the disease have been lower, but there would also have been fewer mental health scars left in its wake. The lack of senior mental health workers in the NHS is another significant problem. In the five years up to 2020, the number of consultant psychiatrists increased by just 4.3 per cent (up from 4,220 to 4,416), while the number of consultants across the rest of the NHS increased by 20.6 per cent to over 45,000.[19] The lack of professionals and the wait for treatment is a huge barrier to self-help and this is not the fault of the individual.

The pandemic added significant strain to health services and in 2021 there were an estimated 8 million people in England alone in need of support who could not get it because they were not considered sick enough to qualify. These included those with conditions such as bipolar disorder, psychosis, self-harm and suicidal thoughts. NHS providers stated that the funding on mental health should rise from £14.3 billion to at least £17.15 billion per year to cope with demand.[20] If Britain did seek to eliminate poverty through a new plan, these experiences suggest that huge social and financial savings could be made through the improvement of people's mental and physical health.

Poverty and Obesity

The connection between poverty, stress and overeating is rarely discussed in public life as a way of understanding the high levels of obesity among people in our country. The focus for politicians has often been to use a sugar tax to price children out of eating too many treats. However, living in poverty involves coping with high levels of stress and overeating can create addiction to high-fat or sugary foods. It is a simple way of gaining an emotional high, even if it comes with a sugar crash later on.

The link between overeating and stress is discussed by the American author Roxanne Gay in her seminal book *Hunger*. Having suffered a gang rape at the age of 12, she used overeating as a way of 'protecting' herself against further attacks by trying to make herself unattractive. When she finally realised this was not helpful, it was too late and she was heavily obese.

If the government wants to reduce obesity, then looking to poverty and stress within society is a vital part of the equation, as well as changing social attitudes to obesity, as people will often assume they know why someone overeats and will judge them accordingly and often abusively.[21]

Gay's experience highlighted how dealing with poverty-related obesity needs a broader strategy than simply focusing on what people eat – the 'why' is just as important. I know this because I have experienced it. Comfort eating enabled me to have small moments of pleasure while living with PTSD. I put on a lot of weight, but I didn't care. The emotional heaviness associated with simple things, like getting out of bed in the morning, was hard enough. I had reached emotional capacity and food kept me going. Once the PTSD was cured, I had the energy and head space to look at my eating habits in a new light. It was only after I realised that it took nine biscuits to get the sugar high I was craving, that I knew something had to change. My body had become too used to those tiny white crystals. I was addicted. It took three attempts to come off the sugar and only happened after a lot of research and planning.

On the first day, I was determined and extremely grumpy. The second and third days involved deep exhaustion and all-over body aches as my muscles began to detox. Then came forty-eight hours of headaches and more exhaustion, but by day six, I finally felt a change. I had more energy and my body and skin felt cleaner than ever before.

To break any addiction and stay off it requires a lifestyle choice. I am not perfect. I fall off the wagon sometimes, especially when faced with a beautiful cake that someone has made for me. It tastes fantastic, but then the cravings return and it can take hours of feeling sick to recover. The key is having alternative foods available and not going hungry. I keep food out of sight and am compassionate with myself when road-bumps happen. I also take time to rest. This final one took a long time to learn. It is easy to forget the importance of rest, and for those working two jobs or living on the breadline, it can feel an unaffordable luxury.

The sugar tax did nothing to dissuade me from overeating; it was all about my mental health. The desserts and biscuits kept me going in the same way that alcohol, drugs, gambling or any other addiction fill a hole in a person's life. They numb the problems and give you something to look forward to during the day.

To help broader society, one option would be to change the way sugary products are marketed to prevent their association with a happy life. In Bee Wilson's book, *The Way We Eat Now*, she highlights how Chile has removed cartoons from food packaging to stop the association between a happy childhood and nutrient-poor foods.[22] The British government could also do more to make healthy foods accessible by subsidising the production of greens, rather than solely taxing sugar, as Wilson found:

> There is clear evidence that price increases have an immediate impact on how many fruits and vegetables we buy, especially for those on low incomes ... On all sides, our food choices are shaped and constrained by economics ... [and yet] there is still a very widespread view that the best way to counteract the rise of obesity is to shame the fat into being less so. These beliefs exist even among policy makers and health care professionals.[23]

Interestingly, Wilson highlights that between 1990 and 2010, the price of fresh green vegetables in Britain went up significantly, while the price of ice-cream fell.[24] In the light of our twenty-first-century cost-of-living crisis, we should not be surprised if there is an increase in the comfort eating of snacks. As energy costs rise, cooking good food in the oven (like a Sunday roast) has become undesirably expensive, and for some utterly prohibitive, and this makes our country's inequality even harder to prevent.

Ultra-Processed Foods

Ultra-processed foods (UPFs) are products that tend to be low in essential nutrients and high in sugar, oil and salt, and are liable to be overconsumed. What characterises UPFs is that they are so altered that it can be hard to recognise their underlying ingredients. UPFs have been found to create new pathways in the brain for dopamine (the chemical that makes you feel good), and this increases the risk of becoming addicted. The same reaction occurs in children's brains and adults of all ages.

In 2019, two large European studies involving over 100,000 people found positive associations between the consumption of these foods and the risk of heart disease and death. Both studies high-lighted the need for further research, as these foods can account for 25–60 per cent of people's daily energy intake. Previous studies have also linked UPFs to increased risk of obesity, high blood pressure, high cholesterol and some cancers.[25] These types of food are often cheap and convenient, and are entwined with deprivation.

In 2021, Dr Chris van Tulleken conducted a self-experiment into the harm caused by UPFs on the body and brain, alongside Professor Rachel Batterham, who specialises in obesity.[26] Dr Tulleken changed his diet to 80 per cent UPF over four weeks. Brain scans, body meas-urements, appetite levels and blood composition were taken at the beginning and end of the trial to check for changes in hormone levels and inflammation within the body. Professor Batterham said:

> Hormones made in the gut play a key role in regulating appetite and body weight. The UPF diet changed the hormones, so Chris felt hungrier and therefore ate more and gained weight.
>
> After four weeks ... Chris' brain connection changed. This could be due to the UPF diet itself or the altered hormones. These changes are likely to have increased his desire to eat more UPF food and also altered his mood.
>
> UPF foods are usually cheaper and we know that people eat the food that they can afford to eat. Several countries (but not the UK) have brought in measures to reduce the consumption of UPFs. For example, Chile has banned the advertising of UPF to children under the age of 14.[27]

This is an important measure, as UPFs are common in the diets of children and may be contributing to the obesity epidemic. In the UK, 21 per cent of children are living with obesity when they leave primary school and this can create problems into adulthood. By eliminating poverty, teaching cooking and nutrition in schools, and supporting adults who are struggling with a UPF-heavy diet, the number of patients needing the NHS for obesity-related conditions could be significantly reduced, and the funding could be redistrib-uted to support other areas of the health service, such as Accident and Emergency departments or clinical research.

Touch Hunger

My physiotherapist held out her hands to support me. Blue plastic gloves stretched over her palms and we stood as far back as possible from one another, our masks strapped to our faces to prevent the spread of Covid-19. As I put my hands forward, it suddenly occurred to me that, beyond my direct family circle, she would be the first person I had touched for months. I had given my friends air-hugs in the street and edged nervously around people in the shops to prevent bumping into them, so when I touched her hands, it was an unusual moment. I felt a small part of my brain burst with energy and the overwhelming desire never to let go. Without knowing it, I had missed the physical contact of others so much that I had developed 'touch hunger' and every part of my body was focused on the comforting stimulation of simply holding someone else's hand. Understandably, she let go quickly. As a key worker she was one of the many heroic souls who kept supporting the public when the rest of us had to stay at home, and yet the comfort was so strong that I felt slightly stung when she moved away.

The lack of physical contact became a serious mental health issue for many people living alone or who were lonely during the pandemic. Touch is a powerful, basic sensation that the human body needs to keep functioning properly. From the moment we are born, humans are instinctively attuned to the sense of touch. It reduces stress levels and depression, slows the heart rate and boosts the immune system. Healing touch therapy and massage are used to relieve the pain that cancer patients suffer and have been found to improve the growth and development of children significantly, when compared with those with touch hunger who have the same nutritional diet.

In worms, rats, premature babies, institutionalised children and adults, the power of touch has been found to be vital for mental and physical health. It is so important that reports have shown that a lack of contact can significantly increase the severity of personality disorders (which are prevalent in the prison population). Massage therapy, manicures, pedicures, pets, foam rollers for self-massage and weighted blankets can all be used to calm the nervous system and ease pressure points.

For parents who work two jobs, are stressed about money, are hungry or are in abusive relationships, the importance of hugging one another can be forgotten in the complexities of life. Young people who enter the care system, live in state boarding schools or suffer bullying and isolation can all be negatively affected by the lack of healthy, consenting touch in their lives. Adults are also not immune, especially when they are in need of physical or mental health care, are in prison or government institutions, or are frail and lonely. This may be an area where AI could be used in the future to make materials for gloves or other products that simulate human touch and benefit medical treatment, or that enhance the rehabilitation of people struggling with stress, burnout or depression.

Stress and Safety

Living in poverty affects all parts of the body. The body and mind are not separate from each other and should not be thought of as separate systems. Dr Gabor Maté highlights this in his book, *When the Body Says No: The Cost of Hidden Stress*.[28] Maté states that, in conditions such as multiple sclerosis, the connection to stress is well established and was first discussed by the French neurologist Jean-Martin Charcot in 1868.[29] For lung cancer, Maté argues that being a smoker alone is not enough to develop lung cancer, as not every person who smokes develops the condition. The disease is caused by the combination of stress and smoking. This was found by David Kissen, a British chest surgeon, who reported in 1962 that patients with lung cancer were frequently characterised by a tendency to 'bottle up' emotions.[30]

There is no safety in poverty. It is an inherently unstable and stressful situation that has a direct impact on an individual's health. When a person's energies are focused on navigating and surviving their situation, stress-related illnesses will increase. Politicians should not be surprised by this and should speak more openly about the biological relationship. Illness inhibitors, such as vitamins and medicines, are also expensive, fresh juice is more expensive than squash, and fresh fruit is more expensive than processed alternatives, so ending deprivation can support our public services by enabling healthier lifestyles.

Social Care

It is often only when people need the social-care system, either for themselves or for a loved one, that they realise quite how disjointed, expensive and inadequate it has become. Questions around how to fund our system properly have been a source of political debate for years and have stifled concrete progress. It seems strange to have a health-care system that is proudly proclaimed as 'free at the point of use' when social care requires tens of thousands of pounds from individuals before the state will step in and help.

The idea of improving the social-care system by ending deprivation has never been part of the debate and yet there are good reasons for it to be included. A more equal society could reduce the need for care as the health of the older population improves. In 2021, analysis from AgeUK revealed that 3.7 million (one in four) older people over the age of 60 in England were unable to eat healthy and nutritious food.[31] Malnourishment is a source of illness, falls and mental health problems, all of which can be avoided. Nourishing food leads to better sleep and lower stress levels, and reduces isolation and pain as people have more energy to move about.

In the future, the combination of better nutrition and new drugs will improve brain health and combat conditions such as Alzheimer's. In 2022, the new drug Lecanemab was designed to remove amyloid plaques from the brain.[32] These sticky proteins are toxic to nerves and kill the surrounding cells, leading to holes in the brain. They also form barriers between nerve endings that prevent messages from passing from one part of the brain to another, leading to forgetfulness and confusion for the patient. These plaques form over many years and are connected to poor sleep: over 60 per cent of patients with Alzheimer's disease also have at least one sleep disorder, such as insomnia.[33]

It has been shown that the onset of Alzheimer's disease can be slowed using sleep therapy. However, as the stress of poverty disrupts a person's ability to get a good night's sleep, it is vital that future governments understand how these issues connect. The social-care system provides support across a huge range of debilitating conditions; however, it is interesting to consider how many long-term degenerative diseases could be avoided or their impact lessened by living in a more equal society. The positive knock-on effects to the social-care sector could be transformative, but we will only know the extent of this uplift in British health by dealing with privation first.

A key part of strengthening our NHS and social-care system is to reduce demand. Research across different fields suggests that, by ending deprivation in the country, the mental health of the population will improve, and waiting times for treatment will reduce as the need for help falls. As the NHS is increasingly pressured into making efficiency savings, this alternative approach could prove more sustainable for some of our greatest public services.

4

POVERTY, HOUSING AND HOMELESSNESS

The best and most efficacious remedy is love and a home ... To make a home for the homeless, yes, it is a thing that must be good; whatever the world may say, it cannot be wrong.

Vincent van Gogh (1853–90)[1]

For a year, our neighbours didn't have a back door; they had a hole where a back door should be. A grey curtain was pulled across in a vain attempt to keep out the cold. I wondered if the foxes came in for a nose-about in search of food. Did they tear open the bins in the kitchen and leave the remnants of dinner on the floor? What did it feel like in winter when snow was on the ground and icy winds blew through the house? Did our neighbours wear thick coats just to toast bread in the mornings? The property was a private rental, paid for by the local council, which is notoriously expensive, so it wasn't for a lack of money on the part of the landlady that it took so long to be repaired.

Housing must be viewed as a serious Cabinet post. The subject is vital to our prosperity and it should not be used as a starter position. In recent years, housing has tended to be a role from which ministers have launched their careers into more glamorous posts. In the fifteen years between 2008 and 2023, there have been seventeen housing ministers.[2] This is hardly a shining example of how to prioritise housing.

The housing sector in the UK is in disarray. There are 1.4 million people on the social housing waiting list and during the pandemic rent arrears tripled in a year. The *Big Issue* magazine stated that this equated to 500,000 households owing an average of £700.[3] During the pandemic, all evictions were halted, but in the autumn of 2021, they began again and many people faced losing their homes. Problems with Universal Credit (UC) delays and housing benefit mean that only the lowest third of market rents are covered, discrimination against benefit claimants is common and renters in arrears can struggle to find a new home. The *Big Issue* suggests a number of options that the government could take to deal with the crisis. (A full list is in Appendix 1.) One option is to create a Covid Rent Debt Fund, to clear the debt that built up during the pandemic as a result of lost income:

> Generation Rent's Covid Rent Debt Fund would cost the Treasury around £288m. That figure may seem high but, given that the chancellor gave away the equivalent of £1.6bn to homeowners through the extension of the stamp duty holiday, it's difficult not to feel that renters have been overlooked by the government. Investing now to fix the rent debt crisis would save the government money in the future, through saving local councils millions in homelessness services.[4]

Local authorities learned a lot about how to improve their homeless services during the pandemic.[5] The seriousness of the situation, combined with extra money from the government under the Everyone In programme, enabled local authorities to work more collaboratively and with greater flexibility, including offering more telephone services, which helped to reduce the stigma of homelessness and ease the process. This is particularly important for people who cannot afford the transport costs of going to a government building for help. A Local Government Association report in 2020 found that:

> Everyone In highlighted the extent of hidden homelessness for single people, in what was often a surprising scale to councils ... some councils are beginning to think longer term about their affordable housing programme and whether it should include a larger proportion of one-bed accommodation.[6]

It is extraordinary that the homelessness of single people came as a shock to councils, but it shows how sofa surfing has covered up serious levels of need. The old proverb 'There's none so blind as those who will not see' may be relevant here, as some councils may never have had the intention to deal properly with the true scale of homelessness in their boroughs. Some local authorities have declared bankruptcy, such as Slough in 2021, Croydon in 2020 and Northamptonshire in 2018, and many more are seeking support while on the verge of it. Councils lost income before and during the pandemic due to poor leadership, chronic financial mismanagement and changes to income streams from commercial rents.[7] It is therefore not surprising that, as some are only just surviving financially, their desire to fully understand and deal with homelessness has dwindled. (For further details, see Appendix 2.)

As a result of the lockdowns, young people under 25 were more likely to lose their jobs and were afforded less financial support through UC due to their age, even though their outgoings remained the same as those of older people. Rent and food costs do not change depending on age, so it is unhelpful that the government safety net is age dependent.[8] In her maiden speech to the House of Commons in 2015, Mhairi Black, a Scottish National Party MP, highlighted the contrast between her situation and the experience of most young people, as she was entitled to a London home paid for by the taxpayer, as well as having her own home in her constituency:

In this budget the Chancellor abolished housing benefit for anyone below the age of 21. So, we are now in the ridiculous situation whereby because I am an MP, not only am I the youngest, but I am also the only 20-year-old in the whole of the UK that the Chancellor is prepared to help with housing.[9]

In response to the homeless deaths in Scotland during the pandemic, the government created a Housing First programme in which homeless applicants are immediately placed into a permanent home and given wraparound support to help maintain it. The idea was to provide stability and have a positive impact on the lives of those struggling with addiction, mental health issues and homelessness.[10] This could be used as a model and expanded across the UK.

The Dying Homeless Project documented the deaths of homeless people during the pandemic. It suggested that a trauma-informed approach to supporting people across services should be introduced, along with the recognition that 'A roof is not enough. People need relationships, meaning and purpose', and new solutions should be designed with this in mind.[11] The link between trauma and homelessness has not been highlighted as clearly in other reports, yet it is a vital concept that should be spoken about more broadly as a way of combating the rhetoric around the undeserving poor. (This is discussed further in Chapter 13.)

Holistic Social Housing

Homeless people in their 40s were most at risk of death during the pandemic,[12] and at that age, for many, having their own individual space – rather than a house share – can be an important aspect of personal confidence and rehabilitation. This suggests that a new form of social housing needs to be developed, one which combines studio flats with a concierge-style support service and a focus on mental well-being, education and savings. Teaching people how to save money and live comfortably in a society that is obsessed with spending money is a vital skill that many generations were never taught at school. It could be particularly important for those who feel keenly the shame of poverty and are often desperate to appear wealthier than they are. A consumerist society does nothing to alleviate this anxiety, but by creating a new type of social housing that helps people to turn away from consumerist ideals and learn how to live without the need for show could help strengthen people's long-term mental health and financial stability.

Savings

Before the pandemic nearly half of all households had less than £1,500 in savings or no savings at all, and in the first month of lockdown the number of families using food banks doubled.[13] If people are to live in accommodation of the type suggested above, then being able to leave with savings is an important aspect of their future prosperity. It is almost impossible to rent a home privately without paying a significant deposit first, and this usually equates to thousands of pounds.

Ed Miliband MP highlighted the importance of even a small amount of savings in his book *Go Big*, in which he discussed the old system of government trust funds. Every child born between 2002 and 2011 was afforded a bank account containing £250 to encourage savings by parents and family members during childhood and adolescence. The money was passed over at age 18. The children who benefited are now reaching adulthood and most accounts have reached £1,000 – the money is often spent on key educational tools like laptops.[14] Having savings undoubtedly leads to liberty and stronger mental health, so the promotion of financial literacy would be an important aspect of any poverty elimination programme.

Housing Market Balance

The basic economic principle of 'supply and demand' has not worked well for the UK housing market. The demand for homes among international buyers has increased house prices and reduced the number of properties available for domestic buyers. The ageing population has also meant fewer properties coming on to the market as people live longer. This combination means that the supply of new homes is unable to keep up with demand and yet many new developments continue to be marketed to foreign investors. There are also serious question marks around how much laundered money is being kept safe in British housing stock. All of this is to the detriment of UK-based workers seeking to get on the housing ladder.

One option is to restrict access to the market to those with British citizenship, who have indefinite leave to remain or who are tax-payers in the UK. This would also limit the number of properties bought by landlords under company names and open up opportunities for individual home buyers. Large housing associations (some have 100,000 properties) are often overloaded with the number of repairs and upgrades that they need to complete on existing properties, and yet continue to build and buy new ones. Some also buy and hoard land that could be used to build homes, but they remain undeveloped until property prices are high enough to make building on the land worthwhile.

This strategy hampers local councils' abilities to build more social homes. An option would be to insist that those organisations found to be hoarding land are made to build social homes or forced to sell the land at a sensible price to local authorities to increase the land available for new homes. This might appear a rather aggressive tactic, but for the 1.4 million people waiting for a council home, serious movement on this issue cannot come soon enough. Broader society would also benefit as the failure to build social homes has increased demand for private rentals and the cost of rents, leaving people vulnerable to unscrupulous landlords or agencies. Having enough homes for everyone would significantly reduce pressures on the housing market and lower the cost of renting, leaving people with more money to spend in their local communities.[15]

An even stronger stance might be the complete cessation of new private housing developments for five years, so that building companies can assist with the production of only social homes during the course of the government. New measures like these may feel imposing at first, but it might be that this is the kind of focus needed to make a significant dent in the social housing waiting list, and as the numbers fall, the measures could be relaxed.

There is also a serious issue with the use of the UK housing market for money laundering and as investments by overseas buyers. The proportion of new-build properties bought by overseas buyers in London rose from 10.5 per cent in 2014 to almost 18 per cent in 2016. In Newham (one of the poorest boroughs in the country and in need of good social housing) up to 20 per cent of all properties were bought by overseas buyers.[16] This keeps property prices in the capital high and means that local councils that are short of properties have to move those in need of social housing out of the city to areas where properties are cheaper. This has a direct impact on people's mental health and increases loneliness, an issue that already affects millions of people in the UK and has been found to increase the risk of mortality by 26 per cent.[17] It affects children's education, takes people away from their jobs and underestimates parents' need for support from their local community. Moving families out of the borough they live in also significantly increases pressure on the public services in the boroughs where people are moved to. Due to budget cuts, many local authorities are already unable to support their local population fully, and all the while more people are being moved into surrounding counties from the cities.[18]

This is not solely a London issue; it is a nationwide issue. Housing has never been properly prioritised, as the reliance on the 'market' to provide what is necessary for the population has been an inadequate response to one of the most important and fundamental parts of a government's job. It also offers up the question: if a government cannot properly house its own population, then what is the government there for?

Creating restrictions on the people who are able to buy property is not a new idea. Switzerland, Denmark and Australia already have policies in place to limit where overseas buyers can invest.[19] The cost of renting is already controlled in cities like Paris and New York, where rent controls prevent local people from being pushed out of the housing market. Rent controls limit the price a landlord can charge a tenant for rent and also regulate the services the owner must provide. They can also limit rent increases.

The lack of affordable housing increases the chances of overcrowded homes being let by unscrupulous landlords, who can make hundreds of thousands of pounds a year by letting properties by the bed rather than by the room. Homes such as these can contain numerous people, sleeping in bunk beds crammed into each room in the house, with mattresses in the kitchen and further unsafe accommodation in the garden.[20] Landlords who are prosecuted risk being given a prison sentence, but if they are not uncovered, then the profits can be huge. In 2021, one landlord in Brent was ordered to pay back more than £700,000 earned from his filthy, overcrowded homes.[21] However, the underlying reason why tenants accept such living conditions, even when they have a job, is often based on immigration status or extremely low wages, which make them unable to access other forms of accommodation. The lack of social homes encourages illegal behaviour by landlords, and the vulnerability of tenants means they have to put up with it or risk sleeping on the streets. The lack of social housing has a direct impact on how poverty is maintained in Britain in the twenty-first century.

New Types of Homes

To speed up the production of new properties, local authorities could proactively use more modern, environmentally friendly techniques. For councils that have little excess space, the creation of eco-friendly micro-homes suitable for one person could be an affordable option; due to their small size, they can be off grid and easy to insulate. These types of properties are already used as UK holiday homes, so the move to permanent social homes would not be impossible. This would also be an important type of accommodation for those people moving from street homelessness and who want to bring their animals with them. The film *Year of the Dog* showed the 'life-line' between homeless people and their pets.[22] The use of dogs in prisons and the rise in pet ownership during the pandemic demonstrate how important animals are to supporting mental health and reducing anxiety. The move off the streets is only made more difficult by the loss of a beloved pet, so social micro-housing that enables people to retain their animals is important.

However, the cost of construction materials is at the highest for forty years, so building new homes will be an increasingly expensive exercise for local authorities with already stretched budgets. The Royal Institution of Chartered Surveyors highlighted that the combination of rising global demand, the impact of the pandemic on logistics, and complications from Brexit have affected all aspects of trade and the availability of labour.[23]

This means that the refurbishment of unused homes will need to be an essential part of any plan to increase housing stocks. Compulsory purchase orders may be used to insist that homes are either used by the owner or sold to the local authority and turned into social housing. In 2018, the BBC reported that there were more than 11,000 Ministry of Defence homes across the UK standing empty and costing the taxpayer more than £25 million a year in rent and maintenance. Homes like these need to be refurbished and returned to local authorities, so that more social housing is made available as quickly as possible.[24] This also shows how every government department has a part to play in the move away from poverty.

Innovation in the house-building sector is essential to reduce the levels of waste and the carbon footprints associated with creating new homes. There are many measures that can be used to create more energy-efficient homes, but bringing an innovative product to market can take years and requires the right timing for when the product is best placed to be bought and used. Batteries that store solar power during the day and then enable the energy to be used during the night can significantly cut energy bills, but if companies launch too early, then the price may not be right for the market, or customers may not be ready to take advantage of the product. If a government was committed to eliminating poverty in conjunction with the green agenda, then entrepreneurs may be more likely to bring innovative solutions to the market sooner and this would benefit everyone.[25]

There are non-governmental structures that can create and maintain inequality and the housing market is one of them. For people seeking to buy a second home to rent out, some banks have added a clause into the mortgage papers stating that the property cannot be rented out to anyone on housing benefit. This bias has led to a scarcity of rental properties just as there is a lack of social housing. In 2018, 90 per cent of the buy-to-let market refused a loan where a tenant was on housing benefit.[26] This banking bias has had a significant knock-on effect on the housing market and was ruled to be an illegal practice. However, while housing bias is technically illegal, it remains down to the private landlord to decide whom they let their property to and this discrimination is an issue that a Department for the Elimination of Poverty (DEP) could focus on (see Chapter 14).

Insulation

On a sunny September day in 2021, an environmental group called Insulate Britain committed the cardinal sin of holding up the M25 (a massive motorway ring road around London) by demonstrating across five junctions, on a busy Monday morning. Thousands of people were affected and many were extremely angry. However, by doing this, the protesters got their point across to the UK government and the media. According to the group, the UK has 29 million leaky homes, some of which are the oldest and most energy inefficient in Europe.

Many people live in cold homes, not just because of the lack of insulation, but also because they cannot afford the heating bill. If poverty was eliminated, then the heating of millions of homes could be on for longer and might cause emissions to rise, affecting global warming. This would be an unexpected consequence of eliminating poverty and highlights the need for a green agenda and a poverty elimination strategy to work in conjunction with each other. A positive aspect would be an easing of pressure on the NHS, as fewer elderly people would contract pneumonia and other conditions during the winter season, saving lives and money. It could be a win-win situation.

Winter 2022

It is a strange feeling to know that between the completion of this book in late 2022 and its publication in the autumn of the following year, poverty rates in Britain will almost certainly rise. The last 'winter of discontent' was in 1978 and the next will surely be this winter as half of all households are expected to be in fuel poverty by the end of it (defined as spending 10 per cent or more of the household income on energy bills). The risks of ill health for people living in cold homes will only increase as the gas stays in the 'off' position and a warm meal cooked on the hob may become a welcome luxury (it already has for some), just as a stroll outside became an exciting novelty during the pandemic.

It is a heartbreaking scenario and one that has not been caused by the people who are chiefly affected. It has been caused by unbelievably high global wholesale energy prices and this has shown the fragility of globalisation. As the government subsidised every household bill to the tune of £400 each, it highlighted the failure of the market to work properly. There should be no need for government intervention as competition between companies should keep prices low. However, for now the public will foot the bill, either through the government borrowing money to pay for the subsidy (which will have to be paid back by the taxpayer later on) or through higher costs to customers.

The supply and demand of energy and clean water are two issues that will concentrate our thoughts during this century. Less access to clean water will increase the risk of international wars, as conflict usually brings with it a rise in the prices of energy and goods. Those countries that are already self-sufficient in both water and energy are buffered from the international changes, but Britain isn't one of them. To prevent fuel poverty in the future, vital sectors will need to be stabilised and that requires new economic thinking. Until then, there are a few things that the central and devolved governments could do to provide more interim support than just a one-off sub-sidised energy bill, which will provide only moderate, short-term relief to this ongoing problem.

The first is to conserve water, wherever possible, on a large or small scale. Every building should be fitted with a water butt that is made in the UK and capable of storing large quantities of water, so that when torrential storms begin after periods of drought, flooding can be kept to a minimum and water can be stored in preparation for the droughts to come. This is a necessary part of planning for global warming, as the weather will become more extreme and unpredict-able. It is a simple policy that could provide relief to flood-prone areas, as the water upstream might not then merge and reach them. The stored water could also become a saleable commodity and returned to the water companies, just as renewable energy can be sold back to the grid by homeowners who have their own systems.

Another option is to help those who are currently in fuel poverty to come off-grid as much as possible. Options include the subsidising of solar panels on the side of social housing blocks (rather than on the roofs, to reduce scaffolding costs) and this would ensure that hundreds of people could have cheaper electricity faster. Where that is not possible, homes could be fitted with lightweight, hanging solar panels on the inside of windows, which feed into a portable battery pack. These batteries could then be used as an off-grid, plug-in power supply for moderate to small electrical appliances, such as phone chargers, lighting, electric heaters, TVs, radios, kettles and electric hobs. The short installation time and lack of scaffolding would keep costs to around £400 per household, and for those in dire need, it could mean a speedy return to hot food from the hob, warmer rooms and a hot cup of tea, all for free and for years to come (most portable batteries last up to ten years). This system is already used by houseboat and mobile home users, so it is not an alien concept.

Another option would be to encourage or subsidise the charity work of electricians and boiler maintenance personnel to provide free services to struggling households. They could check for leaks, ensure people know how to use the boiler timer properly, and install timers to immersion heaters (where they exist) so that people can shut off their gas supply during the warmer months. This would simultaneously reduce the country's carbon emissions from gas and retain hot water for bathing. Much higher fines could also be awarded against companies that continue to contaminate our rivers and seas, and this money could help to pay for the move towards becoming a more self-sufficient country.

It is vital that energy and water supplies are stabilised in the longer term to protect against further unexpected price rises. However, in the medium term, new and practical plans must be implemented to stop poverty from expanding and becoming further entrenched. The ideas discussed above are not the only options available, and policymakers and industry experts can come up with more. However, as you read this book I know life may be really difficult. It doesn't have to be that way. Our future is bright, so long as we stay open to new ideas and don't let the fear of change hold us back.

5

POVERTY, CRIME AND PROSTITUTION

Apothecary: My poverty, but not my will, consents.
Romeo: I pay thy poverty and not thy will.
William Shakespeare, *Romeo and Juliet*, Act 5, Scene 1

Shoreditch is a trendy part of East London, with eco-friendly cafés, chic clothing shops and artistic graffiti – some of which will make you stop and stare, much to the annoyance of passing commuters. However, behind this pleasant aura of city life, round a corner and down a quiet street, is a small property with iron railings across the front. It is a support centre for vulnerable women and prostitutes in the area. I went there with the intention of changing women's lives for the better, but instead I learned far more than I was able to offer.

My work at the centre took place a few years before the pandemic, which saw an acceleration in the number of people, especially women, using the internet to engage in sex work from the safety of their homes. However, it would be untrue to suggest that because of the shift online, vulnerable women have stopped being exploited. In fact, the cost-of-living crisis has forced many into prostitution, including mothers trying to provide for their children.[1] 'Prostitution' is a term often disliked by many because of social sigma and its historic connotations, and yet the social workers I worked with often preferred the term as they felt the phrase 'sex work' obscured the fact that prostitution is not a choice for many vulnerable women. It is a sensitive subject and many people dislike discussing it, not quite knowing what to say. The key is to treat people with respect regardless of their circumstances, and as a whole person with a complex life, rather than through the lens of judgement or embarrassment.

When I sat down to have a cup of tea with a woman at the centre, I sat quietly to let her talk. Being heard is a basic human need for all of us, but especially for those who are treated as a purchasable product on a daily basis. She opened up about her childhood and her violent, controlling brother. It was his abuse that led to her involvement in the trade. Later in life he offered his excuses, but an apology and some humility were what she really wanted.

She worked in a brothel, which she preferred to streetwalking. The owner ensured she got paid and felt relatively safe. Their relationship had become so trusting that the owner became godmother to one of her children. An unusual choice, perhaps, but she had clearly found someone she could rely on and feel safe with and this was special for her.

All four of her children had been taken into care. The youngest was 6 months old. I thought of how small a child is at that age and how much they need their mother. How a little baby had felt the distress of separation. If we lived in a different society, one that was more supportive and focused on rehabilitation, then the pain of loss may never have been necessary. As she spoke, sadness hung in the air, until a light flickered across her eyes as she thought of her eldest son who was studying architecture at university. She beamed with the same pride that any parent would when imparting such good news.

When politicians speak of legalising streetwalking and brothels, I get a sense that they are saying so because it is the easy option. The phrase 'they wouldn't do it if they didn't want to' enables leaders to wash their hands of the deprivation, abuse and complexities of people's lives. Legalising the street and brothel trades also may not be the answer to making women safer. Testimony from women in Amsterdam's red light district has spoken of the extreme violence and abuse used to control them. The city's politicians continue to grapple with the issue. Legalising the sex trade there has not made life simpler.[2]

While it is difficult to gain an accurate picture of the levels of prostitution in Britain, charities estimate that over 105,000 people (the vast majority women) are involved in the trade, with only a small proportion having been trafficked here. When surveyed by the charity Streetlight UK, nine out of ten prostitutes said that they wanted to leave the sector. The reasons for becoming involved included poverty, homelessness, slavery, leaving the care system, poor education, drug use and domestic abuse.[3] These are all significant barriers to leaving prostitution, while the trauma it generates also hinders the creation of a new life.

Streetlight UK found that, irrespective of whether a person has chosen sex work or was forced into it, two-thirds have some form of post-traumatic stress disorder. The disempowerment and disconnection that it creates leads to a split between the mind and body – a dissociation to reality – and people develop complex coping mechanisms, including obsessive-compulsive disorder, self-harm and drug use.[4]

The current law that requires all criminal convictions be cited on job applications, including prostitution, creates another major barrier to finding alternative work. Changing this law and creating a nationwide system of rehabilitation centres offers an alternative to legalising the sector. The Chrysalis Project (2009–19) was created 'to provide high quality accommodation and support for homeless women involved in street prostitution in South London'.[5] A three-phase system was used to rehabilitate women who were either referred to the project or literally walked in off the streets. It was held in a beautiful building with light, spacious rooms and long views down the garden. It conferred a sense that the women who lived there and the staff who worked there were important and valued. There was no sense that people were being judged. Rehabilitation cannot feel that way. It was about the sanctity of physical and emotional security.

The three phases of rehabilitation were:

- Step 1: Providing emergency accommodation and dealing with the individual's benefit and immigration status.
- Step 2: Providing counselling, rehabilitation and education in communal accommodation and restarting family relationships.

- Step 3: Moving out to live independently in a flat with case-worker support and finding employment.

The staged approach provided the structure and flexibility needed to meet individual needs while allowing for long periods of rehabilitation that embedded change. It also provided benchmarks for women as they moved through the programme so they felt the progress they were making towards their new lives.

There is no nationwide system for people seeking to leave prostitution. Approaches for communal living with tailored support services of the type that Chrysalis provided should be developed across the UK and available to everyone. One of the downsides of the project was that it was only available to people within the borough, thereby restricting access to women in other parts of the country. Moving across the country could be an essential part of a woman's rehabilitation by removing them from violent pimps, gangs or from streets that trigger painful memories and panic attacks.[6]

There is a strong argument that this approach to communal living should be used for the creation of a new type of social housing to support people of any age who find themselves in financial difficulties. Social housing centres that focus on a year-long tailored support programme that helps residents leave with savings, a financial education and better mental health could transform the lives of those who might otherwise have spent decades trying to cope or spiralling downwards. These kinds of staged interventions could help prevent an array of other problems arising, which services like the NHS and homeless charities would then have to address.

The link between poverty and crime is well understood. Better housing to reduce crime should form a large part of the plan to end deprivation. The Prison Reform Trust highlighted this ongoing problem in its 2020 report, *Safe Homes for Women Leaving Prison*:

Thousands of women are released from UK prisons with just £46, a plastic bag, nowhere to live and the threat of a return to custody if they miss their probation appointment ... With 65% of people released from prison without settled accommodation going on to reoffend ... secure housing is vital to achieving successful rehabilitation. Without settled accommodation, securing employment, maintaining positive mental health and preventing a return to harmful behaviours, such as substance abuse, are practically unachievable.[7]

So why are so many women prisoners released into homelessness? The Homelessness Reduction Act (2017) gives prisons a 'duty to refer' to their local authority anyone at risk of homelessness on their release. However, the report suggests that the act is failing due to the practicalities that women face when needing to be rehoused with their children if they are the primary carer, problems of relocation due to domestic violence, a chronic lack of suitable social housing, especially for those with complex needs, and being imprisoned so far from home that they lose their local connections.[8]

An essential area of work for the elimination programme would be identifying the governmental and non-governmental structures that create and maintain poverty. The situation of people leaving prison is a clear example of a structure that works against people's ability to move away from poverty and crime. The Prison Reform Trust also highlighted a number of situations that help to create and maintain the poverty of offenders, including low engagement with education, low literacy rates (62 per cent of offenders have a reading age of 11 or lower), the inability to claim UC until released from prison, homelessness (one in seven leave prison homeless) and debt problems built up while they are in jail, such as rent or mobile phone contracts. A lack of access to insurance after release also prevents access to many forms of employment and self-employment.[9]

The cycle of poverty–mental health problems–crime is one that should be properly gripped by politicians and the prison service (which is perpetually underfunded) to prevent the cycle of reoffending, which is unnecessary and expensive for our society.

In Prison with Too Little to Do

On 20 August 2020, Hashem Abedi, the younger brother of suicide bomber Salman Abedi, was sentenced to fifty-five years in prison for his part in the 2017 Manchester Arena attack, which killed twenty-two people and injured over 1,000. Hashem Abedi was 20 when he committed his offences and will likely die in jail.[10]

At time of sentencing, each prison place costs an average of £44,640 per year (although high-security prisoners can cost significantly more).[11] Over the next fifty-five years, Abedi will cost the taxpayer at least £2,455,200. How will he and others like him contribute to our society and the cost of their upkeep while they are in jail? The Institute for Government highlighted that for the prison system:

> Overall demand has grown, with an ageing prison population and increased availability of weapons, alcohol and drugs in prisons ... only 10% of prisoners are being unlocked for the recommended 10 hours per day and 24% spent less than 2 hours a day out of their cells.[12]

With a prison population of around 82,890 people,[13] this suggests that almost 20,000 prisoners are spending twenty-two hours a day in their prison cells. If Abedi is one of them, he will be neither contributing to society nor rehabilitated.

In some cases, unsanitary conditions can leave prisoners with mental health problems that did not previously exist. Reports suggest that infestations of rats in prisons have left some former inmates with PTSD.[14] The Prison Reform Trust also highlighted:

> A failure to ensure decent and humane conditions, as well as respond effectively to the large proportion of people in prison with serious mental health problems, is being paid for in human misery and distress. Too many people are held in overcrowded conditions with too little to do. The government needs a plan to restore purpose and hope to our prisons. Sending more people to prison for longer will make matters worse.[15]

The phrase 'too little to do' is an important one. Prison should not simply be a holding pen for criminals to wait out their time before returning to society. It should be an active place of rehabilitation, learning and preparation for the outside world. The education should be appropriate for each individual and focus on their physical and mental health – such as undiagnosed dyslexia, personality disorders or the long-term effects of drug use on the brain.

The more prisoners understand their brains and why they behave the way they do, the more they can begin to understand why they are in jail and how they can prevent it from happening again. The state and the individual are both responsible; it should be a collaborative effort at rehabilitation, not one-sided. The state is in the position of power, not just over the person's liberty but also in possessing greater knowledge and resources, and the individual must take responsibility for their behaviour. However, extended rehabilitation treatments require money, so innovative ideas are needed.

Indian jails used meditation as an effective and cheap method of helping prisoners to become more reflective.[16] British prisons have been researching the use of mindfulness and providing prisoners with ear plugs to improve their sleep and mental health.

Another novel approach could be the use of bicycle-generated electricity by prisoners. It is generally not deemed worthwhile for an individual to spend time on a specially tailored bike in order to produce clean energy to power their home. However, as so many of the prison population spend the majority of their days in their cells with their energy underutilised, a pilot project to understand the mental and physical benefits of having prisoners generate their own electricity would be worthwhile. It could also bring in money for the prison system through the sale of clean energy. In 2012, a Brazilian prison introduced a system whereby prisoners could reduce their sentences by one day for every eight-hour shift on an electricity-producing bike. This was aimed at tackling overcrowding and reoffending.[17] British jails are perpetually underfunded, understaffed and volatile places, so it is vital that new ways of reducing violence and improving prisoner and prison officer welfare are found.[18]

A single person pedalling a bike can produce around 100 watts an hour. This is enough to power a single lightbulb for an hour – so, not a lot. However, the prison population in 2019/20 was around 87,900 people.[19] That represents a significant amount of electricity that could be produced, even if only a small percentage of the prisoners took part. Alongside reducing the cost of prisons for the taxpayer, the added exercise could also reduce levels of violence and self-harm, and support drug rehabilitation and life skills, which are essential to the prevention of poverty upon release.[20]

Policing

In April 2021, the then chief constable of Merseyside Police, Andy Cooke, spoke openly about the relationship between crime and poverty, suggesting that if he was given £5 billion to cut crime, he would put £1 billion into law enforcement and £4 billion into tackling poverty and increasing opportunity. He noted that aspiration must be boosted to prevent low-paid work and hopelessness from cascading from one generation to the next, where children leave years of compulsory education without qualifications and with no prospect of gainful employment.[21]

It is easy to assume that this is children's own fault for not applying themselves properly, but research has shown that poverty-related stress overloads the brain and prevents learning. Darren McGarvey described the impact of deprivation on children's lives in his book, *Poverty Safari*:

> Poverty is not only about a lack of employment, but about having no margin for error while living in constant stress and unpredictability. And for children growing up in this chaos, the experience can leave them emotionally disfigured ... what is driving many of our current social problems where crime, violence, homelessness and addiction are concerned. It all begins with a child living in social deprivation. When it comes to child abuse, poverty is the factory floor.[22]

This lack of margin of error can be poorly understood by wealthy individuals in positions of power and financial stability. The political argument used to separate groups into 'strivers and scroungers' is an invidious piece of propaganda. Judging those who are already vulnerable is a cynical position to take, especially when the welfare system is complicated, slow and faulty. This view does not take into account a person's physical or mental health, their literacy rate, transport costs, fear of failing at something new, their former attempts at entering the workforce, or the barriers that held them back. The lack of a detailed understanding of the complexities of people's lives, and the assumption that people who live on benefits must have chosen to do so, inhibits positive wholesale action, which is to the detriment of us all.

Traumatic Brain Injury, Prison and Poverty

Traumatic brain injuries (TBI) affect around 5 per cent of the British population, but in prison they affect between 50 and 80 per cent of inmates, with higher levels in women's prisons.[23] Undiagnosed brain injuries hamper a prisoner's ability to rehabilitate and, in early life, a child's ability to learn. They cause a wide range of cognitive, behavioural and emotional difficulties. In prison, women with undiagnosed brain injuries and without specialised support struggle to engage in rehabilitation programmes and are more likely to reoffend.[24]

A study at Drake Hall prison and young offender institution (2016–18) found that over half of female offenders reported a personal history that indicated a brain injury. Almost every one (96 per cent) had experienced domestic abuse, and over half reported that they had sustained a traumatic brain injury due to domestic violence. One in three had sustained the first injury before committing their first offence. Many of the milder symptoms of brain trauma can be masked and yet they cause behaviours that can be seen as 'challenging' and 'difficult' by the criminal justice system. For example, a female offender with a brain injury might frequently miss appointments – this can be seen as the individual being avoidant or irresponsible, but may be due to poor memory as a result of the brain injury. They might repeat the same word over and over again – this can be seen as rude, but may be due to poor self-awareness from the TBI. Or they might say they will do something and never get around to it – this can appear manipulative or lazy, but may be due to poor initiation from a brain injury. (Poor initiation is where a person may experience difficultly in starting tasks unless prompted or assisted to do so.)[25]

It is also important to note that the causes of TBI include road traffic accidents, assaults and falls, as well as a person experiencing several, minor TBIs, which can have a similar impact as having one severe injury. Such minor TBIs might result from being struck by or against objects, as can happen in the case of child abuse or domestic violence.

TBIs are a key factor in crime and psychological difficulties, including excessive tiredness, indifference, obsessive-compulsive symptoms, sexual aggression, lack of social judgement, inflexibility, irritability and concentration/attention disorders.[26] TBIs can be readily screened for and managed in different ways. Understanding their prevalence and impact on children may be an important way of reducing the number of pupils who are excluded from school each year for poor behaviour. Research shows that the younger a child is at the time of an injury, the greater the possibility of long-term difficulties because the brain has not yet finished developing. The damage may only become obvious in teenage years when children fall behind their peers. Brain injuries are also very variable in terms of the duration of symptoms, and the recovery afterwards can be patchy. Common problems show up in four areas: physical, communication, reasoning and behavioural/emotional.[27]

It is difficult to find research on the nexus between childhood poverty, TBI, school exclusions, the care system and prison, but further research could highlight the benefits of focusing on poverty as a way of dealing with the underlying causes of these interconnected issues. Research may also provide extra stimulus to politicians to properly fund schools' special educational needs (SEN) budgets. Combining SEN work with neurological specialists in the NHS could be an important way of identifying and supporting children with undiagnosed TBIs, and preventing future problems, particularly school exclusions, which can make children more vulnerable to gangs and crime.[28]

The American psychiatrist and brain disorder specialist Daniel Gregory Amen spent two decades conducting 83,000 brain scans. When he scanned the brains of over 500 prisoners, he found that people who commit crimes often have troubled brains and that these brains can be rehabilitated. He suggested that, instead of a system of crime and punishment, we should think about crime, evaluation and treatment. For children, brain scans can explain violent behaviour, and for his 9-year-old nephew Andrew, the brain scan identified a golf-ball-sized cyst in his brain. After the cyst was removed, all of Andrew's behavioural problems went away.[29] This may be an important extra aspect in supporting children with difficulties, rather than simply judging them.

In 2020, there were around 100,000 children in care across Britain.[30] In 2016/17 figures showed that cared-for children were four times more likely to be temporarily excluded from school and twice as likely to be permanently excluded. Children's relationships with adults and feelings of safety guide their psychological development. Attachment and trauma awareness training in schools can be used to equip all staff (from headteachers to mealtime supervisors) with the knowledge and information to understand children who have experienced difficult circumstances. Where this has happened, staff and pupils have reported improvements in well-being and behaviour, with most schools also showing rises in attainment. Innovations like 'chill-out' rooms, nurture groups and 'time-out' cards can be used to create a calmer environment for learning and are a more effective way to support children's development than sanctions.[31]

A study by Liverpool University in 2021 found that child poverty has been associated with 10,351 more children (under 16) in England being taken into care (2015–20).[32] The study only covered England, but if extended to the rest of the country, this would suggest that there are currently thousands of extra children in care who would not need to be there if their families had more money. The social-care sector is incredibly expensive and much of this cost is associated with the need for specialist staffing of highly vulnerable children who are being looked after away from home. The average price for a children's home place in England is almost £5,000 per week, but some cost £30,000 per week for a private care home place. There are question marks over whether private companies' high prices exploit the lack of available places for children in state-run care homes or in the NHS, when secure services are not available.[33]

It is moments like this that highlight how important eliminating poverty is, not just for society but for the country's finances. If poverty increases a child's chances of being taken into care, and the state has to pay thousands each week to support them, then ending deprivation and keeping families together is by far the better choice. Wherever possible, children need to be at home, and dealing with inequality will provide a greater chance of this happening.

Marijuana

I unintentionally became friends with our local drug-dealer. My daughter was a toddler and as she stopped to examine the details of a fallen leaf on the ground, I smiled at a young man who stopped to have a chat. He had a tubby, gentle look to him and he talked with pride about his new position in a job centre, helping others get into work. When the pandemic struck, his father died of Covid and his final ask of his son was that he didn't do anything illegal. The young man was left to be the primary carer for his mother, a job that he admitted he was out of his depth doing and didn't enjoy. He had been made redundant from his workplace and spent time hanging around the streets, until one day I saw him with the same bag as all the other young dealers in the area. As he passed by, he was talking eagerly on his phone, unwilling to make eye contact. His shiny trainers and new tracksuit were symbols of his new status and money. I never spoke to him of his father's last words. He knew them well enough. It was sad to watch him fall further and further into the drug-dealer's world. He lived so close to them that it would have been almost impossible for him to get away, even if he had wanted to. I continued to smile as he passed by, but we never really spoke again.

It is easy to buy cannabis in London. The dealers conduct their business openly on the streets and the heavy white smoke lingers in the air. Many in our community use it as an alternative to alcohol. The legalisation of cannabis is a long-running debate in politics and usually spurred on by the attraction that the taxes received would improve the country's coffers and reduce policing costs. However, by legalising cannabis the government would also be suggesting that it is a safe substance for the human body. While alcohol and cigarettes remain legal, they cost the taxpayer millions each year in the treatment of related diseases, so this is not a reason to add cannabis to the list.

Research has shown that smoking cannabis regularly during the teenage years can significantly distort the shape of the growing brain.[34] This has knock-on effects on the individual's health, capacity to learn and future life. Professor David Nutt specialises in neuropsychopharmacology (how drugs affect the brain) at Imperial

College, London, and is the government's former chief drugs adviser. In 2021, he suggested suspending drug testing in jails as it had unintentionally moved prisoners towards harder drugs, such as spice and heroine, and away from cannabis, which is more likely to be detected by sensors and extend an inmate's prison sentence.[35] The government does not provide data on the amounts of spice used in prisons,[36] but it can be easily smuggled into jails by being liquidised, sprayed on to paper, rolled up and smoked. Nutt's concerns have been further investigated by researchers at Middlesex University, who found that a variety of drug treatment options are needed in prisons, not just the abstinence approach. The lack of flexibility has led to some avoidable prisoner deaths, in particular non-violent criminals with a history of substance misuse who have died after moving on to harder drugs, but who may have lived had they been given a community order and drug rehabilitation support.[37]

Professor Nutt's proposal was not a politically palatable one and many retorted that there were other ways of managing addiction in prisons than swapping cannabis for spice. However, what this does highlight is the extreme situation of drug use in British prisons, which, unless it is dealt with constructively, will continue to cause problems for prisoners on release by reducing their chances of gaining employment and increasing their chances of homelessness, poverty and reoffending.

The use of recreational cannabis by those with TBIs has consistently been shown to have negative effects. However, pre-clinical research suggests that medical cannabis can have therapeutic properties on a condition that lacks a treatment or cure. In 2021, researchers highlighted the lack of high-quality studies that examine the effects of medical cannabis on TBIs, and found that some people are using both medical and recreational cannabis to treat their symptoms. This shows the inconsistencies between public policy, perceptions of how well the different substances work and the lack of scientific evidence.[38] Considering the high levels of people in jail who have TBIs and the longer-term goal of preventing poverty in Britain, more research into the effects of medical cannabis on TBIs and prisoners would be useful for politicians and prison officers alike.

Manipulation

If anyone ever says to you, 'It's you and me against the world!' take a step back for a moment. It may sound like a sweet and comforting phrase, but it holds the potential for manipulation, isolation and abuse. Gang members grooming child recruits, extremists recruiting suicide bombers, controlling partners involved in domestic abuse, pimps controlling prostitutes and paedophiles controlling children may all use this small phrase. In each situation, the abuser targets people with emotional vulnerabilities, uses isolation techniques to separate them from their families and friends, may create financial dependence, and can convince people to do things they would never normally choose to do.

These manipulation techniques are used widely, and being able to identify them and remove people from the situation is essential to their personal safety. However, when mixed with poverty, the abuser's power significantly increases. Regarding his work in prisons, Darren McGarvey wrote in his book, *Poverty Safari*:

> When people come here to work [with the prisoners], they often adopt personas that they think will appeal to the participants, forgetting the prison population is filled with some of the most emotionally intuitive and manipulative people you are likely to find … Maltreatment or neglect at the hands of a care-giver appears to play a significant role in triggering the … factors that lead to offending behaviour: low self-esteem, poor educational attainment, substance misuse and social exclusion.[39]

This partly explains why crime reduces as poverty falls. People become less emotionally fragile and so are less vulnerable to manipulation when they are not living in poverty. In their seminal book *The Spirit Level*, Richard Wilkinson and Kate Pickett highlighted the connection between inequality, shame and violence. Wilkinson spoke about it in his TED Talk, 'The link between inequality and anxiety':

> What most pushes up our levels of stress hormones are what is called 'social evaluative threat' – threats to self-esteem or social

status ... Although these social stresses are widely recognised and we're all familiar with them, people fail to see how inequality makes them worse for all of us ... Violence is triggered by people feeling looked down on. Loss of face, disrespected, humiliated – those are the triggers of violence.

Inequality isn't just about unfairness or poverty. It puts us in social relationships of superiority and inferiority. It ranks us from better to worse. It's a really invidious process.[40]

Manipulation is often used by people with an inferiority complex to gain the feeling of superiority that they so desperately crave. McGarvey notes the shame when describing his childhood in the 1990s in a deprived area of Scotland:

Most of the people living in Pollok had a council house but this didn't stop us from acting like we had more money than we did. I suspect the deep sense of shame many of us felt about our poverty – and an overwhelming desire to conceal it – was why the Pollok Centre was so popular. Here you could acquire everything you needed to appear better off than you really were: new trainers, tracksuits, chains, rings, football strips and boots. Such sought-after items and accessories were expensive but the price of looking poor was always far higher.[41]

A Britain without poverty would mean a country without financial shame. The removal of this burden from people's shoulders could transform our society, through less debt, violence, manipulation and crime.

Serious Youth Violence, East London, April 2021

A 13-year-old boy was stabbed near our house today, as he was on his way to school. It happened on a street that I have walked down hundreds of times before. The air ambulance landed on a nearby playing field as little children watched from their swings. A sombre silence hung in the air as crews talked on their phones trying to locate him, a boy whose childhood had evaporated moments earlier.

It takes a long time to recover from the trauma of being stabbed, much longer than the physical wound takes to heal. Anxiety, panic attacks and feelings of insecurity can all be part of the process, and the NHS and the boy's school will need to be there to help him through. The attack made the headlines today, but Londoners know there could be another one in a different part of town tomorrow. The British writer Anthony Horowitz made the observation that 'Childhood, after all, is the first precious coin that poverty steals from a child'.[42]

It is well known that gang stabbings and violence are related to poverty. It is strangely heartening, however, to know that this type of appalling crime is not inevitable and that the elimination of inequality could bring an end to this type of violence. In July 2019, London's City Hall published analysis that confirmed the strong link between serious youth violence and Londoners affected by deprivation, poor mental health and poverty.[43] The figures showed that three-quarters of London boroughs with the highest levels of violent offending were also in the top ten most deprived, while the same boroughs also had higher proportions of children under 20 living in poverty compared with the London average.

Serious youth violence began rising significantly in 2012. A year before, on 4 August 2011, the police shot dead Mark Duggan, a young Black man in Tottenham. It led to the London riots, which spread nationally with thousands of (mainly) young people rioting in cities and towns across England. It led to £200 million of damage to businesses and property from looting and arson, and the deaths of five people. It was the worst civil disturbance in a generation.

Materialism and the herd mentality, along with a police force taken by surprise, perpetuated the violence and looting. A society and economy that have relied so heavily on the principles of consumerism and spending, and where that is not possible, on credit and debt, will not create a peaceful situation while there is also a widening wealth gap. Poverty in a rich person's world is overwhelmingly frustrating. It is not surprising that ignoring poverty during the austerity years fuelled anger and resentment, which eventually spilled over into violence. This is not to condone the events that kept many Londoners at home for a week, but for a government in charge of a society with broad social divisions, it should not be a surprise either.

A year before the riots in October 2010, the Conservative–Liberal coalition announced significant cuts to support services for young people. In September 2011, the Education Maintenance Allowance (EMA), a weekly means-tested payment of up to £30 for students aged 16–19 for being at school or in further education colleges, was cut.[44] Almost half of all students qualified for the EMA and it cost £560 million. It was replaced with a £180 million bursary fund that was distributed by schools and colleges as they saw fit, unlike the EMA, which was distributed according to parental income.[45] It was estimated that after these changes came in, in 2012/13 around 8,000 children left higher education.[46] By 2015, students were legally required to stay in full-time education or training until their 18th birthday, which helped to keep more children at school, but did not prevent them from living in poverty.[47]

Housing support for young people aged 18–21 also changed, as did youth support services, which were either cut or merged, further affecting vulnerable young people. Yet, with all of these changes, society did not improve, crime did not reduce. Politicians' focus on dealing with the national debt rather than creating a society that functioned properly for everyone meant that inequality grew. Poverty is expensive for Britain, not just in terms of a lack of economic growth, but also psychologically and emotionally. It is not inevitable, and if dealt with properly, the long-term consequences for the victims and perpetrators of crime could change dramatically. History has shown that slow political changes are not enough to deal with deeply embedded social problems, but with focus, eliminating poverty could change the lives of people in many unexpected ways.

6

POVERTY AND BARRIERS

Equality matters because, when you have less of it, you have to put up with obnoxious behaviour, insulting suggestions and stupid ideas.

Professor Danny Dorling, *The No Nonsense Guide to Equality*[1]

Heavy gold curtains draped the walls of the Victorian interview room. Wealth dripped from every picture frame and ornament. I perched on the edge of the cushion, buzzing with interview nerves and eager to please. The interviewer sat behind a heavy wooden table, one designed to exude status and wealth. The power difference between us was accentuated further by the low sofa, which forced me literally to look up to him.

'When do you intend to have children?' he asked in a matter-of-fact tone. 'I have no problem hiring women, I just don't want to pay maternity costs a year after hiring you.'

Silence descended. All my interview courage turned into anger at his apparently reasonable question, which was also illegal. It would be ten more years before I would become a mother, so his concerns were as irrelevant as they were patronising, but I knew he would never have asked if I had been a man. It felt like a noose had tied itself around my neck and I had to fight my frustration at being asked about my womb. I felt how much I needed the job after months of waiting for an interview and wondered how much money was left in my bank account. The question squashed me, and no matter how much I pretended to be interested in the role after that, I couldn't summon up the energy. I walked away, wanting to tear down the curtains as I left.

Women's fertility is not the only subject that hinders different people from accessing jobs they could comfortably do. The list extends much further to include race, gender, age, sexuality, religion, nationality, health, schooling, dialect and appearance. To enable social mobility within the workplace, discrimination against employees must be dealt with at every level and good practice should be collated and shared widely. This is important as it will enable senior managers to discuss discrimination within their organisations, and do so in a way that draws on what others in their field are practising and prevent the spread of archaic points of view.

Poverty Premium

Second-hand websites are a minor obsession of mine, as they combine lovely products with less damage to the planet and a low price tag. After buying a smart handbag for £1.50, I wondered why others didn't do the same – it seemed such an obvious way to save money. However, in reality, it hadn't actually cost £1.50. To access the online shop, I had needed a smartphone with internet access and a contract, a bank account with money to spare and a credit card with a good credit rating. To get these, I had needed a stable home address and identity documents. I also needed to be literate and confident in using the internet. Behind the £1.50 handbag was a host of things that really only come with a stable home life. Without any one of these things, the purchase would have been impossible. This is the poverty premium. Access to cheaper goods and services comes at a price and it is easy to forget that.

The premium spans many areas of life, including food. The charity Fair By Design has highlighted that a low-income household can spend an extra £500 a year on bills, and for one in ten of these households, the premium rises to almost £1,000. Considering that £500 can equate to fourteen weeks' worth of food shopping for some families, this is a significant added pressure for those already struggling.[2]

The poverty premium can be found in a variety of different sectors. For car insurance, the amount charged partly depends on the crime rate in the applicant's postcode, and more deprived areas tend to have higher rates of crime. Bank loans and credit cards often have higher rates of interest for those on low incomes or with poor credit ratings, which can leave vulnerable people at the hands of dangerous loan sharks. For accommodation, the cost of a monthly mortgage payment is often lower than rent, yet people can struggle to get on the property ladder because of their income level, even if they have never fallen behind on paying their rent in the past. In the retail sector, the offer of 'buy two and get a third free' is only accessible to those who can afford two products, but it is the families who can only afford one who are often most in need of the extra free food. In the energy sector, the government had to introduce a policy in July 2023 that prevented energy companies from charging customers higher tariffs if they used a pre-payment meter instead of direct debit, at an estimated cost to the taxpayer of £200 million. This is a huge amount of money to be going to private companies on the basis of alleviating poverty. It is unclear for how many years the payment will be made and it could be easily rescinded by a new chancellor at any time. Poverty is expensive for our country and ending it, rather than alleviating it, would be far more productive.[3] (For more ways to combat the poverty premium, please see Appendix 3.)

The poverty premium is being worked upon by many organisations, both within government and outside it, but a focus from government and collaboration within the marketplace could make a significant difference. This is another area where the government could provide leadership and promote collegiate working across different sectors of society.

Literacy

I felt quite privileged to hear him speak so openly. To hear the things he was reluctant to say to his own daughters. At 12 and 15, the girls were full of life and he wanted to keep his dignity in front of them, but the digital age had found him out. As a young teenager growing up in a rough area in the 1960s, his dyslexia had gone undiagnosed and he had left school unable to read. His 20s had been spent in jail, and since then, he had only ever worked cash-in-hand jobs. Now he was in his late 50s, his daughters had internet access and he couldn't keep up. For him, it was alien, scary and embarrassing.

When I began running a digital inclusion programme for a housing association, I wondered if there would be a literacy issue. From my mother's years as a teacher, I knew well that funding for dyslexia testing had varied considerably over the decades, and for those who had been at school before the condition was properly understood, or during a time of low funding, it could easily have gone undiagnosed. For the students involved, it often led to ridicule and bullying, and the idea of returning to education to try again was one charged with difficult emotions. In light of this, I thought that one-to-one tuition would be the gentlest way to ease people back in. I found a quiet room where people could face their fears in private. The job centre offered group sessions, but these were often too imposing and could set people back where they made progress with us.

As I rang round some local tutors to explain the programme, a few of them were completely unable to comprehend what I was saying. The idea that in modern Britain a person could have reached late adulthood without ever having learned to read and write was inconceivable to them. I felt the inequality gap keenly in those moments, as if speaking from another planet – but that is one of the many problems with inequality: it can create chasms between people and groups, and one another's lives can seem unfathomable. This lack of understanding can perpetuate a lack of compassion and trust, and a need to fill the void with stereotypes or hyperbole.

I had to hold back my emotions when the man shook my hand with a wide smile on his face, as he told me that he could finally read well enough to start internet lessons. He would soon be able to help his daughters with their homework and rebuild his standing in their eyes, which was all he really wanted. He was so happy.

The programme worked well for those who went on it, but it came at a price. Good quality one-to-one trainers are expensive, which explains why job centres focus on group sessions. However, the mental and emotional barriers associated with a traumatic school life also need to be considered. Tailored literacy sessions should be viewed as a valuable investment in the human capital of our country and stand in equal importance to our investment in science and technology. Economic growth and a stable society need both types of investment. Plus, we'll never regret teaching someone to read.

Racism

My friend once told me a story from her time as a student in South Africa. It was only a decade after apartheid had ended and debates around equality and the best way to achieve it were rife across the country. One day her lecturer convened her year group and asked everyone to form a line. As the teacher asked a series of questions, the students who answered 'yes' were to take a step forward. What was to come was a hard-taught lesson on inequality.

'Step forward if you have a high school diploma' – everyone stepped forward, chatting and laughing.

'Step forward if you have completed primary school' – everyone did the same. So far, so good.

'Step forward if both your parents have high school diplomas' – only some people stepped forward. The class fell into an awkward silence.

'Step forward if both your parents completed primary school' – again, only some students moved.

'Step forward if you had a car growing up ... if your parents own their own home ... if your parents have always been employed ...'

On and on the questions came, gradually separating out the class until the results were clear for everyone to see. White men were at the front and Black women were at the back. Classmates who, only a few moments ago, had seen themselves as equals were now divided by society's inequalities.

The lecturer raised her voice once more.

'It's a race. The finishing line is over here. Now – RUN!'

Everyone froze. The birds sang through the silence. The harsh reality of the society they had been born into was staring them in the face. They had lost an innocence that had so easily lulled them into a false sense of security with the shock of seeing their friends' lives from their own perspectives. The exercise showed the classmates that if you don't want to see poverty, then you won't. It is a choice. It doesn't make you a bad person, but it should be acknowledged and accepted, so that people don't expect to completely understand the society they live in. It is no surprise that my friend remembered the short exercise years later over a cup of tea in London, as it had a profound effect on all involved. The lecturer had done her job well, by forcing the issue of inequality into the eyes of the next generation, so that they had the perspective needed to push their society towards a better future. Perhaps, as we move forward, this exercise should be repeated in universities across the country, to ensure that everyone understands the lasting impact of privilege?

5 April 1968

The day after Martin Luther King Jr was assassinated, a primary school teacher in the USA, Jane Elliott, conducted a novel exercise on racism with her all-white, Christian students called the 'blue-eyes, brown-eyes exercise'.

The exercise took place over two days and worked by giving extra privileges and praise to one group over another. Elliott found that, within a very short space of time, this led to changes in the children's confidence, educational attainment and arrogance. To her surprise, feelings of superiority among the privileged group led many of them to perform better in class tests than they otherwise would have done. Students also turned from their usual calm, collaborative selves into aggressive children more willing to fight, as the frustration of discrimination bore down on them. After becoming aware of their differences, the students were also more likely to self-segregate into their own groups, even though they knew the exercise only existed within the classroom and the groups switched after the first day.

Elliott's exercise and its impact became a national sensation and she was vilified by many people in her school and country. Today she is regarded as one of the top educators of all time, alongside Maria Montessori. Elliott made her society and the world face the uncomfortable truth that feeling superior feels good. She showed that it requires personal humility and the ability to see the world from someone else's perspective to prevent racism, sexism and all other forms of discrimination. Elliott continues to teach the class to adults across the USA, as she knows that the end of racism has to be actively won. It won't happen naturally through the passage of time or changing generations. In an email, Jane Elliott discussed her views with me:

Racism is a learned affliction and anything that is learned can be unlearned. Racism is not genetic. It has everything to do with power. How long will those who are on the receiving end of it have to be patient with our society's self-imposed and accepted ignorance?[4]

Elliott's work and that of every person involved in anti-discrimination movements continues apace. Racism has been a staggeringly difficult issue for societies to unpick and unlearn. The experiment demonstrated the fragility of co-existence and co-operation, and defining moments from the Holocaust in the 1940s to the riots at the American Capitol Building in 2021 have shown how easily people can be swayed by authority figures.

The creation of a poverty-free Britain could deal with much of the discrimination that exists within our country, as it would create a calmer, less anxious population. It would bring people together and form a stronger, more unified feeling. However, to end deprivation, British institutions will need to determine just how discriminatory they are and put in place measures to tackle it. In 2021, investigative journalists worked with a whistleblower in the social housing sector to highlight the high levels of racism within it. The British reporter Daniel Hewitt said:

It is undeniable [that] race remains a defining feature of Britain's housing crisis and there's very little to say that it's changing ... [The UK has] a government that wants to level up. It will not do that unless it tackles this.[5]

It is the lack of social homes and limited access to them that forces people to live in higher-priced private rented accommodation while earning the lowest incomes. The pandemic brought these inequalities to greater public attention, as disadvantaged communities faced disproportionately high death rates.[6] Gypsy, Roma and Traveller communities also face structural inequalities with a chronic lack of pitches, leading to overcrowding and insecure lifestyles, especially in England. Britain is clearly not as discriminatory as it was half a century ago, and campaigns such as Black History Month continue to highlight the positive impacts of a diverse society, but there remains much to do.

Brexit

The Brexit debate swallowed our country whole for years. Our international allies looked on in wonder and confusion as our once-stable society appeared to implode. As the rhetoric and emotions rose, there was one issue that bubbled under the surface, but was never fully articulated, while the megaphone voices and social media echo chambers steered the debate. Looking back, I wonder, *If there had been no poverty in Britain, would Brexit have happened?* Probably not. You don't need to 'take back control', as the slogan said, if your society already feels in control and on top of its game. If the population's needs are being met, wealth is distributed relatively evenly and there is no blame game towards certain groups, then change for change's sake is not required.

The political rhetoric at the time often portrayed people on benefits and low incomes as being lazy, and with social housing waiting lists at record levels, the debate raged just as austerity curtailed many people's ability to get the basics that they needed. In that situation, why not vote for change? If your current society doesn't work for you, and you're promised better – even without the details – it is an attractive prospect. However, the connection between poverty and Brexit has never really been said out loud. The Levelling Up agenda has sought to pay lip service to it, but a whole-hearted desire to end poverty in Britain has never been mentioned and the centralisation of power in the UK slows down the pace of positive change.

I saw Marvin Rees, the Mayor of Bristol, speak at an Inclusive Growth Conference in 2022 where he highlighted how difficult it was to get hold of money from central government. The allocation of funds was based on the best-written bid, rather than being afforded to areas that needed it the most. Bidding for money is a time-consuming and costly process for local governments. Rees said:

> Competitive funding is an absence of strategy. The costs associated with putting in bids are especially galling when they don't work. The hidden cost of austerity is that planning experts are not a priority compared to supporting social services, and yet, they are needed to access funding. Public money is an

enabler. The current bidding process creates a scramble and this creates uncertainty.

Local government needs to be a stable partner to attract business investment. Bristol did a deal with two foreign energy companies and gained an initial half a billion pounds of investment, but it took three years of work and £7 million to get that deal, and that money could have gone into social care, so it was a huge risk.

Rees also discussed the need for 'place leadership' where decision making and money is better devolved to local leaders. However, he did qualify this:

> Devolving doesn't mean an absence of national government. They can't just dump all the responsibility onto local leaders; it needs to be properly funded. Instead, they should work in conjunction with local government, rather than civil servants in London making centralised decisions about what's best for Carlisle.

Rees suggested the need for an evidence-based approach to better understand how the country works and for the creation of financial mechanisms that would give local governments easier access to private-sector money.

Brexit remains a highly sensitive subject in Britain. People do not want to be proved wrong. However, it should also be acknowledged that inequality makes people vulnerable to alternative options. Should Britain ever try to return to the European Union, a country without poverty would be an attractive member to the group and would be socially and economically stronger. Our population would also be more able to access the opportunities that the EU affords, generating greater prosperity for both sides.

Immigration and Human Rights

The political attitude that has sought to keep migrants out of Britain entirely has created a subgroup of immigrants who have no access to public funds, and this includes homelessness assistance. This does not just involve individuals who are in the country on work, family or student visas, but can also cover situations of slavery and exploitation. While individuals in dangerous situations may be crying out for help, access to support can be limited and this perpetuates poverty and dangerous situations.

For a country that has had a serious lack of workers since Brexit and Covid-19, those who come to the UK as economic migrants (those who come here to work) must be organised sensibly, so that the basic functions of the country are met and in a compassionate and thoughtful way. Considering that many people will be filling low-income roles, there must be available and affordable social housing to support them, alongside the 1.4 million people who are already on the social housing waiting list.

The focus on hardened immigration policies and a desire for government ministers to appear 'tough on crime', combined with a pitiful attitude to the building of social homes, have exacerbated these problems. The Windrush Scandal, in which long standing British residents were unfairly removed from the country due to a Home Office blunder, is an example of the skewed attitudes in government leadership during the 2010s. Rather than focusing on truly important issues, like having a society that works for everyone and eliminating poverty, the government focused on headline-grabbing, unworkable policies and in doing so destroyed many people's lives.[7]

The fact that some politicians have threatened to end Britain's association with the Human Rights Act compounds and exacerbates the potential for discrimination in the country. Human rights enable populations and individuals to hold their governments and other actors to account for their actions. Poverty diminishes people's voice and power, and leaves them vulnerable to exploitation, but access to justice means that a country can stand firm on the values of equality and inclusion. Mhairi Black MP highlighted the danger of losing these safeguards in a speech to the House of Commons in 2022:

> This government literally want to get rid of the Human Rights Act and that begs the question, for whom do they think rights have gone too far? Do you know how scary it is to sit at home and wonder if it's you? Is it your rights that are up for grabs?[8]

Human rights are an essential element of a peaceful and secure society. They ensure a right to food, shelter and dignity. This, of course, is a problem for any government that has not truly attempted to deal with the lack of accommodation in their society. The inadequate provision of social homes and racism within the private sector are key issues that prevent Britain from thriving. There is no way to end poverty in the country without a detailed plan for housing, and discrimination will continue for as long as deprivation prevails.

Swimming and Health

My friend swims in the East End docks in the summer. The still, clear water is a welcome relief from the heat of his tower-block flat. He is not allowed to swim there. The area is peppered with 'danger' signs, but as a grown, middle-aged man he is willing to go slowly and take his chances. He does this because he says the public facilities in the area are dire. The open-water swimming club, which uses the docks legally, costs £15 per year to join and an eye-watering £8 per hour, and is closed when the water temperature drops below 15°C. The cheapest private members' club is well over £100 per month – a financial impossibility for many people in the area.

There is a public pool that the seven local primary schools use to teach the youngsters to swim. This is an excellent use of the facility, but once their lessons are scheduled in, it leaves only two hours each week-day available for adult use, one at midday and one in the evening.

The days of turning up with cash to go for a dip have long gone. Each session needs to be booked in advance, on a smartphone, in the app, and no walk-ins are allowed. This means that for a member of the public to go for a swim, they need much more than just a towel and a costume. They need a bank account with enough money each month to pay the membership fee, to be literate, have internet access, own a smartphone, be able to navigate apps and afford transport to the site, and only work hours that don't clash with the opening times, all the while assuming that the pool isn't full with other customers who managed to book in advance before you. It's exhausting and that's even before you put your goggles on!

Public facilities such as swimming pools are paid for by everyone but are not accessible to everyone. As discussed in Chapter 2, obesity and inflammation are serious and growing problems for our country, especially with an ageing population, and cooling the body through swimming can significantly ease these problems. An accessible pool isn't just important for the young population, or those with chronic ailments; a local pool can improve people's quality of life, make work possible and ease the pressure on the NHS.

Overcomplicated IT systems create unnecessary barriers and this should be acknowledged by politicians and the tech industry. Technology has its place, but having it everywhere does not help everyone, and that is not the public's fault. 'Digital by default' has gone a step too far and needs to be reined in, so that access to local services does not require a level of digital knowledge or expensive products that can exclude people who still have to pay for them through their taxes. Ending poverty is about much more than just putting money in people's bank accounts: it needs a holistic approach where social barriers are broken down and this is as relevant to food as it is to exercise.

Food

Mel was an unusually soft person. Her body had a large, gentle quality and her grey hair was tied back roughly with a scarf into a 1940s knot on the top of her head. Even the way she spoke was soft, as her full lips undulated carefully around her words when she spoke them, slowly and purposefully. She had few teeth and her poise spoke of a woman who had gained her wisdom from life experiences spanning many places and situations, not all of them good.

As I sat listening to her in an office above a huge food bank in London, fork-lift trucks went by below us, redistributing excess food to the city's poorest. In 2021, the food bank rescued and redistributed enough food for a staggering 30 million meals.[9] The scale of the operation was extraordinary. The immense logistical effort and humanitarian care that went into feeding families living in one of the wealthiest cities on earth was a stark reminder of the enormous task that dealing with hunger in our country has become.

I was taking part in a meeting of food bank groups across Tower Hamlets that were all focused on ending food poverty. It was the summer of 2022 and the daunting prospect of rising inflation, food costs and energy prices was only a few months away. Desperate to prepare for the oncoming tidal wave of need, representatives were there to learn lessons from joint working during the pandemic and share best practices. They spoke of the need for clearer information sharing, not just between the public and the support services, but between the professionals themselves. I found this nauseatingly familiar, having left the professional world seven years earlier to have my daughter – joint working had been a key aim back then. It felt like I had been in a time warp, where society had been eternally chasing its tail while I had been away. Why was joint working between organisations and the local council still being spoken of as something new? It was obviously vital and yet, in a world where we have more communication tools than ever before, it still seemed difficult for the right people to communication with each other.

I suggested a simple WhatsApp group to enable the food bank teams to speak to each other, but a groan echoed around the room. People were overloaded with chat and information sharing to the point that it had become difficult to know what was useful and what wasn't. The communication system just wasn't targeted or up-to-date enough to enable practical solutions to practical problems, such as where all the food banks were, when they were open and how to communicate this information to local users who didn't have the spare cash for bus journeys or internet access.

All the solutions required small amounts of organisational skill and money on the part of the local council, such as placing maps on community boards or having a real person to speak to on a helpline, rather than a website or automated phone line, but with budgets in perpetual free fall, this has become a big ask.

People in peril need human connection to make them feel less frightened of their circumstances. With the move to a digital age and the desire for artificial intelligence to fix many social problems, the basic need to speak to another human over the phone is often overlooked. However, those working at the food banks knew this connection was essential because they saw it every day. Food banks didn't have the staff or time to create maps of where the local services were, and yet this would prevent duplication of effort and holes in local services where nothing was provided. The local authority had finally cottoned on to this and had commissioned a pilot project. This seemed to me a more expensive method than just getting on with it, but at least the desire was there.

Due to the plethora of food banks in the borough, one charity had decided to close its doors and move to providing a holistic support service that would stop people needing food banks in the first place. The First Love Foundation offers rapid, trauma-informed, wrap-around support, welfare rights advice and advocacy to resolve an individual's crisis and help carve a path to sustainable living.[10] An important part of its work is ensuring that claimants are receiving all the government benefits that they are entitled to and questioning many unsafe decisions. One mother of three had recently been awarded £16,000 in back-paid benefits after the Department for Work and Pensions had wrongly processed her claim. In five days, she had gone from having to take food bank handouts, to receiving a life-changing amount of money. I can only imagine her relief when the news came through. Having no choices in life is humiliating and she would never have to feel that way again.

However, of all the stories that I heard at the meeting that day, one stood out. A local primary school had resorted to running its own food bank and it was supporting a third of all the families at the school. A mother of three who was fleeing domestic violence had recently asked for food for the children that night. As a mother of one, the stress, fear and guilt of her situation knotted my stomach. That her life had become so dangerous and urgent that there was nothing to put on the children's plates that evening was heartbreaking to hear. Financial problems make domestic violence and child abuse more likely and the number of children being taken into care continues to rise.

The past and the present have too much in common for my liking. I wonder how people 100 years from now will consider the meeting I attended. Will children in schools write essays on 'Life in early twenty-first century Britain' and be amazed to learn that the best way to deal with child hunger was to put food banks on school grounds? Britain has come a long way from the country we thought we would be living in. This situation cannot continue, and it does not require a catastrophe or revolution to deal with it.

The British actor and director Kathy Burke grew up in food poverty in the 1960s and 1970s. As a child, her system for dealing with hunger was painfully innocent and many children will no doubt feel the same way today:

> When I was a kid ... it was a day-to-day survival. I was obsessed with food ... I remember having this feeling that if I eat a lot now, I won't feel as hungry tomorrow.[11]

Crucially, Kathy never felt like 'scum' growing up poor. There wasn't the same shame associated with poverty that there is now as so many families were in the same situation that communities helped each other through. Today, people are more mobile and able to move about in search of work. This can provide opportunities to those with the money to travel and take risks, but for others the lack of work and community can be crushing:

> I think it's incredibly difficult to escape the poverty trap ... it's a lot harder now to be poor. There isn't work for everybody and there isn't help for everybody. Even trying to get help is really f****** hard work.[12]

My discussions with the food bank services show this continues to be the case. If the professionals find it hard to get help for others, what chance do people have on their own?

Kathy visited an innovative organisation called Recycling Lives in Preston. It specialises in recycling waste and provides a rehabilitation programme, accommodation and a guaranteed job for those homeless people who finish its residential programme. The company has expanded and is making a £200 million a year turnover with £2 million of this going to the charity. The chief executive of the charity, Alasdair Jackson, defended the company's position on making money with a workforce of vulnerable adults: 'There's nothing wrong with making money, if you make it in the right way and you treat people with respect and give people the opportunities – it's life changing.'[13] He is right; it does change people's lives and supports the circular economy. This type of industry is vital to Britain's future prosperity, and is significantly more sensible than sending our recycling abroad.

The immense charitable effort that keeps people going in our country is astounding, expensive and should be unnecessary. If we had a government capable of tackling poverty head-on and a population with enough understanding to see past the stereotypes and vote for an alternative future, things could be drastically different. Lord John Bird, founder of the *Big Issue* magazine, summed up the current situation and its ironies:

> We have a situation where 34% of all the money received by the Chancellor of the Exchequer is spent on and around poverty; when we spend 12% of our budget on education and yet we fail 30% of our children in school, who then become 70% of the prison population, who then become 50% of the people who use A&E as a drop-in place. When will the Government and the House [of Lords] get behind the idea that we need a different form of intervention in poverty in order to begin to dismantle it? We are pussyfooting around. We are not dismantling poverty in the way that it should be done. Let us be honest and accept that keeping people in poverty is incredibly expensive.[14]

The barriers that create and maintain inequality in Britain, whether access to food, racism in the housing sector, excessive technology or poverty premiums, are issues that must be considered in a poverty elimination strategy, if it is to be holistic enough to be truly effective. These obstacles show the depth and complexity of the problems that are embedded in our social system. The good news is that, because systems are created, they can also be changed. It is time for a change.

7

POVERTY, EMPLOYMENT AND CARING

Poverty looks grim to grown people; still more so to children.
Charlotte Brontë, British author (1816–55), in *Jane Eyre*

The restaurant closed at midnight. After an hour of tidying up, the manager called me over to discuss the night's takings. I felt sticky as I sat down and could feel how the thick cigarette smoke that lingered in the air had settled on my skin. After a seven-hour shift on £3.10 an hour (minimum wage in the early 2000s), I put my tips on to the table and he counted them up. He took 10 per cent to 'cover the minimum wage', as he put it, and I got to keep the rest. I was tired, angry and completely unable to change the situation. Low wages make people vulnerable; they are vulnerable with the job and vulnerable without it.

In-work poverty is miserable, and people speak of existing rather than living. Since then, the benefit system has changed and Universal Credit is used to top up people's low wages and 'encourage' work, but this also means that the taxpayer props up businesses that pay their staff poorly. Along with a five-week delay for the first payment, which pushes many people into debt, UC also has an unusual system of a high tax rate for those coming off it, so the harder people work and the more money they earn, the less extra cash they can keep. This was highlighted most clearly by the 2020 bonus that was afforded to workers at the bakery chain Greggs. The bakery announced that all of its workers would receive a £300 bonus, but it quickly became clear that, for many staff who were on Universal Credit, the government would take the majority of it and leave them with just £75.[1]

This type of structure disproportionately affects lower-paid staff and is important as the rise of in-work poverty has become a significant feature of the British economy. Over the last fifteen years, all regions of England and Scotland have seen increases in the poverty rates of working-age adults who live in a home where someone works. As of 2020, 68 per cent of working-age adults were in poverty while in a household where at least one adult was employed. Part-time worker poverty rates were more than double the rates of full-time workers. All of this suggests that work is becoming less effective at lifting people out of poverty. The cost-of-living rises in the early 2020s were at their highest level in history and will continue to make this situation untenable as each pound spent buys less and less.

The Joseph Rowntree Foundation's report *UK Poverty 2022* highlighted numerous concerns for the coming years, including:

In terms of … future poverty levels, it seems clear that out-of-work families will fare worse than low-income families in work … it is worth stating that many of the out-of-work families at risk of being left behind are not expected to work due to their disability or caring responsibilities, factors in themselves increasing the likelihood of poverty.

The disparity within the UK was also of concern – the report highlights how the social safety net has become heavily dependent on where in the country each person lives:

The benefit systems in Scotland and Northern Ireland are increasingly different from each other and from the rest of the UK, with mitigations against some of the most poverty-increasing welfare reforms of the last decade … it is noteworthy that these are the two countries with the lowest poverty rates in the United Kingdom, at 18% for Northern Ireland and 19% for Scotland compared with 22% for England and 23% for Wales.[2]

The benefit system has some flawed policies that create and maintain the poverty trap, so this would be an obvious area of focus. It appears unlikely that the poverty levels in Britain during the early part of the 2020s will reduce. As people struggle to afford the basics and cut back on essentials due to rising prices, the benefit system must keep in line with inflation. While eliminating poverty cannot entirely be done through the benefit system, it clearly has a key role to play in alleviating poverty, while a plan for ending it is implemented. (For a list of the difference between essential and basic needs, see Appendix 4.)

The Best Job for You

There are other innovative ways that government departments could help individuals move into employment. Too often, job hunters apply for roles that they are unsuitable for, based on the need to complete enough job applications to gain the following week's Jobseeker's Allowance. An alternative method is for applicants to know which jobs suit their personality before they start applying, thereby not wasting any time.

StrengthsFinder questionnaires could be available for free at employment centres or libraries to give jobseekers information on their five personal strengths and how they could best deploy them when looking for work.[3] The test has no right or wrong answers, but it provides everyone with tailored information on the best role for them and this can help people gain direction in their lives. It promotes positive psychology by focusing on happiness, strength, personal potential and satisfaction.

Job hunting can be a demoralising process, especially in areas of high unemployment, such as the north-east of England. The questionnaire could be piloted in areas like this and used to support people who have been out of work for some time as a way of alleviating the anxiety and insecurity that can come with long-term unemployment. Extra information about an individual's personal strengths can increase the chances of success. The English actor

James Corden once said, 'There's an inner steel that comes from knowing you're good at something.'[4]

The boost in confidence and direction that a StrengthsFinder questionnaire might give jobseekers could be helpful in removing other obstacles to better-paid work. Researchers at the Joseph Rowntree Foundation found that in Scotland three out of ten households had tried to increase their income through work, but that their place in the social hierarchy affected their options. For the top-income households, people were more likely to ask for higher pay or a promotion, whereas those on lower incomes were more likely to ask for more hours or apply for a second job. This disparity in opportunity highlights the precarious nature of low-income work, where a lack of employment security and empowerment within the workplace prevents employees from asking for higher wages. It is unsurprising that trade union membership rates in the private sector are rising, as this is often the only way for employees to ask for a greater slice of the profits, especially where shareholders' dividends are prioritised over wage increases.[5]

For many people re-entering the workplace after a long absence, for reasons such as illness, parenthood, redundancy or a lack of qualifications/skills, it can be a daunting task and this should not be underestimated. New methods that support people back into the workplace should be trialled, rather than continuing the more basic approach of benefit sanctions, which has created significant financial problems for people already in difficulty, and which perpetuates the myth of the undeserving poor.

Britons, and especially women, are socially conditioned to hide their strengths for fear of appearing too egotistical, so knowing what you are good at can be difficult. If the economy is to grow and employment used as a way of taking people out of poverty, each individual must be free to put their strengths to good use. However, this is not always possible if recruitment bias stands in their way.

Marsha Powell, the CEO of BelEve, spoke to me about her feelings on racism and recruitment bias, and how they hold back people with ethnic minority backgrounds:

I used to be an HR Business Partner, so I know how common recruitment bias is. People often don't know they're doing it, especially when recruiting someone who looks and talks like them, or when deciding which bonus should be given to whom. I've been in meetings where I've asked managers to properly justify their decisions and some have just ended up stuttering at me.

Greater transparency on salary negotiations would help, as privacy enables and protects injustices. Some jobs could also have an absolute salary attached to them rather than a pay range, or we could take the Finnish approach and have total transparency, so everyone knows what everyone else is getting paid. It would be a huge cultural shift, but it would break protectionism.

There are also issues around the tests created for graduate schemes. People from ethnic minorities tend to take longer to make decisions because they are more cautious of making mistakes. This is because there are often greater implications for someone from a minority background who makes a mistake, than for someone who is white.

Training to prevent recruitment bias and promote equal opportunities is increasingly used in Britain to reduce discrimination. However, it is not always given the attention it deserves. In 2020, all Members of Parliament were offered free unconscious bias training (as has been undertaken by the parliamentary staff for many years), but some Conservative MPs refused to attend. The training was not compulsory and some felt it was against their working principles as representatives of the people. Sadly, these MPs were ignoring the part of their role involved in leading by example and were signalling to other organisations that tackling racism and unconscious bias was not essential.[6] It is a priority for the country, not just because it is morally important, but because without it we will all face discrimination at some point in our lives, either from genetic illnesses or disease, or as we move into older age and become more physically vulnerable.

Poverty and Disabilities

After a few moments of talking to Debbie Brixey, you know she is someone who has her feet firmly on the floor. With her pink, spiky hair and no-nonsense approach, she can appear slightly intimidating, and yet her deep compassion for others and her immense life experience (of which she remembers almost everything, whether she wants to or not) means that to sit and listen to her is an education in itself. As an IT trainer for people with disabilities (either lifelong or newly acquired), she does vital work helping people into employment or to continue their role when life has changed unexpectedly. This maintains employees' dignity, liberty and financial independence. In a digital age, easy access to online shopping, banking and employment significantly improves the lives of people with extra needs and can give them a far better quality of life than was the case for previous generations.

Debbie trains people in their workplaces and hears many stories of how people have been treated, both the good and the bad. Some employers have made huge changes to keep their staff employed by putting in new lifts to improve access and providing new technologies to enable people to keep working. Some of the costs can be quite low – only a few hundred pounds – and this is easily returned to the business through low staff turnover and high morale.

However, other employers can be less forthcoming. Many assume that they will need to pay vast amounts for the adjustments and so don't bother to find out what support is available, even when government grants will often cover the expense. If an individual is nearing retirement age, then they can be faced with the insulting suggestion of taking early retirement, rather than being seen as a valued employee and helped to stay in work.

Assumptions are also sometimes made once an individual has the extra tech they need. Employers often assume that staff can do their work faster and hence increase their workload. This lack of understanding can be grinding, as it overestimates what an individual is capable of doing with their condition. An unsupportive boss can also prevent promotions and affect a person's mental health, increasing the amount of sick leave taken, all of which edges them closer to leaving the workforce, moving on to benefits and into poverty.

For those who do manage to work from home, a lack of proper support can also be a hindrance. Debbie said:

> My friend is a psychotherapist and has cerebral palsy. She can work from home, but needs help to do the basics around the house. She can't work evenings as her carers put her to bed at 6 p.m. at night. A grown woman! If they didn't come in, then she would have to sleep in her chair.
>
> She earns good money, so the problem isn't an inability to work. It's the logistics, especially extended travel times which can lead to much longer working days for the same amount of money. This makes working extra difficult, and if people aren't properly supported, then gradually they can't face the commute and move out of the workforce.

I wondered what other barriers people face when trying to work with a disability. Debbie said that there are three main predicaments:

> Some people will do whatever they are given, irrespective of whether they want to do it, but that is hard because everyone wants to do a fulfilling job. Historically, blind people were only trained as typists on the assumption that it was all they could do.
>
> Some people take jobs, but have a poor experience filled with discrimination and decide not to continue. Or people can't get an interview in the first place and after filling out hundreds of applications they give up trying to get into the workforce.
>
> This means that when people do get a role, they rarely give it up, so there is very little churn, which should be a good reason to keep people happy, but so much of this is about employers' assumptions and a lack of experience of working with those living with disabilities. Part of the citizenship programme should involve learning what life is like with a disability, as young people are employers of the future. If we truly understood the barriers people face, then we might all be a bit kinder to each other.

AI has played an important role in helping people live more independent lives. Voice-activated technology like Alexa and Siri can help people with mobility issues use lights and electrical equipment without the extra movement required. Self-drive cars will also help (assuming they are accessible) and will reduce dependency on public transport and mobility buses, which often have unhelpful timetables. Some tablets now respond to mouth or blinking stimuli, but training is essential, so having properly qualified teachers is vital to improve self-confidence and employment opportunities. Logistics, discrimination from employers and financial problems can all hinder an employee's independence and ability to use their skills in the workplace. Indeed, we all lose out from the disappearing talent in the economy and low morale within organisations, as the entire staff know that they will not be supported properly if anything unexpected happens to them.

Caring

Tending to another person's needs is hard work. It often requires long hours, physical and emotional strength, and the patience to deal with often relentless demands, night and day. Those who cared for relatives at home in 2023 received £76.75 for a minimum of thirty-five hours a week.[7] This equates to a maximum of £2.19 an hour, as caring doesn't stop at 5 p.m. on a Friday. This is a fraction of the national living wage and a comment on how poorly the government values and understands the work of carers.

Caring for someone living with dementia can take a heavy toll on the carer's mental health. In the latter stages of the condition, the brain fails to recognise the difference between night and day. This can lead to sleep loss for the carer, which increases the onset of depression. The loss of personal independence and identity can also affect a carer's emotional health. The Alzheimer's Society's training package has shown that by professionalising the work, it can significantly reduce levels of depression in carers.[8]

A job with many complex facets should not be valued so poorly by society. While ending deprivation cannot be achieved through the benefit system alone, there is a strong argument that the role of a carer should be financed properly by the state. Yuval Noah Harari highlights this in his book, *21 Lessons for the 21st Century*. He envisages a society where AI could replace jobs in banking, transport and law, but he argues that there will be no shortage of work as the caring sector will expand, especially as the population ages.[9]

The caring work of a stay-at-home parent with children below school age should be acknowledged and supported by the government as well. It is perverse that a nursery worker can have their role classed as a career, but the role of stay-at-home parent is not valued in the same way. Providing financial support to stay-at-home parents could help reduce poverty for families with young children, while also reducing pressure on nurseries, which are often teetering on the brink of collapse because the cost of caring for children in a nursery can be more than the amount the government is prepared to pay. For those people who earn too much to qualify for nursery vouchers and must pay private fees, it is often cheaper to leave the workforce entirely and stay at home with the children (usually the mother).

In 2022, the Joseph Rowntree Foundation canvassed the views of over 4,000 people living in Scotland. Its report highlighted how the lack of adequate childcare forms a large part of the poverty trap:

It is not possible to speak to parents who are experiencing poverty and not discuss the subject of childcare. Childcare needs to urgently be more flexible, more accessible and more affordable.

Childcare should be a means for children to receive excellent nurture, play and learning. For some, it can be, but it is also acting as part of the poverty trap in Scotland due to cost and a lack of flexibility.[10]

The piecemeal nature of childcare provision means that it depends very much on where a person lives as to what they can access or afford, and this is not solely a problem for Scotland. A definitive solution has yet to be implemented by central government, and it will need to be found if a future government is to end poverty nationwide.

Currently, parents who return to work after a period at home will often find the time has inflicted a heavy toll on their returning income. Researchers at University College London focused on women who became mothers between 1995 and 2005, and found that the motherhood penalty for women's own earning is around 45 per cent less compared with how much they would have earned if they had remained childless.[11] These lost earnings can prevent stay-at-home parents from re-entering the workplace and can lead to financial dependence on their partners. This can increase the opportunity for domestic, emotional or financial abuse, especially in religious patriarchies, where women can be prevented from having their own bank account and stopped from controlling their own lives.

Keeping women in the workforce or valuing their newly acquired skills when they re-enter it is essential to maintaining balance within society and the economy. The best-performing FTSE100 companies are often those that have a good balance between men and women at the top of their organisations. Christine Lagarde, as head of the International Monetary Fund, wrote of the need for more women in the banking sector and how this had impacted the 2008 global financial crash:

> A key ingredient of reform would be more female leadership in finance. I say this for two reasons. First, greater diversity always sharpens thinking, reducing the potential for group think. Second, this diversity also leads to more prudence, and less of the reckless decision-making that provoked the crisis ... As I have said many times, if it had been Lehman Sisters rather than Lehman Brothers, the world might well look a lot different today.[12]

Lehman Brothers was an investment bank that collapsed during the crash and created a ripple effect across the financial sector, causing it to seize up. Writing on the tenth anniversary of the collapse of Lehman, Lagarde considered how far the changes had come:

> The bottom line is this: We have come a long way, but not far enough. The system is safer, but not safe enough. Growth has rebounded but is not shared enough ... We are now facing new, post-crisis, fault lines – from the potential rollback of financial

regulation, to the fall-out from excessive inequality, to protectionism and inward-looking policies, to rising global imbalances. How
we respond to these challenges will determine whether we have
fully internalized the lessons from Lehman. In this sense, the true
legacy of the crisis cannot be adequately assessed after ten years –
because it is still being written.[13]

Eighty per cent of British businesses are classified as 'small' and they
are often set up by parents trying to fit work around school hours.
Ensuring that stay-at-home parents' caring work is acknowledged,
valued and supported in the early years could help them create new
businesses and access job opportunities, rather than see their prospects shrinking (J.K. Rowling wrote her first Harry Potter book as
a single mother on government benefits).[14] Pre-school childcare,
whether provided by a nursery or by parents, should be properly
supported. A large number of nurseries have closed in recent years
as government subsidies have failed to keep up with inflation. This
means the wages of nursery workers are often below the national
living wage.[15]

The lack of funding from government has also had a significant
effect on private care providers used by local governments to provide
at-home care for vulnerable people. Home care workers give vital
support to millions of people, including those with physical disabilities, learning difficulties, chronic illnesses, or the elderly. Their
role can include the most intimate of tasks, such as helping people to
wash, get dressed, eat, take medication and go to the toilet. For some
people, their care workers are the only human contact they have all
day. The Bureau of Investigative Journalism researched this topic
in 2021. It found that, for some carers, up to a quarter of their take-
home pay is spent on petrol, and if they end appointments early to
allow for travel time, they have their pay cut as a result. A care home
director stated:

> The rate paid by councils made it impossible to offer a living wage.
> Councils across the North of England pay ... for each hour of care
> needed, but ... do not factor in travel time in between calls, nor the
> company's other costs of doing business.[16]

Renationalisation is a dangerous word for many in political circles, conjuring images of the 1970s union strikes, but the current situation is untenable and has been for decades. It may now be worth considering bringing the home care sector in-house as the most effective way of ensuring that staff are paid and treated properly, do not work on zero-hours contracts and are in receipt of sick and holiday pay.

The trade union UNISON has encouraged all councils to sign an Ethical Care Charter, which promises all commissioned care workers the real living wage. However, in 2021, out of forty-three councils who had signed the pledge, researchers at the Bureau of Investigative Journalism found home care worker adverts offering below the living wage in thirty-seven of them.[7]

An alternative option could be for care staff themselves to decide how many hours a day they are prepared to work, how many clients they take on and where the clients are, so they can visit people who live close to each other to reduce travel times. If care staff were in charge of their own schedules and pay, like self-employed people are, then they might have better control over the situation. The main problem will come if people are prepared to do the work for less money, as has been the situation under globalisation for decades, and if carers are undercut and unable to compete. Bringing the sector in-house is an easy way for local councils to ensure that carers are paid properly and treated well.

It is a dangerous and absurd situation that so many people are working in roles that do not facilitate a decent life. Employment rarely makes millionaires, but it should provide a stable and secure home, and a future for the country's children as well.

8

POVERTY AND EDUCATION

The ability to read, write and analyse; the confidence to stand up and demand justice and equality; the qualifications and connections to get your foot in that door and take your seat at that table – all of that starts with education.

Michelle Obama, former First Lady of the USA, and author[1]

Harry Leslie Smith grew up during the Great Depression in the 1930s and worked part time from the age of 7 because his family were destitute. While child labour has been abolished in the intervening period, some of his experiences remain close to those of many teachers and children in Britain today:

No matter how hard I worked at my part-time job, there hadn't been enough to afford a pair of shoes ... I was reduced to trying to patch my old ones with newspaper and cardboard but, when the bottoms fell apart, I stopped regularly attending school. I was ashamed and humiliated and didn't want to listen to the taunts from other students who had more resources but less humanity ...

My maths teacher noticed my absence and ... one day when I did turn up, he asked me to stay after class ... He presented me with a new pair of shoes. This teacher didn't want a fuss made over something that he thought should be second nature to any civilised person, but his act of kindness allowed me to continue my schooling and leave school at fourteen with my certificate.[2]

How is it possible that a situation during the Depression could have any similarity to the education system 100 years later? Yet, there is accumulating evidence from teachers across the country that they are using their own money to support children and families, from providing the basics of food, clothing and mattresses, to paying funerals costs where children have died unexpectedly.[3]

Period poverty is well known for keeping girls away from school, in the same way that a lack of shoes did for Harry. The Red Box project was set up to help solve the problem by providing sanitary products in girls' toilets. In 2020, the government rolled out a new scheme to provide period products to all state-maintained schools and colleges. Estimates suggest that around 137,000 girls were missing school each year because of a lack of access to sanitary products. In some schools, providing them increased attendance levels by nearly a third.[4] This hidden problem ended with positive government action, but it also highlighted the fact that, if there were no deprivation, these kinds of provisions would not be needed and the Department for Education's budget could focus more on school equipment than on the very basics of what girls need.

Working for Free

Grandad looked at me through the eyes of someone who was increasingly baffled by the world. 'They're going to pay someone, so they can work ... for them... for free?' I couldn't help but smile at his clear-minded logic. The year was 1998, I was 18 and many of the teenagers from my school were organising their gap years before going on to university. Companies were advertising placements abroad in developing countries to the tune of thousands of pounds per person. The lure of new life experiences, content for the CV and a better chance of a good job in the future meant that many families were prepared to pay for the placements on offer.

My grandfather's work experience had been forged on the East End docks. He had worked there from the age of 14 until the Second World War arrived, when he drove petrol tankers in support of the advancing army lines. His family had been bombed out of their home three times during the Blitz, so working for free was an absurd notion to him.

Today, young people seeking well-paid jobs often need a CV filled with unpaid work experience, especially if they want to enter the journalism, acting or charity sectors. These industries are dominated by the middle classes, as free work is not an option for many people from struggling families. To help, placements are arranged by some secondary schools. My friend who organises internships spoke to me of her despair at the number of teenagers who were returned to class, having been dismissed for refusing to complete the tasks that their employers had set for them.

'They're so entitled!' she said indignantly.

I pondered this for a moment. *Perhaps some are entitled*, I thought, *but how many simply don't want to work for free?*

There is an obvious value in sitting in a class and learning, but where is the true value in forcing a child from a poor background to sweep floors and empty bins in a hair salon, unpaid for a week, if they then have to return to a cold home with no proper food? Are they 'entitled' or are they traumatised by the stress of privation and feel overwhelmed, afraid and angry instead? The shame of poverty can bind people's lips, so if children are unable to articulate how they feel, then the label of 'entitled' can be placed upon a young person without properly understanding their emotional or practical situation.

The ability to articulate what does and does not work for a person requires many years of nurture and practice, and the earlier it begins, the better. BelEve is a charity in South London that provides mentoring and support to girls and young women to help them navigate some of life's major transitions, such as the move to secondary school, self-care, toxic relationships, leadership and career options. This type of emotional education and self-reflection offers a resource to help young people better handle life's challenges when they arise. It has the power to prevent difficult situations from spiralling, and reduces the need for support afterwards to pick up the pieces.

This charity is part of a growing trend in modern education concerning how best to equip young people with the skills they will need in their future lives. It is arguably much more valuable than the free employment 'opportunities' that children from poorer backgrounds are encouraged to fulfil. In interviews, employers look for articulate and self-aware people, and the type of mentoring that BelEve offers is an important way of helping young people from deprived backgrounds into higher-paying roles.

I asked Marsha Powell, its CEO, why she began the BEAM project (Beautiful, Empowered And Me), which is for 8-year-olds, and she explained that her daughter had been called disruptive by her after-school club teacher for talking too much. Marsha knew the history of suppressing Black, female voices and decided to create a loving and supportive space where Black girls could become used to hearing themselves speak publicly and learn how to use their voices to best effect. Since then, the charity has supported over 9,000 young people and it has plans to continue to help many more in the coming years.

I asked if the girls ever spoke about money or how they felt about living in such an unequal society. She said:

> They don't talk about money because for the girls that we work with, poverty is the norm. All their friends are in the same situation. The norm for them is not having three meals a day, so they don't expect it. We run holiday clubs where we give them fruit and most of them have never eaten exotic fruits.
>
> There's a school in Deptford [in South London] where you can see Canary Wharf and yet, even with free travel, many have never gone to visit it. They just don't know why they would go there and assume that it's not for someone like them. That is why we focus on boosting their self-esteem, so that when opportunities do arise, they have the self-confidence to take them.
>
> It is really important that youngsters in poverty can articulate themselves. Imposter syndrome is a huge barrier. I've been into homes where they don't even have a dining room table, they eat dinner on their laps on the sofa, watching TV. Without a table, they can't learn how to have a proper conversation, expand their vocabulary, grow mentally and learn about the society they live in.

Marsha's background as an HR business partner in finance makes her well placed to know what employers need from school-leavers.

I wondered what she would want to hear from a government intent on ending inequality:

> The education system needs to change. There is too big a dispar-
> ity between school lessons and the core competencies that young
> people need in job interviews. It would help if there was more
> funding for collaboration with grass-roots charities, as this would
> engage more youngsters, rather than imposing rigid policies onto
> schools. Policies need to be co-created with young people. Schools
> have a duty to provide diverse learning which provides kids with
> the basic skills to make informed decisions, rather than a total
> focus on grades.
>
> The best qualification to get nowadays is an Apprenticeship
> Degree. It is the best qualification out there. It provides a degree,
> help with tuition fees, a paid job during the holidays and a guar-
> anteed job at the end of it. The more companies that can provide
> these, the better it will be for young people trying to get out of
> poverty. We need this type of commitment from businesses all
> over the country and especially from those who earn billions of
> pounds in profits. They need to give back to the community.

The combination of free work experience for young people from wealthy families, alongside a school system that does not provide a broad enough education to enable access to the wealthier roles in society, and parental inability to buy the basics for their homes, are all barriers to social mobility. These obstacles are not insurmount-able, but they need to be realised and understood by politicians and policy-makers, many of whom will have been on expensive gap years and free job placements themselves.

The Cost of the School Day

Today, a teacher must switch skilfully between educator, therapist and social worker, while permanently walking the fine line where too much support could be viewed as grooming, despite the innocu-ous intentions of those involved. Some schools provide free food in the playgrounds for parents to take what they need, while others try to support children who are hungry, but too embarrassed to ask for help. Teachers must be on the lookout for children who are borrowing money from friends to buy food, falling asleep in class or moaning with tummy ache because they couldn't have breakfast. They can spend hundreds of pounds of their own money each year providing the basics for children in their classroom.[5]

In 2019, Public Health Scotland and the Child Poverty Action Group published a report: *The Cost of the School Day*. They worked with a variety of teachers, parents and experts to determine the practical things that schools could do to reduce the financial pressures on students. The Cost of the School Day Toolkit follows a five-step process to help each school identify the barriers that costs create and how to tackle them. The report highlights:

> Uniforms, trips, school lunches, gym kits, pencils and pens, and dress down days can be difficult to afford for low-income families. When children and young people can't take part in opportunities because of cost, they miss out and feel excluded, and it is harder for them to learn, achieve and be happy at school.

The process requires a whole-school conversation and involves extra work to understand and mitigate the effects of poverty on the school community. It encourages the sharing of ideas and good practice from schools across England, Scotland and Wales.[6]

In Northern Ireland, the Commissioner for Children and Young People (NICCY) highlights the significant divide between students. Their report in 2016–17 found that the average spend per child on schooling by families was around £1,222, and this rose to £1,900 in grammar schools. These are huge sums for parents on low incomes and create considerable problems:

> For many children, access to critical educational opportunities and key entitlements are based on their parents' ability to pay. There is an increasing disparity between schools not only in terms of what provision is offered, but also how much it costs to access this provision, and this is increasing inequality.[7]

The NICCY also highlights that the practice of charging school fees and requesting voluntary contributions are discriminatory against those who do not have the means to pay, and it should end immediately. It also suggests that a larger proportion of the education budget should be allocated to schools, so they are not dependent on parents to provide funding. In 2017, spending on pre-school, primary and secondary education in England was 18 per cent higher than in Northern Ireland; in Wales it was 31 per cent higher and in Scotland it was 46 per cent higher. However, subsidiary services to education, such as home-to-school transport, school meals and pupil support, were significantly higher in Northern Ireland compared with the rest of the country.

In 2022, the NICCY again called for transformational reform, urging a move towards a single education system that can address the segregation and inequalities that have arisen from academic selection. From an early age, around 90 per cent of children in Northern Ireland attend schools that are largely segregated along religious/ethnic lines.[8]

School places based on tests like the 11-plus are seen as one of the most significant factors in persistent educational underachievement. This has created a school system that supports children from more affluent families and reinforces the social divide. The NICCY stated, 'This is evidenced by the fact that 37% of children in non-grammar schools and only 14% of children in grammar schools are entitled to free school meals.'

Selection has exacerbated issues, as many parents who can afford it will pay for their children to receive extra tuition for the tests outside of school hours. This pushes lower-achieving pupils into a small number of schools and the density of disadvantage further aggravates the social divide. Feedback from young people also reinforces the sentiment that there is not enough funding on education initiatives in certain communities and so students in these areas experience lower educational outcomes than others.[9]

Data from the NICCY states that 77 per cent of the difference in performance between schools can be explained by the difference in the socio-economic background of pupils.[10] Academic selection clearly acts as an instrument that allows issues like poverty to dictate the opportunities available to children. Any system that creates and maintains inequality should be a key priority for central, devolved and local governments working to eliminate poverty.

The statistics also highlight the flawed nature of school league tables, which are published annually across Britain. These focus exclusively on academic achievement and do not consider the background of the students. They also cannot highlight the extraordinary ability of those schools that do provide the type of education capable of nurturing children from deprived backgrounds to high achievements. Furthermore, league tables do not give a rounded picture of everything that happens in each school and can shame those that face the most challenging circumstances. They can also form a barrier to sharing best practices from the genuinely top schools, such as the Mayflower primary school in East London, which has a high number of children on free school meals, but also uses evidence-based methods to help children achieve consistently high results. Inequality divides communities across school lines and this is not helpful for anyone.

•••

'Well, you are the white one,' she said quietly, not wanting to offend. It was the first time anyone had ever commented on the colour of my skin. It felt bizarre to me, but for her it was a statement of fact as I was one of the few white parents in my daughter's class. I had suggested a playdate at our house where the girls could play in the garden, but she turned it down. Unable to reciprocate, she explained that she was living in a single room with her husband and two children in his parents' flat, and they were waiting for a social home, so she couldn't invite anyone over. The longer she talked, the more she physically curled inwards, so her head hung low enough to prevent eye contact. She didn't want our unequal situation to be shone brightly into her daughter's face and have to deal with awkward questions on the way home. I understood, and she was by no means the only person who didn't want to face that situation. At the end of the year we moved schools and the segregation gap widened a little further.

When politicians talk about integration in our country, it is often couched in terms of language, clothes, religion or values, but we rarely speak about how the money divide creates barriers to even the simple things, like a playdate. The mesh of interlocking issues that are affected by inequality is immense. This was a small example, but one that may be replayed hundreds of times across the country. Each failure to connect between communities is a lost opportunity for shared understanding and perspectives. This doesn't strengthen our society, it weakens it, and for our future to be bright, it needs to change.

The Important Early Years

One of the major challenges for the education system is the experiences that children receive in the first few years of life, before they begin Year 1. Those children with relatively affluent parents are more likely to be exposed to extra conversations and more nurturing experiences, such as baby massage, museums and children's centres. If home life is poor, chaotic, busy and stressed, the children are less likely to develop language skills and can arrive at school with monosyllabic English and a severe lack of words. The education system is then expected to raise all children up to the same level of academic achievement, with all of them sitting in the same space. Mixed-ability classes can teach advanced children patience and interpersonal skills as they help struggling classmates, but the pressure on staff is intense.

The Pupil Premium is designed to provide extra support to the less privileged children in school and this can provide better resources for all students in the class. However, there is a clear link between poor attendance and difficulty in learning maths, as the child has to acquire knowledge step by step in order to progress. Teaching becomes more difficult if children miss school, and for households in poverty where both parents are out of work, there can be less urgency to ensure their child attends regularly.

Rebecca Abrahams is an executive head teacher in Tower Hamlets. When I asked her what she would like from a government that chose to focus on poverty (beyond the obvious end to budget cuts), three core issues came through clearly:

The first would be a reduction in class sizes. Mixed-ability teaching can be great when done well, but it is extremely challenging.

The second would be a Reader Recovery Programme, which involves one-to-one tuition and requires specialist training for the teachers. It can be extremely effective, but it is also expensive. One teacher over a year may move only 10–13 children up to the standard needed for their year group. The National Tutoring Programme which was set up to deal with the impact of Covid-19 has extremely high expectations, but has not been funded properly.

The third would be Nurture Groups for early years.[11]

In 2020, researchers at Queen's University Belfast analysed the effectiveness of using nurture groups to support children in Northern Ireland. The approach is a short-term intervention targeted at individual children beginning school who are already displaying social, emotional and/or behavioural difficulties, such as internalising problems, or displaying phobias or aggression.[12] These difficulties can be an understandable response to poor emotional bonds with their main carers that emanate from a difficult home life, including familial neglect, abuse, violence, family separation/death, inconsistent parenting, racism, poverty and social exclusion/marginalisation.

For children in care, these psychological issues are exacerbated by experiences of poor attachment in the pre-care home and difficulties forming strong bonds while in care. Without feelings of security, a child will struggle to soothe themselves, regulate their emotions and form relationships. Their self-esteem and confidence can also be harmed by not believing themselves to be worthy of attention or love, and not believing others to be trustworthy and dependable. These issues are then amplified in the classroom when a child lacks the basic skills needed to learn.

Nurture groups were first developed by Marjorie Boxall in the 1960s as a response to high levels of early childhood psychosocial disorders. The system sets out to provide a safe, welcoming and caring environment for a small group of children (ten to twelve maximum) for a certain period each day and for a limited length of time over the course of one school year to provide opportunities for social learning, emotional literacy and raising self-esteem.[13]

However, it is not just in children that unhelpful behaviours have arisen in response to inequality. The focus on school statistics can create unhealthy policies from senior leadership teams as well. Some schools without academic selection have found alternative ways to sway the types of families who apply to their school. Prohibitively expensive school uniforms have been used to such an extent that the government had to ban these types of policies. Educators understand that children from poorer backgrounds can bring with them extra difficulties, and some schools are disinclined to deal with them. It is encouraging that the government has issued statutory guidance on this issue, but it remains one of many problems that promotes division and inequality within the British education system, and these will need to be faced if poverty is to be successfully prevented.[14]

PART TWO

OUR MONEY

9

THE GREEN AGENDA

Humanity's twenty-first-century challenge is clear: to meet the needs of all people within the means of this extraordinary, unique, living planet so that we and the rest of nature can thrive.

Kate Raworth, Oxford economist, 2018[1]

November 2021

Glasgow is heaving with diplomats from around the world. All are desperate to negotiate a deal to reduce global climate emissions without damaging their government's credibility and plans. Outside the conference centre, demonstrators noisily keep up the pressure on politicians to act, and the press avidly awaits the latest news. The impact of global warming feels closer than ever. Over the past twelve months, there have been deadly floods in Germany, vast wildfires in Australia and snow in Texas (to name just a few incidents).

The Chinese and Russian governments have failed to attend in person and India has promised to reach net zero by 2070, twenty years after the UN's main target. The climate is 1.1°C warmer than its pre-industrial temperatures, and if emissions are not curbed then it will reach 2.7°C warmer by 2100.

A look down the list of topics under discussion at the climate change conference (COP26) reveals the immense desire for innovation and change. Yet, plans to incorporate inequality elimination into the strategy are not obviously on the agenda.[2] One part of the conference focuses on education and young people: Action for Climate Empowerment. It wants everyone to understand and participate in the transition to a low-emission, climate-resilient world:

> Sustainable lifestyles, sustainable patterns of consumption and production, are fundamental to reducing greenhouse emissions and enhancing resilience to the inevitable effects of climate change. Success will require broad collaboration between all levels of government and all sectors of society.[3]

While undoubtedly true, the statement fails to acknowledge that, for people in developed nations who have serious financial problems, global warming is not necessarily their primary concern. In the UK, gas is cheaper than renewable electricity, organic food is more expensive than regular food, many cheaper products use more plastic, and imported goods can be cheaper than similar ones made at home. To suggest that everyone in society is equally responsible to behave in a more environmentally friendly way is to dismiss reality for millions of people who are living on or below the poverty line. If climate change is to be dealt with effectively, then we must also deal with deprivation. This is well understood internationally, but it has yet to be discussed domestically in the same way.

A question I have been asked many times while writing this book is: what would it feel like to live in a Britain without poverty? The obvious places to look for clues are the Scandinavian countries, where a good quality of life is valued beyond all else. However, Britain is different in one important way – we do not want to pay higher taxes, and certainly not at the levels that our neighbours do, so there is no blueprint. Fortunately, as our history has shown through the invention of the London Underground, the steam engine and the internet, Britons are quite happy to be the first to try something new and learn the lessons afterwards.

In 1946, George Orwell predicted that if we did manage to create a stable and prosperous society, we would go on to enjoy lives that were more focused on nature, rather than material goods. As the move towards decluttering our homes and promoting biodiversity continues, his predictions appear to be apt for our modern era:

I have always suspected that if our economic and political problems are ever really solved, life will become simpler instead of
more complex ... I think that by retaining one's childhood love
of such things as trees, fishes, butterflies and ... toads, one makes
a peaceful and decent future a little more probable, and that by
preaching the doctrine that nothing is to be admired except steel
and concrete, one merely makes it a little surer that human beings
will have no outlet for their surplus energy except hatred and
leader-worship.[4]

While Orwell was writing in the aftermath of the Second World
War, the hatred seen on social media today and the leader-worship
of social influencers, celebrities and politicians like Donald Trump
show that humanity has not evolved far enough. Twenty-four-hour
news cycles and endless scrolling on smartphones can make us feel
like life will continue to be a frenzy of new innovations and excess
information forever more.

However, in a refreshing contrast to this view, Oxford University
professor Danny Dorling has detailed how, in many ways, our society has been slowing down since the 1970s. In his book *Slowdown:
The End of the Great Acceleration – and Why It's a Good Thing*, he
discusses how the deceleration is already upon us and how we are
either poorly prepared for it, or utterly blind to it.

Today the shock is not change. The shock is when the change stops.
When the cranes are taken down, and we are building mostly to
repair and renew what we first built a long time ago ... just as we
find it hard to understand change, so too will we find it hard to
understand a state of very little change – until it becomes normal.

He suggests that we may also struggle to accept this as a positive:
'Optimism tends to be viewed as naïve, so we prefer to postulate
dystopia.'[5]

Dorling's final point here is interesting. Most futuristic stories
and films usually feature a dystopian fantasy, where a façade of
perfection hides evil social norms underneath. It is no wonder that it
can be difficult to imagine what it would feel like to live in a country

without deprivation, as there is not enough drama in it to make a film worthwhile. Leading emotionally quieter lives, filled with less fear, anxiety and crime, and no hunger, could come with an explosion of art, culture, music and design. This may not be the excitement that film-lovers want to see, but it sounds like a wonderful place to live in reality. The Italian Renaissance era, which produced Leonardo da Vinci and Michaelangelo, could not have happened without wealthy families investing in art. This could happen again in Britain once deprivation ends, but on a broader scale as exceptional artists could come from any section of society and all would have the opportunity to shine.

Dorling argues that the last three generations have already lived through the greatest periods of technological change and that, since then, we have been slowly decelerating. He acknowledges that there is still change, but the pace of it is different now. The shift from having no phone, to a landline, to using a mobile phone, was an enormous leap forward. The phones from now on may change in shape and characteristics, but these original shifts in technology cannot be replicated, and teleportation will only ever be a fantasy: 'Within just one century we went from the horse being the fastest mode of transport to the jet plane. We cannot do such a leap ever again.'[6]

He also highlights that we should be pleased with these changes, compared to the alternative:

Today, the passing of the era of acceleration is something to be very thankful for. The alternative to slowing down – an ever-growing total human population, ever more divided societies, ever-greater consumption per head – would be a catastrophe. Without material economic growth, capitalism as we know it is transforming into something else, something far more stable.[7]

Dorling predicts a future with more women leaders running more equitable societies, the evolution of capitalism to a more stable state, and the decline of migration as population rates fall through better access to contraception, women's education and improved infant mortality rates, all of which reduce the need to have a large family.[8] Dorling's final prediction is quite comforting:

Great economic inequalities will be very hard to sustain during and following the slowdown. As things change less, it will become much more difficult to make money out of a shrinking and aging population who may also become savvier and harder to fool with the allure of the 'new' ... Slowdown means goods lasting longer; it means less waste ... Slowdown gives us time to reflect, and time to change what really matters. It gives us time itself.[9]

Dorling's vision of our future concurs neatly with a new economic model that is being taken increasingly seriously by leaders across the world. In 2012, British economist Kate Raworth developed Doughnut Economics, a new model for the creation of a thriving – but not necessarily growing – economy. Raworth argues that perpetual economic growth, measured by gross domestic product (GDP), cannot continue to be the main benchmark by which societies and economies progress. GDP is a measure of the size and health of a country's economy over a period of time, normally a year or a quarter (three months). It is possible to argue that GDP-led economies have, in part, created the current situation of climate breakdown through unsustainable economic systems.

Raworth's Doughnut offers a more modern and balanced view of the future. It can be used as a way of measuring a country's overall performance in relation to the needs of humanity and the environment. The Doughnut shows where we would wish to be, where the needs of the planet and humanity are in balance between the foundation of basic human needs, and the upper limits of what our environment can maintain.

Raworth explains that the hole in the middle is where people are struggling to maintain the essentials of life. The aim is to move everyone inside the doughnut while not overshooting the outer circle – the ecological ceiling. The diagram can be used as an indicator dashboard to show current progress on environmental and social issues. Raworth argues against growth for growth's sake and calls for economies to be redesigned. She explains what we really need: 'No longer an ever-rising line of growth, but a sweet spot for humanity, thriving in dynamic balance between the foundation and the ceiling.'[10]

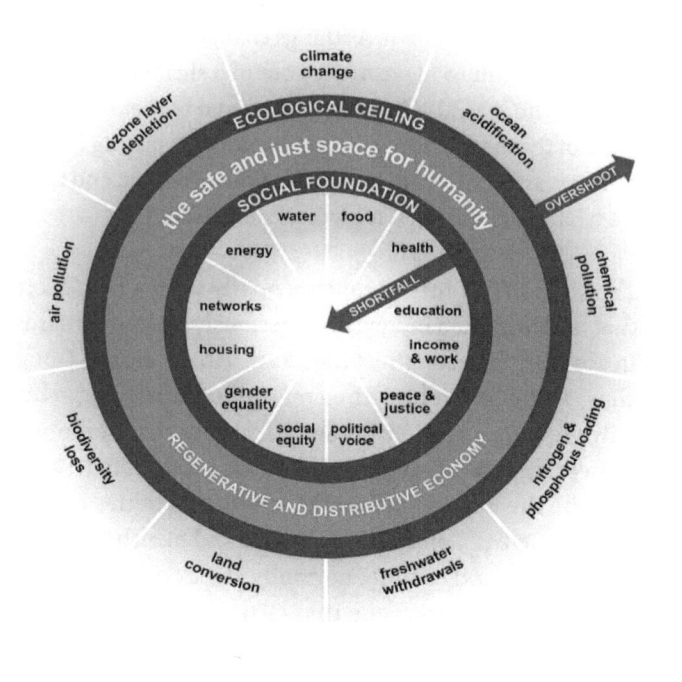

The Doughnut model has spread around the world. While it is not yet a global phenomenon that G20 leaders are prepared to embrace, it is being used on a smaller scale in regions, cities and towns for local leaders to understand their area more clearly. Amsterdam has put the Doughnut at the heart of its policymaking and aims to create a fully circular economy. This has drawn interest from other city leaders, including in Copenhagen, Glasgow, Nanaimo and Brussels.[11] Raworth argues for more developed thinking, which challenges old economic assumptions when the issues we face are unique to modern human history: 'We need ideas of our own because we are the first generation to see this, and probably the last with a real chance of turning this story around.'[12]

I am not an economist, but after hearing Raworth's rationale and after living through the 2008 global financial crash, austerity and the pandemic, it seems obvious that the old economic theories will not fit our future world, and yet they are stubbornly held on to by politicians and international organisations. It is true that we have never before faced this combination of economic and environmental instability, so new ideas are inevitably needed. How long it takes to use them, however, is another question.

There is an old joke that states that if you put ten economists in a room, you'll get eleven opinions, such is the complexity of the topic. Their job involves examining a huge range of moving parts and trying to make sense of them all. Many say the answer is essentially an educated guess because macroeconomics (understanding how global and national economies work) is too complex a discipline to be understood completely. This makes Raworth's model even more attractive as economic policy decisions are often in the hands of politicians, so a simple diagram that explains to them and the public the rates of progress over different areas is a helpful tool for communication and action.

I have been asked what would happen to the fabled British productivity rate if deprivation ended. My educated guess is that productivity would rise significantly and, in so doing, grow the economy – whether that is something we actually care about or not. Poverty is humiliating, exhausting and leaves people will little energy to go the extra mile at work, pay for new qualifications, or think deeply about new business ideas and innovation. Poverty gives no space for manoeuvre or mistakes and this inhibits the freedom to take risks, start a new business, create a new product (which may take years to bring to market) or even move to a new area to get a different job. All of this constrains and depresses our economic potential.

France and Germany have traditionally been similar-sized economies to Britain and yet both are significantly more productive. Their companies spend more money investing in new technology and abide by the European working time directive (an EU initiative that prevents employers from requiring their workforce to work excessively long hours, to protect their health and safety). Britain, by contrast, has an opt-out mechanism where employers can write into a person's contract that they must be prepared to work extra hours if needed to complete their tasks.

There is, however, a growing backlash in the UK against the long-hours culture, and some companies are researching the effects of a four-day working week for their staff, while still paying for five days. Companies have found that staff are happier, just as productive and use their spare day to enrich their lives in other ways, such as spending more time with their families or doing voluntary work, often benefiting the environment. Staff in these companies are usually happier and so less likely to move jobs, which reduces the amount needing to be spent on recruitment, freeing up money for business investment. All of these effects benefit the economy and our broader society, so long as the focus on perpetual and extreme profit is not the main aim of the company. If an employer wants long-term stability with a productive workforce, low turnover and low sick leave rates, then this may well be the path to choose.

The idea is discussed in detail in Dr Pedro Gomes's book, *Friday Is the New Saturday: How a Four-Day Working Week Will Save the Economy*. Gomes draws on a range of economic theory, history and data to show that a four-day week will stimulate demand, productivity and innovation, while reducing unemployment and ending populist movements. The move to a two-day weekend happened in the 1900s, but now that we have an ageing population that will have to work later in life before taking retirement, a four-day week may be the most sensible option for everyone. Many are already doing it by moving to flexible working hours to deal with childcare or adult-care arrangements, but in doing so they currently lose a chunk of their income. To retain all of your income for a four-day working week and stay productive would be an extraordinary step forward. Gomes states:

> The concept of marginal productivity [is] how much more a worker produced if he works one extra hour per day, or one extra day per week. Economists think that most jobs face diminishing marginal productivity. The last hours of the day are typically less productive because a worker is already tired. Also, fatigue kicks in on the last day of the week, so workers tend to be less productive, working more slowly and making more mistakes.[3]

If workers are already exhausted from the struggles of poverty, this last day becomes even more pointless. How much of the diminishing returns relate to poverty, stress-related fatigue or clearing up mistakes?

Gomes states that 'Several recent studies on the performance of medical interns, nurses and police officers find a positive association between long hours and low efficacy, accidents and injuries'.[14]

The UK's public services are regularly underfunded, but they also spend huge sums of money on dealing with mistakes. Between 2020 and 2021, the NHS spent £7.9 billion on clinical negligence claims and the majority (60 per cent) were related to maternity services and the provision of long-term care for children with brain damage caused by negligence during childbirth.[15] This is a vast sum of money and, though relatively small in relation to the total scale of the NHS budget, it is ironic that the money used to pay for clinical negligence could have been invested in providing safer care for patients.[16]

The idea of a four-day working week is in confluence with the slowdown that Danny Dorling discusses. The extra free time could improve our environment and society by increasing the time spent volunteering or improving our health, which in turn would reduce the burden on the NHS and other services. Productivity has been a long-term goal of senior politicians, especially during the disastrous weeks of Liz Truss's premiership, where her desperate ambition for higher economic productivity led to a serious economic crash after only a few weeks in the job. A move towards a more balanced Doughnut economics model could provide the structure that our politicians need to help them focus on the holistic picture rather than working on a single issue.

Gomes makes a compelling case for change and highlights that, while a four-day working week may feel counterintuitive, that does not mean it is wrong:

> Both jobs and demographics are putting pressure on mental health and making workers less productive. The economic motor is running too fast, but we are not getting any more speed. We need to change gear. The four-day week would reduce this pressure and raise workers' productivity. This idea is counter-intuitive, because we would be working less to produce more, but don't be fooled. Anyone with a creative job knows that inspiration doesn't come when someone is exhausted. It is better to switch off and come back with a fresh mind.[17]

Politicians talk a lot about wanting a high-skill, high-wage economy, but what about the lower-paid jobs? Jobs that are not necessarily productive in terms of stuff made, but that enable our huge institutions to function – jobs done by the key workers during the pandemic, such as cleaning. If the hospitals weren't disinfected, the NHS would grind to a standstill with spreading diseases. Will cleaners be paid more through rises in the minimum wage? Will they be paid the same amount for a four-day week? Will their household outgoings be reduced by rent controls? How would it work for those at the lower end of the wage scale who are exhausted through poverty, but don't do particularly creative jobs? A government focused on eliminating poverty could find answers to these questions and this would benefit everyone.

•••

Clearly, there is much to be done to reinstate balance into the economy and how humanity works within the environment.[18] Anti-poverty strategies and the green agenda need to work in tandem if there is to be significant headway on both subjects, and the plan to eliminate poverty from Britain (as described in later chapters) shows how this can be done in a holistic and realistic way.

In October 2021, renowned naturalist Sir David Attenborough and Prince William introduced the Earthshot Prize awards. In his opening speech, the prince said:

> We're alive in the most consequential time in human history ... The actions we choose or choose not to take in the next ten years will determine the fate of the planet for the next thousand.
>
> Each year for the next ten years we will award five prizes ... to those who are bringing hope to our future and can protect and restore nature, revive our oceans, clean our air, build a waste-free world, and fix our climate ... we need everyone from all parts of society to raise their ambition and unite in repairing our planet.[19]

It is a good concept and undoubtedly needed, but a brief glance down the comments on the attached social media stream found that it was far from an obvious win.[20] While many people were supportive of the new initiative, there were many for whom his words rankled. The cause of their disquiet was inequality. The sight of one of the wealthiest individuals in the world asking people in every section of society to help repair the climate (which has been broadly damaged by the wealthy) was too much to bear, especially for those who were already struggling to put food on the table and heat their homes.

For many people, concerns over poverty outweigh concerns over the planet and this is not an unreasonable point of view. The challenges of climate change must be dealt with while also dealing with poverty, or progress will continue to be slow. This is not because people don't care or don't understand, but because they have too much to deal with already. It is vital that environmentalists and politicians understand this. The Joseph Rowntree Foundation highlighted this during the COP26 summit:

> A vocal minority of politicians and media commentators are challenging the cost of the transition to net zero and how these costs – through levies, taxation and direct costs to households – will impact those on the lowest income, using this to frustrate progress to net zero.
>
> There is a cruel injustice that those who currently pay proportionately most in green levies on their energy bills are the ones most likely to be rationing their energy costs because they cannot afford to keep their homes warm. But leaving these inequities unchallenged, and failing to take advantage of the opportunities that a transition to net zero should create, would be a political choice, not an inevitability.[21]

(See Appendix 5 for the Foundation's proposals for tackling these issues.)

The former Irish president Mary Robinson, in her book *Climate Justice*, discusses the need to develop transition plans for workers, such as those on oil rigs or coal mines, for whom the fight against climate change means the end of their profession and the break-up of their communities. It can be a painful process and the impact should not be underestimated.[22] The closure of the British coal mines during the 1980s led to immense social pain and lasting deprivation for the populations involved.

Looking forward, there must be strategic planning for vulnerable industries and communities that are likely to suffer as a result of climate change in our country. There are also opportunities in the move to net zero to create a more balanced economy, with a stronger manufacturing sector and a move away from cheap imports that come with a larger carbon footprint. The sectors of private jet travel, the rural economy and sea fishing are examples where transition plans are needed.

Private Jet Travel

Private flights are known to produce significantly higher emissions per kilometre than any other form of transport due to the small number of passengers on board. While commercial flights use more fuel per hour, they can fly far more passengers than a private jet and therefore produce fewer emissions per person.[23] Since the pandemic, the private jet industry in the UK has been booming, with over 90,000 flights a year from fourteen private airports – equivalent to a flight every six minutes. This is more than any other European country. London to Paris is the most common route, which is also unnecessary given the regular trains available. In 2021, France banned the use of private internal flights for journeys that could be taken by train in under two and a half hours (environmental groups wanted four hours).[24] Considering the levels of pollution involved and Britain's net zero target, the closure of the private jet industry should be anticipated and prepared for. Central and local governments would need to work closely to ensure that any impact of the closure did not cause a domino effect on surrounding communities and businesses.

Leo Murray, Director of Innovation at the climate charity Possible, has suggested that the closure of the private jet industry could help accelerate the introduction of electric flight, by incentivising the super-rich private jet users to invest in emerging solutions. This could create new opportunities to boost innovation within Britain's aviation sector, while supporting the move to net zero, enhancing economic growth and creating high-paid jobs that protect against poverty. Given the wealth of those involved, the results could happen extremely quickly.

Rural Poverty

The British countryside is some of the most beautiful in the world, but it holds some of the poorest populations in the country. The needs of rural populations are often overlooked, and yet with investment in internet services, which have enabled better home working, some rural populations are growing. This has good and bad implications, as it can boost local economies but also increase house prices in areas such as Cornwall or Wales, and price the local population out of affording their own home.

Around 12.5 million people live in rural Britain, where poor access to health and transport services is often cited as a major problem.[25] In Wales, a quarter of the rural population is over the age of 65 and many of the triggers of isolation are related to the triggers of poverty.[26] Local shops are often more expensive than larger supermarkets, and travel poverty prevents access to services. A robust rural transport network, easier access to health care and better social connections are all key areas to prevent privation. One area of extra support may be the expansion of air ambulance services. These helicopters are currently funded through charitable donations and offer a lifeline (literally) to hospital care for the most seriously injured in rural areas. Where this isn't available, waiting for an ambulance can take many hours as they travel across the narrow or busy rural road network to reach each patient. This situation makes a mockery of the idea of a free health-care system, if patients in need are literally unable to access it in a timely way.

Rural businesses are particularly reliant on good internet access and a thriving local economy. Before the pandemic, only 42 per cent of businesses in Wales were still operating after five years.[27] Such a low success rate will not attract investment into the country, or help reduce poverty by maintaining employment rates, so policies must be put in place to help businesses survive or adapt. This is particularly important for industries that are vulnerable to climate change.

Sea Fishing

The fishing sector is highly vulnerable to a warming planet through rising sea temperatures and freak weather events. A government intent on ending inequality must look ahead and prepare fishing communities in advance to prevent rising deprivation and unemployment as problems arise.

The fishing industry has been in decline in Britain since 1895 and the future effects of climate change and overfishing must not be ignored. Since Brexit, the UK government has gained full responsibility for managing fisheries in the UK's Exclusive Economic Zone (EEZ) and has greater powers to protect its waters. (The EEZ is an area of the ocean extending 230 miles beyond a nation's territorial sea, and within which it has jurisdiction over both living and non-living resources.)

Rising temperatures and changing ocean currents may have a significant effect on the breeding patterns of some species and cause them to move to cooler waters. However, these are complicated ecosystems to understand. Researchers at Aberdeen University and the Scottish Marine Institute have shown that, while there have been higher rates of poleward migrations due to rising sea temperature, some species are more vulnerable to barriers in the ocean that prevent them from moving away from warmer waters, including physical barriers (currents or trenches), a lack of suitable habitat, competition and predation. Predicting how ecosystems may change, even using complex modelling, can produce uncertain results – for example, warming seas may negatively affect local cold-water species, but in their place may come a rise in the number of warm-water species.[28]

Research conducted in Scottish waters in 2021 found that global warming is affecting the size of commercial fish species. It found that juvenile fish are getting bigger and adult fish are getting smaller as sea temperatures rise.[29] However, it is not clear how this change may affect reproduction and long-term population sizes, as more juveniles may be taken from the sea before they spawn.

There are contrasting reports around how sustainable the sea-fishing industry can be and whether the use of large trawler nets should be banned as they churn up the sea floor, release carbon and destroy fragile ecosystems. The oceans are the world's largest carbon sink – far greater than the rainforests – so protecting the biodiversity of the oceans is important not just to prevent climate change, but also to protect those communities that rely on the fishing industry for employment, such as fish-processing plants that employ tens of thousands of people. This is a cause for concern as social deprivation could easily swell if fishing in the sea becomes unsustainable.[30]

An obvious option in the protection of fisheries is to change the uses of sea-caught fish. Estimates suggest that one-third of the world's fish catch is intended for animal feed, which goes into the pet industry and fish farming. This equates to 31.5 million tons of fish taken from the world's oceans each year, and 90 per cent of that catch is turned into fish meal or fish oil.[31]

The omega-3 oils that are extracted from fish come from the algae that they eat and can now be produced directly from plant life. Banning the use of fish to produce this oil would be a positive step forward in protecting wildlife. Mealworms are also a more environmentally friendly alternative to fish food. These two changes would be manageable if well planned within the industry and would also be effective at reducing pressure on wild populations.

A more forceful stance would be the banning of all nets used in British waters for five years and the creation of a new, land-based fishing sector, as found in the USA. Jobs could be transformed to focus on sea protection and monitoring, as sea angling would become the only legal method of fishing. Marine conservation organisations have highlighted that fishing boats that trawl the ocean floor can release levels of carbon equivalent to the entire aviation industry.[32]

Many will disagree with curtailing the use of nets, stating that it is unnecessary and harmful to food production. However, it is also important to consider that, when I studied pandemics for my biology degree in the early 2000s, no one gave them much serious thought and the idea of preparing for one seemed excessive. Twenty years later, the exact same methods of air travel and close living quarters that we discussed all those years ago came to dominate how Covid-19 spread around the world. When it comes to our environment and food security, I would prefer preparation and protection over a scrambled response of the likes seen during the vaccine and personal protective equipment (PPE) sagas. It would be helpful if we learned the lessons from Covid-19 and planned ways to protect the fisheries sector now, rather than fumbling for answers in the future should our marine ecosystems unexpectedly collapse.

Hydroponic fish farms are being used in the USA to give low-income residents access to cheap, local fish. In New Orleans, a small aquaponic farm, fuelled mostly by solar power and rainwater, farms catfish alongside greens, tomatoes, cucumbers and melons. In the past, the farm has sold fish to restaurants and bags of fruit and vegetables to local residents. It is situated in a low-income area and the primary focus of the farm is to provide food for the poorest residents.[33] Land-based fish farms are not perfect, but they may be an alternative way to support the restoration of fish stocks and broader ecosystems in the sea, while also protecting jobs that rely on the fishing sector, such as our beloved fish and chip shops.

The fishing industry is a billion-pound sector, so its decline could be disastrous for local communities if the government does not support new ways of adapting to climate change. Jobs in the fishing sector are some of the most dangerous in the world, so changes could protect vulnerable workers as well.[34]

However, questions remain about what the aim should be. How many fish should there be in the sea? Have people become used to seeing empty waters, in the same way that urban skies are often empty? A tantalising clue comes from a record in 1847 from St Ives in Cornwall, when the largest recorded catch in a single day was 57 million pilchards.[35] This would be an impossible catch today, where a ton of fish can be collected over the course of a year, not a day.

The knock-on effect of changes to biodiversity across the world have been detailed in many of David Attenborough's programmes. In *Extinction: The Facts*, he highlights how the UK may be affected by unforeseen changes in other parts of the planet. The changes could come extremely quickly and with little warning:

> Extinction is a natural process. Things come, they grow, their populations get huge and then they decline. But it's the rate of extinction, that's the problem. So, when you look at previous groups in the fossil records, then it's over millions of years they go extinct. Here we're looking at tens of years … Studies suggest that extinction is now happening 100 times faster than the natural evolutionary rate, and it's accelerating.[36]

The complexities of the marine environment, and our incomplete understanding of how the seas will change as temperatures rise, highlight the vulnerability of the fishing industry in the UK. However, it also means that the government can implement policies and support new industries to prevent areas of deprivation arising as global warming continues.

Green Innovation

In her TED Talk, 'Why climate change is a threat to human rights', former Irish president Mary Robinson highlighted the need to combine solutions for the environment with social change, and considered the future lives of her grandchildren in 2050:

> We know that inevitably it will be a climate-constrained world, because of the emissions we've already put up there, but it could be a world that is much more equal and much fairer, and much better for health, and much better for jobs, and better for energy security, than the world we have now, if we have switched sufficiently and early enough to renewable energy, and no one is left behind.[37]

Considering that the developing world is drowning under the problems caused by global warming (in some cases literally), solutions need to be cheap, fast and local. We should not assume that complex and expensive emerging technologies will be able to sort it out for us. Danny Dorling highlighted this in his book *Slowdown*: 'Future technological innovation will not make the poor better off. Only redistribution and social innovation can do that now.'[38]

While the scientists work on methods to capture carbon out of the air and store it underground, there are other options that can be taken to make our world more comfortable for humanity than is currently the case. Summer days of 40°C in Britain were inconceivable only a decade ago, and yet England reached this milestone for the first time on 19 July 2022. During the heatwave, our country slowed to a standstill, schools sent children home early and the roads became sticky as they began to melt. They are warning signs of what is to come, so we must have a diverse set of options to mitigate the ongoing warming. These include using artificial shade to prevent evaporating streams, expanding the use of hydroponic systems to grow more food here instead of importing it, expanding rewilding methods, which can stabilise threatened ecosystems, supporting the production of hemp to reinvigorate the rural economy, building green structures that will clean the air in pollution hot-spots, and using easy water storage systems to prevent flooding and droughts. We have options that do not need expensive machinery, and while we wait for technology to provide the answers, the options discussed below may offer more immediate and affordable solutions. They may not be perfect or spectacular, but if they are effective, then they are worth considering.

Dappled Shade

Simple solutions are being used in India to cool down concrete homes. White paint is used to cover the flat roofs of houses in slum areas, and these can reflect enough light to turn the inside temperatures from unbearable to habitable.[39] Could a similar concept be used in forests to prevent drought, maintain moisture in the topsoil and prevent wildfires? Obviously not by painting the forests, but by enhancing the amount of canopy cover between trees, using waterproof, non-flammable material with drainage holes. Dappled light and water could reach the forest floor and help recreate temperatures normally found at the lower levels of the canopy. If they are used all year round, the undergrowth may become rich enough with fungi and deep water reserves that the hot summer temperatures may not lead to droughts and harm wildlife.

Scientific research would be needed to check how effective the material would be at reducing broader temperatures, either locally or nationally, and how it affects biodiversity and the reintroduction of species. Could shading materials also be used in cities between apartment blocks to cool buildings and the air below them, improving air circulation on what would otherwise have been still, baking-hot days?

Life at 50°C has become less inconceivable as the number of extremely hot days increase worldwide,[40] so there is an urgent need for new, simple ideas. British scientists could research the effectiveness of such materials, and their production could be used to create sustainable jobs in deprived areas of the UK. This could contribute to our international aid package and the fight against climate change both in developing countries and at home.

A variety of complex scientific innovations are considering the need for more shade. Researchers at the University of Leeds used computer models to assess different ways to limit the amount of sunshine that reaches earth, including artificially changing the amount of cloud cover and spraying particles into the atmosphere to block sunlight (called solar radiation management, a type of geoengineering). They found that every idea reduced temperatures, but they also worsened floods or droughts for 25–65 per cent of the global population.

Clearly, difficult technological answers are not always the best way forward, and they could be used as a way of maintaining the status quo for energy companies.[41] The move towards renewable energy will create stranded assets, such as unusable oil rigs and abandoned coal mines, and these will become an enormous expense for businesses to incur when the world does finally stop using fossil fuels.[42] As developing nations need support now, new ideas need to be simple, effective and affordable. Britain could be at the forefront of producing them and in turn create sustainable employment for those living in financial difficulty here as well as abroad.

Green Towers

Growing up in London during the 1980s and 1990s meant experiencing balmy summers up to 28°C. Two decades later and the peak last year (2022) was 40°C. The heat thickened the air, stilled the wind, closed schools and created a deep brain fog for those of us unaccustomed to it. It was unpleasant and unnatural.

Before Covid-19 stopped the world in its tracks, the view across central London on a blue day was often tainted with a brown smudge of air pollution that hovered midway across the city skyline. Having spent years commuting into the centre, I had become accustomed to the smell and taste of traffic pollution. My skin felt grimy and I held my breath as buses and lorries passed by. The congestion zone worked well to reduce some of the traffic, but it was only when I saw the smudge across the city – as if an artist had smeared paint across a photograph – that I realised how polluted the air had become.

The issue of carbon capture remains a hot topic of research. Taking carbon dioxide (CO_2) out of the air and storing it to prevent further global warming feels like the perfect idea. However, the technology has yet to be scaled up to countrywide levels and there are constraints on the storage of CO_2 as only certain types of porous rock will accept the gas without it escaping back into the environment.[43]

A lot of effort has gone into artificially recreating processes that plants do naturally. London has been trying to clean up its air for decades, and for people with respiratory problems this cannot come soon enough. In 2013, Ella Adoo-Kissi-Debrah, a 9-year-old girl from south-east London, became the first person to have air pollution cited on her death certificate. The coroner found that the fumes from nearby roads had significantly contributed to her death.[44] Thousands of people across Britain are affected by dirty air each year. The British Lung Foundation found that children are more vulnerable to breathing in pollutants than adults, as their airways are smaller and still developing, they breathe more rapidly than adults, and buggies are often at the level of car exhausts.[45]

Simply planting vegetation and assuming that plants will do the rest is not enough for cities and towns with high congestion. Various types of green infrastructure can be used to limit the levels of emissions that affect human health. However, this is mainly based on how green spaces are built within an urban area, so that the prevailing wind can blow the pollution away or barriers prevent the pollution from spreading to pedestrians. In 2018, researchers at the Air Quality Expert Group found that green infrastructure does little to take pollution out of the air altogether, but it can have an impact by generally improving biodiversity and people's quality of life:[46]

> Urban vegetation typically removes only a low percentage of emissions by a process called deposition, which is when pollution sticks to the surface of a leaf and is removed from the air. However, urban vegetation can greatly reduce the amount of emissions people are exposed to by changing the distance they must travel ... to reach people.
>
> The benefits of green roofs include, sustainable urban drainage, mitigation of the urban heat island effect (cooling buildings and reducing energy used for air conditioning) and increased biodiversity. However, their potential for reducing exposure to road transport pollution is limited.[47]

Moss is extremely efficient at removing pollution, and green benches are being used in some areas to clean the air in local pollution hotspots. The CityTree is a combined bench and hedge, which contains a 4m-high vertical garden and is claimed to do the work of 275 trees in 1 per cent of the space. Each bench holds 1,682 pots of moss, which extract pollution from the air.[48] They are a fantastic invention and form part of the solution to air pollution, but they do little to support and promote biodiversity. It is vital that new green structures in urban areas are able to do both. It would be even better if these were to line major arteries through towns and cities and remove the particles at source.

In the Italian city of Milan, two skyscrapers have been built with plants in mind. They are the Bosco Verticale (Vertical Forest), colloquially known as the city's Green Lungs. The buildings provide food for the local residents at ground level and wildflowers at different times of the year to promote biodiversity.[49] These structures are extraordinary but expensive. Could there be an easier way to create aerial forests in Britain's cities, while reducing poverty through the creation of new jobs and supporting local manufacturers and plant producers? The Gherkin in London is 180m tall. Could Britain's vertical forests be of a similar height and used to cool the cities while also promoting wildlife? They need not be the breadth of a skyscraper, but a 5m² steel structure designed to foster plant life may be affordable and could provide jobs, cool urban heat islands and promote tourism in town and city centres.

An urban heat island (UHI) is caused by the combination of buildings, narrow roads, reduced vegetation, air pollution, traffic, domestic energy use and industrial processes. Cooling Britain's inner cities is important for global warming containment. Research has shown that London, Manchester and Birmingham have been 5°C warmer than their surrounding rural areas over the past two decades. With 90 per cent of the UK's population projected to live in urban areas by 2050, it is important that the UHI effect is dealt with. Cooler air means fewer air-conditioning units and fewer heat-related deaths.[50]

Some buildings have beehives on their roofs to support biodiversity, but without the plant life to sustain them, some colonies have been found starving. A new array of green towers in towns and cities across the country could provide part of the solution to the rising temperatures that urban areas will face in the coming decades.

Hydroponics and Rewilding

Isabella Tree and her husband Charlie inherited a huge farm, the Knepp Castle Estate, in the south of England in the 1980s. After decades of difficulty farming the clay soil, which morphed from impenetrable earth in the summer to sticky mud during the rest of the year, they decided to try an alternative approach and let nature take over.

In her book *Wilding: The Return of Nature to a British Farm*, Isabella describes the transformation of Knepp towards a home for biodiversity by removing intensive farming techniques and leaving the land to rewild itself through the introduction of large herbivores, particularly deer and traditional cattle breeds. These animals churn up the soil and bring more nutrients to the earth, creating habitats that enable smaller mammals and plants to grow. To the owners' delight, twenty years later, the biodiversity at Knepp is flourishing and their ecotourism business is bringing in more money than their traditional farm ever did:

> Knepp is but a small step on that road to a wilder, richer country. But it shows that rewilding can work, that it has multiple benefits for the land; that it can generate economic activity and employment; and that it can benefit both nature and us – and that all of this can happen astonishingly quickly.[51]

This is a comforting thought: that nature can rebalance itself and thrive within twenty years. Rural areas of Britain often struggle with access to good jobs and amenities. Knepp's success shows that a new approach to farming could rejuvenate even the most damaged areas of land and bring ecotourism into deprived parts of rural Britain. Knepp has become a focal point for demonstrating a new way of dealing with some of the most serious environmental issues facing our planet, including global warming, biodiversity, food supplies, pollination, soil restoration and water security.[52]

However, if we are to rewild much of our country and restore its biodiversity, we must still be able to feed our population. Stable food supplies are vital and imported food brings with it a large carbon footprint. As global warming continues to cause a more unstable climate and freak weather destroys crops, we must create parallel systems.

Hydroponics is a method of indoor food production that has leapt forward in the last ten years. Crops are often grown vertically to use less space and water, while the plants are also protected from pests and so need fewer chemicals. They can be produced in disused Underground stations or on small rooftops, and provide local restaurants and shops with fresh produce and a small carbon footprint. They create stable jobs and businesses for local people and free up more land for rewilding. This is a technological advancement that will be vital in an unpredictable world, and government intervention can help this industry thrive by affording it lower taxes and building rents. Due to the high summer temperatures last year (2022), gardeners were able to grow more Mediterranean fruits, such as watermelons, figs, lemons and avocados. This is a new opportunity, but we must have the correct water supplies to be able to support it.

Water

An outsider's view of Britain is often of a place where it rains a lot, a country of umbrellas and warm country pubs, but this is not always the case. The drizzle that kept our rolling hills green does not come as often, or last as long anymore, and hosepipe bans are more prevalent. Many water companies in England have not prepared properly for changes to the climate, and when great storms come their systems are often overwhelmed, so untreated sewage enters our seas and waterways, creating appalling pollution. Building new infrastructure will create jobs all over the country, but it will take decades.[53]

As the temperatures rise, more freshwater from rivers and reservoirs will evaporate. Startlingly, in summer 2022, the source of the Thames dried up. New innovations need to be created to cover our waterways during periods of extreme heat, and one option is to build moveable solar panel 'trees', which mimic the dappled shade of natural trees but simultaneously cool the reservoirs and generate electricity for the landowners. A ban on the cutting down of mature trees would also help, as they are more able to survive periods of drought than younger ones.

The need is urgent as we can see our future being played out through the lives of others on the planet. In 2019, Australians living near the Darling River in New South Wales witnessed the effects of hotter summers and poor water management. As the water levels fell, the river deoxygenated and killed vast shoals of fish in what was described as 'an ecological catastrophe'. A scarcity of clean water will cause water bills to rise and this will not help struggling households either. Britain needs to prepare for hotter times to come.

Hemp

I foresee the time when industry shall no longer denude the forests which require generations to mature, nor use up the mines which were ages in making, but shall draw its raw material largely from the annual produce of the fields.

Henry Ford, American car manufacturer, 1935[54]

Hemp is not the same as cannabis/marijuana. It looks the same and feels the same, but it does not contain enough of the chemical (tetrahydrocannabinol – THC) that is needed for drug use. Hemp production is not illegal in Britain, but it is regulated and requires a licence and background checks for the licence-holder.[55] The plant can be turned into a range of products, including paper, hospital-grade swabs, building materials, insulation, food and drink, fibreglass, animal feed, textiles, oils and wood chips (which contain enough cellulose to make plastic bags and textiles similar to nylon). With a growth rate of 4½m in three to four months, it is also easy to produce at scale and quickly. This rapid development enables the plant to outcompete most weeds and reduces the risk of diseases, which avoids the need for pesticides, herbicides and fungicides, and supports biodiversity while also reducing costs.[56]

Britain has a long history of growing hemp and it has been used for thousands of years to provide communities all over the world with food, clothing, shelter, medicine and fuel. Henry VIII reportedly imposed a penalty on farmers who didn't grow hemp and later Elizabeth I declared that for every 60 acres of land, farmers must allocate 1 acre to the plant. Everything changed in the 1930s with the emergence of the plastics and petrochemical industries, but today, as we face extreme ecological problems, a return to hemp could be a major part of the answer we are looking for.[57]

It can also be a highly profitable sector. The British Hemp Company went from zero to a £1 million turnover in just three years. I spoke to Steve Glover, the company founder, and asked him what he would like to see from a government focused on using hemp as a way of expanding the rural economy to reduce inequality. His answers came quickly.

We need a Hemp Marketing Board to raise the profile of the product, promote networking and educate the public on its uses.

It is a weird industry at the moment. On the one hand, there are activists who want a free-for-all to grow hemp anywhere without regulation and who really don't understand what goes into a clean product, including mycotoxin and heavy metal testing. If hemp is grown on poor land, it will absorb whatever is in the soil and that can be deadly for humans, so good testing is vital. At the other end of the spectrum are people who want to make millions without doing the graft. Then here we are plodding along in the middle, getting on with it.

We are the largest vertically integrated company in the UK, which means we do the farming, testing, processing and sales, but there is a big gap in infrastructure. The problem with hemp is that the stalks are not compact and so are difficult to transport to processing facilities before they go off.

We want mobile processing facilities which can be taken to rural farms and the hemp can be processed there at low cost to the farmer. Then they can either sell the product to us or store it and sell it when they are ready. Farmers need to be able to store their wealth (not in cash terms, but in the product they produce) in their sheds and fields and sell it when the market is right for them.

Steve also highlighted the unnecessary carbon footprint associated with some current practices:

We would also like regional hub processing facilities so the produce doesn't have to travel far. At the moment, hemp seeds can be grown in Poland, processed in China and then sent back to Europe for sale.

This seems an excessive environmental cost for a product that can do so much to support biodiversity. Steve's company has created a way to empower communities through the growing of hemp in rural, deprived areas. He educates farmers on how to sow and harvest the plant using normal farm machinery, which makes it an accessible crop for those who are currently eking out a living on poor-quality land and who often earn less than £10,000 per year. Keeping costs low for farmers is vital, as it can be difficult for them to compete with European farms which receive financial support from the EU under the Common Agricultural Policy.[58] A national system of hubs would avoid importation costs, paperwork and expensive machinery. This could create a range of truly British products from field to shop, and the low costs will be necessary to compete with cheaper imported products.

Hemp has the potential to transform the British landscape and our manufacturing base while simultaneously supporting the green and social agendas. By working directly with the farmers, Steve is also able to ensure reliable and safe working conditions for the factory workers. On a trip to eastern Europe in 2022, he described a visit around one factory where the staff looked malnourished, badly dressed and with no health and safety measures, which would be standard requirements back home. With a good industrial strategy, the government could turn hemp into an internationally recognised British brand with trusted, ethical working conditions, while also supporting biodiversity. A version of this model has worked well in Holland and the small country is now a top global exporter of the plant.

Hemp could also create a British textile revolution as materials made from it are four times stronger than cotton and use significantly less water. The company's environmental argument for using hemp is compelling:

Today, 99.95% of paper and card comes from trees, but this was not always the case. Up until 1883, 75–90% of all paper in the world was made with hemp fibre. Deforestation is a global problem with approximately 80% of the world's forests already destroyed, and paper production accounts for 35% of all felled trees.[59]

Imported bamboo products are often marketed as being eco-friendly, as they do not require the cutting down of trees. However, the majority of bamboo used globally is from China and with it comes a large carbon footprint. Crops that are made in Britain will be increasingly important as the country moves towards its net-zero target. An increase in hemp production nationally could spur on a variety of new industries, which complement both the green agenda and a poverty elimination programme.

Going forward, we must think creatively if we are to protect vulnerable sectors and create new ones. The weather will become increasingly erratic and biodiversity rates will continue to fall for a while yet. As they do, poverty rates could easily rise as the economy becomes more unstable, but this is not inevitable. Solutions can be found and many do not require expensive, high-tech solutions. By mimicking nature with more dappled shade over fields and waterways, by creating larger hemp and hydroponic industries, by building green towers and changing government policies around sea fishing and private jet planes, we could find that working to a sustainable economic model, based on the Doughnut, is quite possible. In doing so, we would be sowing long-term stability within our society to defend against inequality and climate change. For the next generation, this is not an unreasonable request.

10

FINANCE

When opposition politicians discussed the size of the national debt before the 2008 global financial crash, they were often faced with a barrage of derision from the Labour Party benches in the House of Commons, as they cited the years of economic growth that Britain had benefited from and how this was a buffer to any concerns around the national debt. For someone who had grown up during the economic turmoil of the 1980s and early '90s, I was wary of anyone who said that stability was here to stay, and, as we found later on, beneath the lauded economic growth lay a mesh of problems that almost brought down the entire financial system. Had the banks not been bailed out, money would have turned to mere paper in our hands.

It was the speed, variety and complexity of problems that led to the crash. One at a time would not have done so much damage, but they fell like dominos as the interconnected system, which had once been a strength, turned into a hazard. The problems included illegal changes to LIBOR (the London Inter-Bank Offered Rate), the instability of huge financial institutions like Lehman Brothers, the Royal Bank of Scotland's disastrous takeover of ABN Amro in 2007 and the bursting of the American housing bubble. All lending between banks and to the public effectively stopped. In Britain, the knock-on effect led to the collapse of Northern Rock, a bank that had a viable business model as long as the financial system remained unchanged. The result was the worst global economic crisis in history, even more extreme than the Great Depression of the 1930s.

Those of us who weren't directly involved in the financial sector were watching it with confusion and horror on the television. It became easy to clump 'bankers' together and afford group blame to anyone in the sector, irrespective of role or salary. The level of anger within the country was significant, but there were people at all levels within the financial sector who worked solidly to prevent an even greater catastrophe from happening.

The crash highlighted how the interconnected nature of economies, which had brought prosperity to many in the world, could also inflict immense damage on sections of society who had no knowledge of the money markets and no funds to invest. It showed the darker side of globalisation and unfettered capitalism. In the UK alone, the declining rates of suicide reversed around the time of the recession. There were an estimated 1,000 extra deaths from suicide between 2008 and 2010, and similar rises occurred in many other countries, especially in Europe and North America. Unemployment, financial difficulties, debt and eviction all increased the risk of depression and suicide, especially for young men.[1]

The 2008 British bank rescue package was formed of two parts, £137 billion of taxpayers' money and £1 trillion of government guarantees to restore confidence and stabilise the banks. The cash element included buying shares in Royal Bank of Scotland and Lloyds Banking Group, among others. In 2018, the Office for Budget Responsibility estimated that the interventions had cost the public £23 billion overall, with the rest of the money being recouped over the years.[2]

Since the crash, government finances have always been tight and the 2020 pandemic created further huge costs. Yet money has still been found for new projects, large and (relatively) small, such as High Speed 2 (a railway network estimated to cost £72–98 billion)[3] and the Garden Bridge across London (discussed in Chapter 11), so funding can be found in the system when needed.

Any plan to deal with poverty in Britain will require money. New departments, systems and projects are expensive to set up, and without tax rises, new cash will need to be found elsewhere or moved from existing projects. Normally, new money is gathered through tax receipts gained from a growing economy, but Britain's economic growth has been poor and unpredictable over the past decade.[4] To get an economy to grow sustainably, people need money in their pockets to spend and this is difficult if a quarter of the population lives around or below the poverty line.

A major issue is the UK's national debt. The House of Commons Library summarises the scale of the debt caused by the Coronavirus pandemic:

> In 2020/21 government revenue (income) ... was £794 billion while government spending was £1,112 billion (£1.1 trillion). The deficit was therefore £318 billion ... which is a peacetime record ... equivalent to around £4,800 per head of the UK's population.[5]

By the spring of 2022, UK government debt was £2,365 billion, which was almost 100 per cent of our GDP.[6] This is not a comfortable situation, so where could the money come from to instigate a new programme to end deprivation? A few options are described below.

Royal Bank of Scotland Shares

During the 2008 global financial crash, the UK government bought a significant stake in the Royal Bank of Scotland (now known as NatWest Group) for almost £46 billion. Since then, the gradual sale of these shares has provided a usable income for the Treasury. In 2022, the government's stake in the bank was valued at around £11 billion (although this changes depending on the share price).

In 2020, the Office for Budget Responsibility suggested that, from the money spent to prop up the bank during the crisis, the taxpayer would make a loss of £38.8 billion.[7] If this is accurate, it is a staggering amount of money to lose, especially given the serious problems that were caused by the post-crash austerity measures. It is only appropriate that the sale of the shares should be directed towards the creation of a fairer society. The money will not last forever, so it should be put to good use while it is available.

A Small Reduction in the Nuclear Arsenal

In 2021, the UK government decided to expand the size of its nuclear arsenal in the belief that this would strengthen its international standing in a post-Brexit era. The world has around 13,000 nuclear weapons (although some are waiting to be dismantled). The vast majority are owned by the USA and Russia, with around 4,000 active warheads each. In 2021, the UK raised the cap to 260, having previously planned to reduce the total to 180 in 2010.[8]

If the UK reduced its arsenal and spent the money elsewhere, the impact on the UK's international standing would be negligible. With 180 nuclear warheads, the UK would still have the ability to end around 200 million lives, depending on the population density of the sites hit and the number of deaths caused by the after-effects of radioactive rain, exposure, starvation, disease and suicide (the mental health implications for survivors are rarely included in statistics).

Each warhead has an explosive power of around 100 kilotons. The atomic bomb dropped on Hiroshima was 15 kilotons. Nuclear weapons are powerful enough to destroy both social and environmental support systems, so the numbers affected are difficult to estimate. However, the key question is this: how many people does the government need to be theoretically able to kill for its population to feel safe? A reduction in the size of Britain's arsenal could provide some of the money needed to create and sustain a poverty elimination programme, without compromising our national security.

International Development Money

The money that Britain gives to developing countries to promote its soft power and reduce extremism, migration and climate change is a perpetually contentious issue. The sums given from the nation's budget are extremely small: in 2022, it was only 0.5 per cent (around £11 billion) of the national income.[9] However, when people are living in relative poverty or there is an economic downturn, questions are regularly asked about why people are being supported abroad when so many are struggling at home.

The benefits of the aid budget have not been well advertised to the public and so the budget is consistently under pressure and in need of justification. If the UK government wants to find money to invest in a poverty elimination programme, the international development fund would inevitably be raised as a candidate.

In their podcast *The Rest Is Politics*, Alastair Campbell (the former Downing Street head of communications) and Rory Stewart (former Conservative secretary of state for international development), discussed the foreign aid budget in relation to Brexit:

> Rory Stewart: 'When people were leading the Brexit campaign many ... claimed they were doing it because they wanted a bigger role for global Britain, but actually in truth the real dominant trend in Britain is about us having less to do with the world, not more ... Many people want to say "charity begins at home, we're not giving any more money to poor people overseas ..."'

> Alastair Campbell: 'That is a failure of leadership and a failure of political education as well, because real political leaders ... would be explaining convincingly why our interconnectedness ... matters more, not less.'[10]

We live in a heavily connected world with around half of the food on our plates produced domestically and only 16 per cent of the fruit we consume. As of 2020, 71 per cent of the country's land was used for agriculture with the majority being used for grazing animals. As the climate changes, the spread of plant diseases and inclement weather events will make global food supplies more unpredictable and raise prices, so supporting the political and social stability of developing countries around the world that produce our food is vital.[11] Global warming is also expected to increase migration, as countries become less habitable, and in turn create the political instability that allows violent extremism to spread. All of this means that Britain's international aid commitments will matter more than ever as we move through this century.

As developed countries across the globe are the greatest polluters, they bear much of the responsibility for the creation of climate change, and the international development budget is often used to prevent it from getting worse. An example of this is Britain's support for the Great Green Wall, a new forest of trees that is gradually being planted across the Sahel region of Africa to prevent desertification, strengthen water supplies and maintain social stability.[12]

Supporting developing countries does not have to be an either/ or option. The UK economy is large enough to provide for both social groups. Constraints and laws on how the overseas aid budget (also known as Official Development Assistance – ODA) is allocated through its tendering process could be changed to prioritise British businesses and manufacturing, and help to maintain jobs and reduce poverty in the UK, rather than continue with its global competition rules.[13] The cheapest options are not always the best, and if a British business can provide a good product and create jobs, while it may be at a higher cost, the twin benefits of reducing poverty at home and overseas means it remains an effective use of public funds.

There are concerns that this approach could lead to 'tied' aid, which the Organisation for Economic Co-operation and Development (OECD) describes as:

> Offering aid on the condition that it be used to procure goods or services from the provider of the aid ... this can increase the costs of a development project by as much as 15 to 30 per cent. Untying aid, on the other hand, avoids unnecessary costs and gives the recipient the freedom to procure goods and services from virtually any country.[14]

This structure is understandable, as wealthy countries can use aid in a predatory manner to gain access to developing countries' natural resources through unfair contracts. Such an example is the Hambantota port in Sri Lanka. In 2018, the port was signed over to the Chinese state-owned bank because the Sri Lankan government could not repay the Chinese loans it had taken out to build the port in the first place.[15]

The UK has laws against this type of predatory action, but a loosening of tied-aid policies could be allowed if it also helps in the fight against poverty in Britain, such as printing books here for a developing country's education system. It is not just about the amount of money that is provided abroad, but also the number of people who benefit. This may be particularly important to boost the British rural economy, as manufacturing firms often move out of the cities in search of cheaper premises and labour.

An alternative school of thought is to put money directly into the hands of people living in extreme poverty in developing countries. Give Directly is a charity spearheading this change. It provides funds so that people can choose what to buy and when, so they can plan ahead, rather than be told what they need by a foreign government or charity. However, while the idea is controversial, it can offer good value for money as the running costs are small compared with traditional charities and produce faster results. Research has found that recipients use the cash carefully and spend it on essentials such as medicines, solar lights, irrigation, school fees and agricultural stock.[16]

There are question marks about how the funds would affect inflation within a country, but if the money is given in instalments, this may reduce the risks. Giving cash directly may also have a significant impact on women's rights, as the power of money would be in women's hands rather than male family members or corrupt local governments. The sums are relatively small in Western terms, yet, for example, in South Sudan, where the average yearly earnings are less than $800, small amounts can make a significant difference to a person's quality of life. It is likely that a combination of both development projects and direct cash payments may be the best way of ensuring social stability in developing countries in the future.

It is worth noting that much of the international development budget is passed directly from the Treasury to organisations like the United Nations peacekeeping programmes and is never given to the civil service to support development projects, so much of the UK's international development budget is not usable cash. While potential changes to the procurement system may support many UK businesses, ODA should not be seen as a 'cash cow' from which all the money can be found.

Politicians may also find that civil servants working on international development push back against any involvement in the UK's internal politics. However, the technical expertise that is held in analysing, understanding and responding to poverty could be of significant benefit for a new Department for the Elimination of Poverty. The Ministry of Defence often works closely with its partners in international development on the logistics of large-scale projects. These skills may also be helpful when working on fast-paced domestic programmes.

For the public to accept that international development matters and support the government's aid budget, it is vital that people understand how vulnerable our economy and food supplies are to international shocks, and that using government money to support others will help to create a more stable world for all of us.

Issuing Government Bonds

Government bonds are known as gilts in Britain and are a loan from the buyer of the bond to the government. The government pays a fixed interest rate to the buyer until the bond reaches its end date and the loan is repaid.

One option to raise money for a new anti-poverty agenda would be to offer ring-fenced gilts that would guarantee the money only being spent on socially positive activities. This would enable investment fund managers to advertise their investment portfolios as socially responsible. This guarantee would be important. Today, governments around the world fight against 'greenwashing', where investment funds advertise that they are investing their clients' money in environmentally friendly businesses, but then fail to do so. Ring-fenced government gilts could prevent the equivalent of 'poverty-washing' and provide an extra layer of certainty for investors, while raising much-needed funds for new projects.[17]

An International Shipping Tax

Shipping is one of the world's largest industries and is responsible for more than 2 per cent of global emissions (if the industry were a country, it would be the sixth biggest polluter in the world). Noise and pollution caused by ships' engines are having a major impact on wildlife. The shipping industry has been calling for a new global tax to incentivise shipping firms to invest in greener energy.[18] The tax would likely be passed on to consumers through the products they import, but industry experts have stated that the cost would be a few additional pennies per item.[19]

Water is an excellent medium for the transmission of sound waves and enables marine life to communicate across long distances. Ships' engines are filling the seas with sound, and some are audible underwater for hundreds of kilometres. The British marine company Hydrosphere states, 'Short, loud blasts can cause physical damage, whereas persistent background noise – such as that from anchored cruise ships – can alter communication and feeding behaviours in marine animals.'[20] The combination of underwater noise and ocean poisoning may be a significant contributor to the sharp rise in mass beaching of sea mammals in recent years. In 2020, 7,000 cape fur seals beached on the coast of Namibia. Unusually large mass strandings of marine mammals were also found in Australia, Britain, Ireland, Sri Lanka, France and New Zealand.[21]

Many ships choose to remain at sea rather than pay fees to berth in ports, or they find there is no space in the ports, as happened with Felixstowe in 2021. This causes ships to use their engines for much longer than would normally be the case, decreasing the air quality for coastal communities.[22] When compounded with the chemical pollution and oil spills that come from poorly maintained ships, this strongly suggests that the shipping industry needs a speedy change of direction. Noise pollution can be dealt with by changing the position of engines on boats, and cruise ships are starting to use electric motors to drive their propellers. For the UK to reach its net-zero carbon target, ships will need to use cleaner alternatives to petrol or return to wind power using engineless, sailing cargo ships or wind-assisted technologies, such as the towing of ships by enormous kites.[23] It will also take an international effort, as the United Nations highlighted in 2020:

> If shipping companies, ports, cargo owners, and governments opt to pursue wind propulsion as part of their emission-free shipping

strategies, it will require a concerted effort in both policy and action to make that shift viable.[24]

The creation of a global carbon tax on shipping combined with the creation of new shipbuilding industries could create long-term funding for the green agenda, protect biodiversity and stimulate British manufacturing, while also releasing other government funds to deal with inequality.

When it comes to financing a poverty elimination strategy, there are options available and it is likely that more than one approach could be used. How the government spends its money is always a choice. Politicians who suggest that poverty elimination should not be attempted because of the expense have not thought deeply or innovatively enough about the options available. Civil servants with expertise in the financial sector at the Treasury, Bank of England and Financial Conduct Authority could also help to make the system financially viable and stable over the long term.

11

PROCUREMENT

The nine most terrifying words in the English language are: I'm from the government and I'm here to help.

Ronald Reagan, president of the USA, 1981–89[1]

I sat down in a huff and looked between the faces of my despondent colleagues and the rolling news headlines on the TV. Everyone was angry. It was the quiet kind of anger that left people seething and afforded little relief, other than to vent to a sympathetic ear when the opportunity arose. It was 2009 and we were in the midst of the MPs' expenses scandal. Every day new details were being published of cases where elected Members of Parliament had taken, or had tried to take, taxpayers' money for expenses that they had no right to claim. One Conservative MP infamously filed a £1,645 expense claim for an ornamental floating duck island. Even though it was never paid, the arrogance of the request became an emblem for the whole affair.

Some parliamentarians were sent to jail for false accounting, others were suspended or forced to resign, and many had to repay the money they had received. This included £2,200 for the clearing of an MP's moat on their country estate, £2,000 to repair a pipe under a tennis court and £5,000 for gardening. Others made hundreds of thousands of pounds in profit from the sale of their flats, which had been bought with the help of taxpayers' money.[2]

One of the reasons for the public anger was that the scandal came only a year after the global financial crash, and the chaotic behaviour of those who had created it was being reflected to us in our own Parliament. It shattered the illusion that we were being governed by honest people, and while some MPs never took a penny, the trust between the public and the political elite never really returned. In the following years, more reports of incompetent leadership and financial losses reignited the anger within the battered relationship. They also highlighted that there was always money available, even though the government said otherwise, and all the while those on the lowest incomes struggled the most.

The decade of austerity after the crash was defined by the Conservative government's belief that private companies, which offered almost impossible deals for government contracts, were best placed to run key services in the country. This decision quickly began to fail as companies found their tenders were unsustainable in the long term.

The high-profile collapse of Carillion in January 2018 had a huge impact on the country's ability to function properly. The company employed 43,000 people for services in defence, education, health and transport. A parliamentary committee stated that the government's overriding priority for outsourcing had been to spend as little money as possible, while forcing contractors to take unacceptable levels of financial risks.[3] The constant race to the bottom, to pay companies less for doing more, showed how British society was working to an unsustainable theory.

Money in the Pot

You don't have to dig very far to find staggering levels of financial waste by the British government over the years. This is important as it debunks the myth that poverty would be too expensive to eliminate. The various projects and political priorities discussed below highlight that there is always money in the pot to spend.

The plans to create a London Garden Bridge never came to fruition and yet cost the taxpayer £43 million, including £161,000 on a website, £417,000 on a gala, £9.5 million on designers, £2.3 million on legal costs and £1.7 million to pay the Garden Bridge Trust executives' salaries. London is an innovative city, but it already has so many tourist attractions that it never needed this one. The global kudos of having the only capital city in the world free from poverty would have been significantly more interesting than another bridge over an already world-famous river.

Another questionable use of public money was the Marble Arch Mound, which was constructed next to the famous landmark. It cost £6 million (2021–22) and was mocked for being 'London's worst attraction'. It only lasted seven months.

These two examples are at the lower end of the scale when it comes to wasted money. The Ministry of Defence was found to be so poor in its accounting that it wasted £64 million between 2010 and 2021 in administrative errors and fines imposed by the Treasury. Poor procurement processes ranged from £5.7 million on earplugs that were found to be 'not fit for purpose on operations', to cancelling a research and development project for new armoured vehicles to the tune of £600 million (2021).[4]

The Covid-19 Test and Trace (NHS T&T) system cost £37 billion over two years. It was designed to prevent further national lockdowns, but after it was created in May 2020 there were two more. A Public Accounts Committee report in March 2021 stated that:

> While NHS T&T clearly had to be set up and staffed at incredible speed, it must now 'wean itself off its persistent reliance on consultants' ... and it's not clear whether its contribution to reducing infection levels ... can justify its 'unimaginable' costs.

Meg Hillier MP, chair of the Public Accounts Committee, lambasted it, saying that 'Test and Trace still continues to pay for consultants at £1,000 a day'.[5] The top price was £6,624 per day.[6] The pandemic was a crisis situation and, in those circumstances, governments will often open the coffers and spend money on anything that sounds like a good idea. However, turning to private companies for essential services has been a longstanding position of the British government and has caused the costs of many services to spiral. The assumption that a country can be well run by a small government and a large private sector has not been reliable and greater balance is needed in the future.

As our technological advances create increasingly complex ideas, simple projects that will last are often not given the status that they deserve. Some basic Victorian and Edwardian swimming pools are still in use and yet more modern ones have been built and destroyed in short order because the repairs needed to wave machines or poorly constructed buildings were deemed too expensive. (The Moseley Road Baths in Birmingham opened in 1907 and is still in use, yet the Minehead Aquasplash in Somerset only lasted fifteen years and is now a Lidl.)

The National Audit Office stated that one of the reasons why the London Garden Bridge wasted so much money was because the then prime minister, David Cameron, ignored the concern of his senior civil servants and allowed the planning to continue, which eventually led to a £56 million shortfall in the trust's accounts.[7] All politicians, whether in local or central government, should not be hailed for their 'vision' at investing our money in risky ventures, but for the provision of safe and well-functioning public services.

The public can often feel an arc of emotions, from hope to cynicism to despair, over the course of a government's term. The hope that a new, better leader will bring with them fresh ideas that will provide social stability and a more prosperous future for all often turns sour as promises are broken and reality sets in. So, why does the green field utopia rarely materialise? (I should say that this is not just a British problem.) When politicians run out of ideas, they may start to experiment. The desire to look bold and visionary combined with actual power appears intoxicating, but, as any scientist knows, most experiments don't work, and if they have never been done before then the results are rarely as expected.

While introducing a plan to end privation in Britain has never been done before, the difference is that no one would truly be hurt. There may be some people who would be miffed that tax cuts for the wealthy wouldn't happen again, but they would not get hurt to the point of homelessness or hunger. There are also many rich folk who would rather have a properly functioning society than more money in their bank accounts.

In September 2022, the then Chancellor of the Exchequer, Kwasi Kwarteng, gave a large and unapologetic tax cut to those earning over £150,000 per year in the hope that they would either spend the money and boost economic growth, or invest it in the country and the money would then 'trickle down' to the rest of society. At the same time, many millions of people were concerned about sharp rises in energy and food bills caused by Brexit and the war in Ukraine. The LBC radio host James O'Brien gave his assessment shortly after hearing the news:

> Kwasi Kwarteng's calculation is that by giving me thousands of pounds, he's really helping you ... Don't tell me to give it to charity or volunteer, I want a better and a fairer taxation system and today we got the opposite ... He's just given me thousands of pounds and you don't know how you're going to pay your bill(s) next month ... talk me through why that's fair, because I don't think it is and I'm winning![8]

Trickle-down economics is widely regarded as a poor idea and it is particularly bad when funded through debt. The policy was reversed the following month, but there were many journalists in the right-wing press who hailed the new policies. This saga has highlighted that a plan to end poverty in the future may not be universally welcomed.

The British government is one of the largest procurers in the country and spends around £290 billion each year. In 2021, the rules around procurement and public contracts shifted away from concentrating on the lowest cost, to a more socially responsible scope that takes into consideration levels of job creation, investment in skills, and opportunities for local growth, especially in deprived areas.[9] This is a complete turnaround from government advice for the preceding decade. It is a positive development, but with local government budgets continually stretched and a large national debt, it will be interesting to see if it is implemented properly. The level of need in the country is so great that transforming it into a truly prosperous nation cannot be done through trickle-down economics or a change in the procurement system alone. It will take compassion, focus and a plan.

PART THREE

OUR FUTURE

12

ELIMINATING POVERTY FROM BRITAIN

If you want something hard enough, you'll find a way of getting it.
Stanley Thear (Grandad), dry cleaner and
Second World War army veteran

Poverty is unacceptable and yet, if we are honest, it is accepted. For all the poverty alleviation measures that exist in British society, such as charity work and welfare support, they are still only alleviation measures, they're not elimination measures. As we seek only to alleviate poverty, we accept the fact that some people will still have to live in poverty; it has become acceptable and accepted.[1]

Why should that continue to be the case? If a political party attempted to end poverty in Britain, how could it be done? The causes are complex and varied, so a holistic approach from government would be essential. It would also need actively to incorporate new ideas grounded in reality that would not take decades to bear fruit. Furthermore, there would be some unpalatable truths that any leader involved in the task would need to accept.

First, there is the issue of time. The UK Parliament has five-year sessions, so eliminating poverty would need to be to completed in five years as there would be no guarantee of re-election. This timescale would be vital. History shows that prime ministers cannot rely on their successors to continue their work. Much of the progress that Labour made in reducing child poverty in the late 1990s and early 2000s was subsequently undermined during the Conservative austerity years, after the 2008 global financial crash.[2] There is also the issue of public trust. It is easier for voters to put their faith in politicians' promises for five years rather than ten. An air of suspicion and mistrust can surround a politician who suggests that they need two terms to complete their work.

Five years to change British society is not a long time and partly explains why eliminating poverty has never been attempted. An aim that appears so difficult that it could be viewed as an inevitable failure is hardly political nirvana. However, that also depends on a society's definition of failure. If, after five years of trying, a government had reduced poverty by 50 or 60 per cent, it would technically have failed, but the endeavour would still have been worthwhile and not just for those released from the poverty trap. With lessons learned, future governments would be in a more experienced position to continue the work and less hindered than they were before. The Centre for Homelessness Impact defines the type of country they are working towards as 'a society in which any experience of homelessness is rare, brief and non-recurring'.[3] This aim should be used for the elimination of poverty more broadly. As people's lives change and flux, poverty may still occur, but it should not become a permanent situation, or intergenerational.

Social scientists have found different ways to measure poverty in a developed country. The spare cash a household has left at the end of the week, after housing costs have been paid, is one way of deciding if a family is living in poverty. If they cannot afford a basket of essentials (the contents of which can vary), then they are living in deprivation. It is important to include housing costs, as prices vary significantly across the country. When it comes to fuel poverty, it is currently impossible to gain an accurate picture. The devolved governments and charities that collect data do so at different times and use different measurements to decide what defines fuel poverty. We simply do not know how many people are struggling, but estimates and modelling suggest it may be 7.39 million in England,[4] 614,000 in Wales,[5] 980,000 in Scotland[6] and 197,000 in Northern Ireland.[7] The figures are generally based on whether a household spends more than 10 per cent of their net income on domestic energy, after housing costs. (For more details of how poverty is measured, see Appendix 6.)

The poverty situation in Britain has been difficult for many years. During the 2010s, levels increased for both adults and children. This was caused by a combination of cuts in benefit levels, rising housing costs and limited opportunities to improve earnings through work. In 2019, the United Nations published a report into British poverty that was roundly rejected by the Conservative government, led by Theresa May at the time.

Although the United Kingdom is the world's fifth largest economy, one fifth of its population (14 million people) live in poverty ... Close to 40 per cent of children are predicted to be living in poverty by 2021. Food banks have proliferated; homelessness and rough sleeping have increased greatly; tens of thousands of poor families must live in accommodation far from their schools, jobs and community networks; life expectancy is falling for certain groups; and the legal aid system has been decimated.

The social safety net has been badly damaged by drastic cuts to local authorities' budgets, which have eliminated many social services, reduced policing services, closed libraries in record numbers, shrunk community and youth centres and sold off public spaces and buildings including parks and recreation centres ...

Brexit presents an opportunity to reimagine what the United Kingdom stands for ... And social inclusion, rather than increasing marginalization of the working poor and those unable to work, should be the guiding principle of social policy.[8]

All the main political parties committed to eradicating child poverty in Britain by 2020, and this shared commitment was enshrined in the Child Poverty Act (2010). However, even by 2013 it was clear that the target was likely to be missed and that progress on social mobility was being undermined by the twin problems of youth unemployment and falling living standards.[9] The predictions have turned out to be right. In the early 2020s, children are more likely to be in a low-income household compared to the overall population. Government statistics highlight the mess we are in:

- 75 per cent of children in poverty live in a working household.

- There were 3.9 million children living in poverty in the UK in 2020–21. That's 27 per cent of children, or eight in a classroom of thirty.
- Nearly half (49 per cent) of children living in lone-parent families are in poverty. Lone parents face a higher risk of poverty due to the lack of an additional earner, low rates of maintenance payments, gender inequality in employment and pay, and childcare costs.
- Children from Black and minority ethnic groups are more likely to be in poverty: almost half (46 per cent) are now in poverty, compared with around one in four (26 per cent) of children in white British families.[10]

This situation has been exacerbated by the coronavirus lockdowns, which caused the UK national debt to run up to £2.14 trillion and exceed the size of the economy.[11] This has been caused, in part, by a combination of enormous falls in government income from tax and national insurance as the economy slowed during lockdowns, as well as spending more on support measures, such as the furlough scheme to protect businesses and jobs.

Tax rises should therefore be inevitable. However, it is one thing to raise taxes while you are in power and quite another to tell the public that they need to rise during an election. This is the second reality. The aim of eliminating poverty would need to be offered to the British public on the understanding that taxes would not rise. Political history has shown that, for parties to be elected into power, taxes can only be held at the current rate or cut. Those parties that seek to raise taxes, even for important reasons such as funding the NHS, are not elected into government. Britain's first-past-the-post system does not lend itself comfortably to coalition governments, so for significant change to happen and laws to be passed, the government would need to have a majority.

Five years to eliminate poverty without raising taxes appears to be a Herculean task and yet those are the realistic constraints. There are also three fundamental requirements upon which all else would stand: the need for a compassionate society, government focus and a detailed plan.

13

POVERTY AND COMPASSION

I believe that unarmed truth and unconditional love will have the
final word in reality ... I have the audacity to believe that peoples
everywhere can have three meals a day for their bodies, education
and culture for their minds, and dignity, equality and freedom for
their spirits.

Martin Luther King Jr, Nobel Prize speech, 1964[1]

I can't remember where I was in the country when it happened, but
in truth it could have been anywhere. The high street was busy with
cars and commuters. The evening had drawn in and transformed the
road into a nightscape of flashing brake lights and neon signs from
the nearby clubs. The street lamps shone yellow halos down onto
the pavement, and among the bustle, a young woman in dirty jeans
and a high ponytail sat quietly at the side of the pavement begging.
She pulled out an old-style mobile phone and read her messages.
Walking out of the crowd came two strong, middle-aged men. One
commented indignantly to the other, 'She's got a mobile phone!' and
they walked on scoffing in camaraderie.

As I passed her, I wondered how long it would be before she
entered prostitution. I knew homelessness was the biggest driver into
it. She was so young – 20 at most. I wasn't surprised she had a phone;
in fact, I was glad of it. It meant she had access to the police, or family
and friends. Her homelessness might only have been a week or a day
old. The fall into desperation does not mean she must immediately

don an old sack and be covered in muck to warrant compassion or help. Not only would I want a mobile phone if I were on the streets, but I'd also want a dog as well. All that love, protection and loyalty in one small animal, and a welcome hug, too, when loneliness set in.

The men who passed the young woman gave her situation less than a second's thought and their primary motivation was not wanting to be taken for fools. It is well known that criminal gangs ship people into Britain to earn money by begging on the streets or public transport. The number of beggars on the London Underground has significantly increased since the pandemic and it is hard to know who is genuinely homeless and who is in the hands of a gang. In truth, both groups need help, but in the snippet of time spent with people in those situations, commuters must make a split-second decision as to whether to give money or not, and people don't want their empathy to be taken advantage of.

Compassion is an emotion that has taken quite a pounding over the last century. The concept of the 'undeserving poor' is very much alive in the country's psyche and dates back to pre-Christian eras.[2] However, for modern Britain, the idea was cemented into our social conscience by the Victorians. The great philanthropists of the day found that there was a section of the poorest in society that could be helped, and another for whom no help was possible. From then on, this latter group became the 'undeserving poor'.

The Victorian prime minister Benjamin Disraeli wrote his own description of the separation between classes, and it has uncomfortable parallels with life today. Clearly there have been huge improvements in the intervening years, but the way people are labelled or discriminated against, based on income or any other distinction, continues to act as a barrier to the creation of a poverty-free country and needs to be reversed:

> Two nations between whom there is no intercourse and no sympathy; who are ignorant of each other's habits, thoughts and feelings, as if they were dwellers in different zones or inhabitants of different planets; who are formed by different breeding, are fed by different food, are ordered by different manners, and are not governed by the same laws ... THE RICH AND THE POOR.[3]

The huge disparity in housing across Britain today is a clear example of this ongoing imbalance, and the Grenfell fire tragedy in 2017 highlighted it in the most heartbreaking way. Grenfell Tower was a twenty-four-storey block of social homes, with only one escape route for over 350 residents. Seventy-two people died in the fire, which took over sixty hours to extinguish. Yet, in the same borough there were privately owned blocks of flats with fully functioning fire alarms and sprinkler systems that would have prevented the kind of inferno that Grenfell created. Watching the tower smouldering at sunset was an unforgettable moment in our history, a moment that crawled under your skin and embedded itself in your core.[4]

The fire fuelled many people's anger and resentment towards the austerity cuts to public services and the Conservative government's attitude towards those living on low incomes. It is ironic that these attitudes were then flipped during the 2020 pandemic, when low-paid hospital cleaners, care home workers and NHS staff were suddenly lauded and praised as extraordinary individuals, when it became obvious how much we needed them.

The undeserving poor is a perception that has been reinforced by many politicians over the years. In 1978, Margaret Thatcher made her views clear:

> Nowadays there really is no primary poverty left in this country. In Western countries we are left with the problems which aren't poverty. Alright, there may be poverty because people don't know how to budget, don't know how to spend their earnings, but now you are left with the really hard, fundamental character-personality defect ... Even when you've been taught all the right things, all the best things, it doesn't mean to say you will do them.
>
> Every person, whether high or low born, whether they get to high places or they have a very simple straightforward life, earning an honest wage for an honest job, each has that human dignity, each has that choice ...[5]

An alternative view, which is demonstrated in Chapters 2 and 3 of this book, is that poverty removes human dignity and choice. It erodes and exhausts people's abilities, it raises stress levels and fear to such a point that people won't take the sensible or obvious option. When people are in love, we accept that they are unable to think 'straight', and yet when under extreme financial pressure, they are not given the same latitude to make mistakes. The high-interest credit company Wonga provided loans with an annual percentage rate (APR) of 1,509 per cent (a bank loan is usually below 15 per cent) and lent money to thousands of people, many of whom would never be able to repay. This type of loan was only taken up by desperate and vulnerable people, and after an investigation, the firm agreed to compensate 45,000 customers for unfair and misleading debt collection practices.[6] Assuming that everyone behaves rationally when under extreme pressure is naïve.

In 2005, the then MP for Henley-on-Thames, Boris Johnson, wrote a newspaper article that insulted and belittled the poorest 20 per cent of society.[7] On becoming prime minister, he refused to apologise for the comments he had made towards the populace he had been elected to serve. When politicians express their views so strongly and with so little compassion and understanding, and are still elected, it highlights the need for a leader with an Obama-like level of ability to turn believers away from the 'undeserving poor' stereotype.

Poverty removes the liberty and flexibility of choice from a person's life. The old phrase 'beggars can't be choosers' remains as true today as it was in the 1500s when it was first recorded. As a teenager, I was taught little in school about poverty and the structural inequalities that create it. As public ignorance and social stereotypes continue, they can be used by some politicians to justify the concept of the undeserving poor. By blaming an individual's poverty on their personal decisions, politicians are then able to wash their hands of any real responsibility to deal with it. Indeed, it is much easier to run a country if social attitudes revolve around the idea that other people's pain is not your pain to deal with. Many politicians over the years have stated how they care deeply about poverty, but their actions regularly fall woefully below the levels needed to end it.

Other politicians have the equation between poverty and social problems entirely the wrong way round. In a speech to the Conservative Party conference in 2015, the then prime minister David Cameron stated:

We need to tackle the root causes of poverty. Homes where no one works, children growing up in chaos, addiction, mental health problems, abuse, family breakdown. We will never deal with poverty unless we get to grips with these issues.

Most of the time, poverty causes these problems. Remove the deprivation first and family life becomes instantly easier, and children don't then grow up in chaos. Family breakdown is less likely in situations where arguments about money are not commonplace. Addiction and mental health problems reduce because the poverty-related stress decreases. This is particularly important when it comes to access to food. Hungry people's brains do not work effectively and making informed decisions ceases to be a priority when the basics of life are not easily available.

Food bank donation areas in supermarkets are now a regular sight, but they were unseen during the 1990s and early 2000s. The Trussell Trust is the UK's largest food bank charity and it saw significant increases in the numbers of food parcels it was providing between 2010 (around 100,000 a year) and 2018–19 when it provided over 1.5 million.[8] These statistics show that, while we may assume that things will get better as we progress through the modern era, it is not always the case. We can go backwards, and it is the realisation of this that often leads to angry protests and riots, which seem to appear out of nowhere, but are in fact the visualisation of an unbalanced society in need.

A 2020 study carried out on the characteristics of food bank users at the Trussell Trust found that almost every person (94 per cent) was 'facing real destitution' (unable to buy essentials to stay warm, dry, clean and fed); 23 per cent were homeless; two-thirds had experienced a problem with the benefit system in the year before they needed emergency food; and seven in ten people had reported at least one 'challenging life experience' (such as eviction or divorce).[9] The reasons behind poverty are hugely complex and the support that government provides must be flexible and responsive to a variety of needs. This does not mean that poverty cannot be solved, it just needs politicians who genuinely understand the nation they are leading.

Child Poverty

> No matter how hard my mother tried to clean me, there would
> always be a smudge left on my soul from the hunger, poverty and
> drudgery I'd already experienced by the age of five.
>
> Harry Leslie Smith, English writer (1923–2018)[10]

Sadly, there is one form of deprivation that has become the 'new
normal' in some parts of the country: child poverty. Data published
by the End Child Poverty Coalition in 2019 showed that it was
becoming a standard situation in some parts of the UK, affecting
more than half of children in certain areas.[11] In 2019, the chair of the
End Child Poverty Coalition said:

> We know what causes child poverty and we know how to end
> it ... we know that work alone does not guarantee a route out of
> poverty, with two-thirds of child poverty occurring in working
> families. Yet in many areas growing up in poverty is not the excep-
> tion it's the rule, with more children expected to get swept up in
> poverty in the coming years.[12]

Eliminating child poverty has been an aim for many political parties
over the years, which suggests it is a more appealing and manageable topic than the broader issue. However, children are not immune
to their parents' deprivation. During the pandemic, over one in ten
adults living with children reported skipping meals because they
could not afford or access food.[13] Living with adults who have high
poverty-related stress is harmful for children as it causes mental
and physical health problems for the whole family and can lead to
domestic violence or substance abuse. It is vital to deal with adult
and child poverty together to protect young people from the broader
impact of poverty on family life. It is also miserable for a child to
watch their parents struggle without the power to change the situation. (For further information on food insecurity, see Appendix 7.)

Those families who rely on food banks must eat whatever has
been donated, and this tends to be long-life, cheaper foods, which

can often have a lower nutritional value and higher levels of salt and fat. A lack of access to fresh food at home and a reliance on cheap, fast foods can create addictions in the growing brain. Local authorities need to be aware of how this affects their populations, as over a third of children are obese by the time they leave primary school, and this figure is higher in some deprived communities. Figures from Public Health England reveal:

England's poorest areas are fast food hotspots, with five times more outlets found in these communities than in the most affluent … Some local authorities have developed 'healthier zones' to help tackle childhood obesity by limiting the number of outlets in areas with high concentrations of fast-food outlets, high levels of deprivation, or where children gather – including near schools, community centres, playgrounds etc. … while not all fast food is unhealthy, it is typically higher in salt, calories and saturated fat.[14]

To change child poverty, financial problems within the home are not the only issue – local areas must be supported as well. However, this requires the central government to provide the funding to make change possible for cash-strapped councils.

The longer that views on the undeserving poor are spread, the faster is the route towards inept decision making, as was seen in October 2020. In the midst of the pandemic, 321 Conservative MPs voted against plans that would have compelled the government to extend free school meals to over a million children during the holidays. Only five Conservative MPs broke ranks and voted for it. The government spokesman, Gavin Williamson MP, said he wanted to 'help through the Universal Credit System and by ensuring that the welfare system worked for everyone in the country', but it was well known that UC was a system riven with problems and this was a crisis. He went on to say that everyone in the House of Commons was 'united in their commitment to drive out poverty and to make sure that children do not go hungry'.[15] So why then vote against it? It is hardly surprising that the public is cynical about the games that many politicians play. Other MPs stated that they were voting against the motion because of questions over how it would work in practice (Tom Randall, MP for Gedling), but another argued that head teachers were capable individuals and, once given the money and a loosening of the eligibility criteria, they could cope with the extra responsibility (Barry Gardiner, MP for Brent North).

Other MPs didn't want temporary measures to continue indefinitely, preferring a longer-term debate on sustainable solutions (Jo Gideon, MP for Stoke-on-Trent Central). Yet, hungry children don't need a debate, they need food immediately. Another MP saw the issue as a political football: 'I will not be voting for a Labour motion that is just one more action by those intent on undermining and derailing the response to this national crisis with yet another strapline' (Suzanne Webb, MP for Stourbridge). Another MP spoke of his desire to live in a utopian society where neighbourliness and local charities deal with poverty rather than support coming from central government:

> The opposition parties are advocating for us to live in a world where the state caters to every need and every challenge and mitigates every consequence ... That is not the kind of country I want to live in, where generosity of spirit, kindness and support for our neighbours are somehow surplus to requirement ... The combined wealth of some of the individuals and businesses who think this can all be fixed with money means that they are very well placed to make that change themselves if they think it is necessary. Do not tell me these problems only start and end with government.
> [Dr Kieran Mullan, MP for Crewe and Nantwich]

The problem with this attitude during a crisis is that it fails to deal with the immediate needs of the children involved, and more broadly creates a piecemeal society where deprived families are reliant on the charitable mood of the wealthiest in their area. It also suggests that the public doesn't already support local organisations, when in fact the UK charity sector is a multimillion-pound industry, and yet poverty remains.

Other MPs argued that parents were responsible for feeding their children and it was not the role of the government or schools to do so.[16] The issue was discussed for hours in the House of Commons, costing the taxpayer thousands of pounds, only for the policy to be reversed eighteen days later when Downing Street discovered how appalled the public was at the decision and opted for a multimillion-pound support package instead.[17]

This debate shows how difficult it may be to transform the concept of the undeserving poor in many people's minds. Alexander McLean, the founder of the African Prisons Project, offered this alternative:

> The lowliest-looking person is filled with gifts and talents beyond your imagination ... Those living on the margins of society do not need to have their problems solved for them, they just need to be given the opportunities to solve them themselves. And in doing so, they will often also solve the problems of others.[18]

By this argument, the government should act as a facilitator to enable people to live manageable lives. Parliament should not be used as a place of all-powerful judgement. Instead, it should provide a social safety net for when things go wrong and, crucially, remove the barriers that prevent people from helping themselves.

It is clear that the Victorians were missing a piece of the social puzzle, which we now understand. It is the piece that relates to the links between mental health problems causing poverty, and poverty causing mental health problems. The social taboo around mental health has prevented people from seeking help when they most need it, and prevented the services from being properly invested in. Those with mental health problems who were blamed for their poverty were also unable to seek the help that would have enabled them to get out of poverty, and so the cycle continued.

As of 2019, there were an estimated 14 million people in poverty, including 4 million children, and the 2020–21 pandemic and lockdowns have added further economic and psychological impacts on to an already stressed society.[19]

A holistic, government-wide approach to eliminating poverty is essential to dealing effectively with its interconnected problems. In the ancient book *The Art of War*, Chinese military strategist Sun Tzu wrote, 'Strategy without tactics is the slowest route to victory. Tactics without strategy is the noise before defeat.' Whether on the battlefield or for society, this remains true. The aim will fail if the 'tactical' details of the policy are not implemented properly. Similarly, failure will also occur if central and local governments do not support and act on the overarching strategy.

There will be some people who believe that eliminating poverty should not be attempted, that it is a pointless endeavour, conducted by utopian idealists. History has shown that idealism should be avoided at all costs, as it can cause irreparable damage to humanity and the environment. However, the aim of ending poverty is different.

First, in order to eliminate it, the plans must be practical, realistic and strong in the face of scrutiny. In a democracy with a free press, there is no way of covering up failures and there should be no desire to do so. Lessons must be learned.

The second difference is that nobody gets hurt. Poverty elimination strategies should be socially positive and introduced with consideration. This is an important point as it requires a level of self-awareness and concern for others, which sadly some politicians do not have – the former US president Donald Trump having been a classic, but by no means singular, example.

Turning compassion into a positive emotion, rather than one that suggests people and society would be taken advantage of, is important and likely to take time. In today's fast-paced society, people's lives are complex, so a more understanding outlook from leaders and society towards those in difficulty is essential.

Compassion is at the core of every major religion. Humanity has been trying to imbed this concept into its societies for thousands of years, and yet we continue to struggle with it.[20] In 1845, Benjamin Disraeli wrote, 'Christianity teaches us to love our neighbour as ourself, modern society acknowledges no neighbour.'[21] If it cannot be assumed that the public will vote for dealing with poverty based on compassion alone, then the policy would need to be presented in other ways, especially in terms of how it will benefit everyone, whether they live in poverty or not.

14

THE PLAN

Equality is the soul of liberty; there is, in fact, no liberty without it.
Frances Wright, Scottish author (1795–1852)[1]

It would be remiss to ignore universal basic income (UBI) as an option for dealing with poverty in Britain. The Stanford Basic Income Lab states that, 'At its core, UBI is a cash transfer given to all members of a community on a recurrent basis regardless of income level and with no strings attached'.[2] The method has been studied for decades across the world, and the Welsh government has considered conducting its own pilot as one in five children in Wales in 2021 were living below the poverty line.[3] However, a Welsh government report in 2019 noted that deprivation is a broader issue than often considered:

> Deprivation does not just mean being poor. It refers to unmet need which is caused by a lack of resources of other kinds, not just financial. It can mean having fewer resources and opportunities than we might expect in our society, for example in terms of health or education.[4]

UBI provides the public with a basic level of financial stability, irrespective of personal wealth. However, it is politically contentious as politicians often worry that it will disincentivise work. In pilot studies in Canada and Finland, UBI has been found to reduce stress and improve mental and physical health, reduce crime and in some situations improve job prospects.

Alaska has provided a Permanent Fund Dividend since 1982. It affords an annual income to every woman, man and child, and is funded by the $70 billion Permanent Fund, generated by Alaska's mine, oil and gas reserves.[5] The British benefit system is complicated and problematic, so a similar approach to UBI is attractive. However, Britain does not have Alaska's disposable income and will struggle with its national debt for decades to come, so an alternative option is needed. In the future, the spread of new technology will change the workplace and for employees this will mean more periods of unemployment, retraining and the need for a flexible welfare system that supports the population through the transition.[6]

How should Britain transform its economy and social system without fomenting instability or political revolution, which will frighten voters away from supporting policies that could end poverty? The answer is: with calm clarity. A plan to end deprivation needs to be communicated and implemented in a way that ensures everyone can understand the benefits of a more equal society and feels they can contribute. This is particularly important for those living in poverty, who often feel marginalised from the debate. Darren McGarvey highlighted this in his book, *Poverty Safari*:

> Lack of insight often leads to the creation of myths as people pour hyperbole into the gaps in their understanding ... What I soon learned was that no matter your background, you are cast out the second you offend the people who're in charge of your empowerment ... Look out for these people. The people who pay wonderful lip service to giving the working class a voice, but who start to look very nervous whenever we open our mouths to speak.[7]

Transparency and thoughtful debate are key to maintaining public trust. The former British prime minister Tony Blair has spoken of his concerns around the public's waning faith in the 'generational promise' – the social understanding that the next generation will do better than the current one. He considers that the best way to re-establish lost trust is to have strong political leaders with a unifying vision, who offer radical solutions that are both reasonable and based on evidence.[8]

The need for a focused, centralised approach that promotes collaboration between local government, charities and the public was recommended by the UK's Social Mobility Commission 2020, as it reviewed the Johnson government's progress:

A major worry for the Commission was the lack of joined up thinking across government departments, which is why it is now calling for a central unit to support its work and to help ensure action is taken.

The Prime Minister has set as his goal 'levelling up opportunity' across the country ... but there remains work to be done to understand what levelling-up will mean in practice.[9]

As with many government plans, the key to whether it will be effective is in the detail. Levelling up sounds positive, but if it is not the elimination of poverty, then what is it? The broader truth is that there is a huge difference between a moderately competent government seeking to *alleviate* poverty, and an extremely able and ambitious government seeking to *eliminate* poverty. Alleviation is much easier and far less effective. We know this because we have been doing it for decades.

A Warlike Focus

In 2003, I joined the Foreign and Commonwealth Office. At that time, Britain was at war in Afghanistan and had just started the war in Iraq a few months previously. I entered a civil service that was completely immersed in a war mentality. Teams sprang up, budgets were found and new postings were created. The wars were all that team leaders and senior managers wanted to talk about, and it was all that politicians talked about. It seemed as if the entire civil service did nothing else of any value at all.

That period showed that when the British civil service is given genuine direction, it can be an extraordinarily powerful tool for government. It is that type of focus that is needed to end poverty in Britain. This would be a vital element because if ministers told the civil service that its aim was, for example, only to halve poverty rates in five years, then it would become just another target for civil servants to work towards, among hundreds of others. And what would happen if the target was missed? Frankly, not a lot. No one would lose their job and the civil service does not give large bonuses, so there would be little incentive either. However, should the government's main aim be to eliminate poverty, then the civil service and ministers would need a similar type of focus to that shown during the Iraq and Afghanistan wars.

Day One

If a prime minister were elected on the basis of eliminating poverty, where should they begin? The first week of any premiership involves creating a new Cabinet. A new post of Minister for the Elimination of Poverty would need to be created and viewed as one of the most important roles in government, alongside the Chancellor of the Exchequer and Prime Minister. The new position would need a department, the Department for the Elimination of Poverty (DEP). An endeavour on this scale cannot be solely conducted from a top-down standpoint, so collaboration with communities, charities, social researchers and local governments would be essential.

What would a Minister for the Elimination of Poverty actually do?

The DEP's strategy would need to be the most important overarching strategy in government, and one into which all other departmental strategies fed. No area would be exempt from having some part of its strategy aimed at helping to deal with poverty. All government and non-governmental policies (where applicable) would need to be reviewed and analysed to understand if they create or maintain poverty. Those policies found wanting could be put on the government website for consultation and debate, and then dealt with methodically one by one.

Beyond this, the DEP could also analyse and publish findings on the raft of social barriers that prevent people from accessing jobs and services. Employment discrimination and the poverty premium are key examples of this and have been discussed earlier. Publishing the findings alongside best practices would help to educate the public against the 'undeserving poor' stereotype, while clarifying the issues and enhancing broader debate.

The DEP could also have the power to create new nationwide policies that combine the green agenda and poverty elimination. One of these could be a new system of exchange for children's goods, such as clothes, shoes, toys and books – a system that has been at work for over a decade in Tower Hamlets.

The Exchange Project

An unassuming building set back from a main road in East London became one of the most important places I found as a new mother. From the moment you walked through the doors, you knew you were in a safe, child-friendly space. Your little one could walk around and take an interest in things in a way that would have been unacceptable in other shops; in here, friendly, wise faces simply smiled. On one side of the large room were rails filled with children's second-hand clothes and other items, ready to be exchanged for free for the ones you had in your bag. If they were in good condition, and you wanted to exchange no more than six items each week, you could take your pick. Bring in a babygrow and take away a blanket. Bring in a pair of shoes and take away a book. As long as it was for primary school-age children or younger, it was a free swap. Children grow out of their clothes so quickly that some are never used, so the flexibility of the service was one of its strengths.

The area was spacious and had one entrance and exit, which was essential to prevent little feet from wandering too far. Some larger toys were conveniently placed in the middle of the room, which meant that parents could browse at ease, while always able to have one eye on what their child was up to.

By the time I started using it, the Exchange Project had been in place for about eleven years. It was set up by a small group of East End midwives who were seeing new mothers enter their postnatal check-ups with almost nothing for themselves or their babies. The project became a lifeline to hundreds of families and was sorely missed when it closed during the pandemic. It was a place to social-ise and meet other parents, which was vital in a big city where so many of the inhabitants are transient visitors and creating of a sense of community can be difficult. The staff in that room made every-thing easier and that is no small thing.

The Exchange Project won the Queen's Award in 2019. The cere-mony was a genteel affair, with pretty cakes and bone-china cups. There was a small assembly of trustees, volunteers and supporters who all felt passionately about the project. As the ceremony drew to a close, two elderly gentlemen in neat shalwar kameez stepped forward and uncovered their own award for the project. It had been donated by the local British-Bangladeshi community to say 'thank you' for all the support they had received. A gasp of surprise and delight echoed around the room at the unexpected gift. Until then, no one had real-ised the impact that the small charity had had on that particular community as everyone was welcome, but it should not have been a surprise. Tower Hamlets has one of the highest levels of child poverty in the country, with over half of children living below the poverty line, many of whom are from minority ethnic communities.

The Cost of Children report by the Halifax building society in 2017 highlighted that parents spent around £47 per month on children's clothes and £33 per month on toys. (In 2023, adjusted for inflation, this equates to £60 on clothes and £42 on toys.) Toddlers are the most expensive group.[10] For families living around the poverty line, the ability to spend less and still provide for their children would create a significant boost to family finances and morale. The environmental impact of reusing products would also be significant. Reuse is a better remedy than recycling in the fight against climate change, as Sir David Attenborough highlighted during a BBC interview:

We are going to have to live more economically than we do. And we can do that and I believe we will do it more happily, not less hap-pily ... the excesses the capitalist system has brought us have got to be curbed somehow. I believe that ordinary people worldwide are beginning to realise that greed does not actually lead to joy.

Our economic system has been based on the profit principle that you have to come out at the end of the year having made a profit ... and in the short term that works, but then it ends with disaster. So that, at last, you have to have the wisdom to realise that you can live sustainably, that it is possible that your economics could work on a rather different system ... if you help the natural world, the world becomes a better place for everybody.[11]

A national system of exchange would not just be an essential way of reducing child and family deprivation, but would also offer an additional and very practical way of reducing waste and pollution from the fashion industry. Children's clothes would still be bought new in shops, but there needs to be a greater balance in what is newly created and how much we recycle and reuse.

This is a comfortable example of how the poverty elimination and climate change agendas can complement one another. This harmonious way of creating government policies could rapidly speed up the change that Britain needs. As a national system, products could be more easily spread out across the country. If one area has a glut of baby clothes and another of children's shoes, mixing the pool of products would be easier and spread the wealth more evenly across the country. Part-time jobs could also be created and used as a stepping stone for parents returning to work or in need of jobs that fit around school hours.

However, proponents of the system should note that there may be serious pushback from the fashion industry over concerns of lost profits in the children's clothing market. The sector is worth billions of pounds to the UK economy and employs hundreds of thousands of people, but this cannot be used as an argument against setting up a system that will help every family in the country.[12] There were doctors who opposed the creation of the NHS after the Second World War and yet it is now an essential and well-loved service.

For businesses to survive the changing economic times, they must adapt. Size and strength do not always lead to longevity. Woolworths was a high-street staple for decades until the retail sector changed, and the giant went into administration with the loss of thousands of jobs after the 2008 crash. Adaptability as a form of economic resilience will be increasingly important as the calls for a more equitable and environmentally friendly society continue to grow.

In the Italian town of Prato, sustainable fashion has become an integral part of the local economy, and Britain is in a good position to learn from its extensive experience and best practices. There are hundreds of companies in a small district, each specialising in a different aspect of the process of transforming old clothes into new ones, such as spinning, weaving or designing. First, the clothes are sorted by colour, then they are torn apart, washed and the new recycled material is transformed to make new garments with minimal waste. The town says it processes 15 per cent of all recycled clothes in the world.[13] Alternatively, Ghana receives many of the clothes that the UK throws away. Those that are saleable are sold in the local markets, and those that cannot be sold are burnt on large tips, causing serious pollution in the surrounding areas. This is an expensive and destructive way of treating the excess resources that come from our country.[14]

The processes involved in creating recycled cloth in Prato are relatively labour intensive, but could potentially be mechanised if given the right impetus. Either way, the fashion industry needs to change direction at some point in Britain, and for regions that are vulnerable to climate change, new industries will need to be developed to prevent unemployment and destitution, and to support a more renewable economy focused on people and reuse, rather than consumption.

Yuval Noah Harari suggests in his book *21 Lessons for the 21st Century* that people may eventually become surplus to requirements as AI takes over industries that do not specifically require the human hand or heart. He suggests that innovations in the life sciences and social sciences could enable computers to become better at analysing human behaviour than people currently are, and that any new jobs developed will require a high skill set that would leave holes in the labour market for unskilled workers. Harari suggests that governments will need to support these workers actively through a lifelong education sector and financial safety nets during inevitable periods of transition between careers.[15]

Social media's algorithms already decide what comes up on a person's feed by predicting what they are most likely to enjoy watching, and AI systems are also used to trade on the stock market. The extent to which this will spread to other sectors is unclear, as is whether governments will intervene to protect jobs, rather than support people through retraining services and unemployment support. Either way, it is clear that the speed at which technology is being developed has overtaken the speed of social mobility and this is where the danger lies. If poverty already exists in a society where more jobs can be automated, and the government does not act to acknowledge the risks and protect the vulnerable, then the consequences could compound an already difficult situation. However, if strategies are in place to prevent destitution, then the social system will be able to deal with the changes that technology brings.

Harari suggests that job losses may not result solely from the rise in technology, but also through our evolving understanding of neurobiology, which may enable computers to outperform human psychiatrists and bodyguards by the middle of the century.[16] The idea that people will no longer need to talk to a human psychiatrist seems unlikely, especially as the rise of social media and the internet has not prevented loneliness, as many had predicted. Harari acknowledges that just because something is possible does not mean it will become popular: for example, today there could be a market in human organs given the demand, but this has been prevented through international laws. Similarly, automated answering machines and customer service teams based abroad are often less popular than speaking to a person in-country, and this has led many companies to reintroduce UK-based call centres. A society free from deprivation is key to helping employees flex to an unpredictable future by providing the stability they need to guide them through the coming changes, whatever they may be.

As the population ages, new materials and styles in fashion should be innovated to take into account everyone's needs. For people living with disabilities, new fashions need to be accessible and attractive for everyone to wear, as not all clothing is suitable, for example, for someone sitting in a wheelchair all day or with limited hand function. There are opportunities available to reform old industries and create new ones in ways that are appropriate for an environmentally friendly and inclusive future.[17]

Just a Phone Call Away

To deal with the intertwined issues that create and maintain poverty, the DEP would need an anti-poverty hotline, staffed by trained professionals with a deep understanding of how to talk compassionately to people with mental health problems or addiction issues, while also having a good understanding of the benefit system, housing, finances and more. This hotline would be similar to Childline in being there to support people in difficult or abusive situations, and would need to operate with the same compassion and aim to serve.[18] Northern Ireland's Department for Communities has a 'Make the Call' service that connects people with the benefits and support services available, and the Citizens Advice service provides similar support throughout the UK.

The anti-poverty hotline could expand on these models. After a discussion with the caller, the staff could create a 'life map' for each person that could contain two lists. The first would contain what the government could do to help – for example, sorting out a Universal Credit claim or finding local support centres (such as Age UK, children's centres or domestic violence shelters). The other list would highlight what the individual could do to help themselves, such as requesting mental health support from a GP, or getting internet or financial/literacy training at a job centre or library. Each plan would be tailored to the individual's needs and sent to them. It could also be kept on record so that, if they called the helpline again, the responder could have their details to hand to speed up the support process.

There must also be greater use of the low-cost and natural treatments available in our country. It is not just talking therapies and anti-depressants that can reduce the impact of stress on the human body; it is well known that access to blue spaces, green spaces and vandalism-free areas can all contribute to better health.

Blue Spaces

Research has found that access to areas of open water significantly reduces stress levels in the human body. To take advantage of this, a greater variety of outdoor bathing options could be used to draw out the medicinal benefits for the whole population. In Iceland, hydrothermal pools are used for outdoor bathing as the weather is often too inclement to swim in the sea. The pools need not be large or expensive to maintain – the one I visited in Iceland was a large, concrete water channel and free to use. The combination of warm water, cool air and open sky was exhilarating. While the UK's hydrothermal activity is not as widespread as Iceland's, water can be heated using a combination of underground heat pumps and renewable energy.

Sea bathing is also helpful in reducing inflammation and supporting mental health. There are around 100 sea pools in Britain's coastal towns and, considering the medicinal effects of saltwater, the building of these lidos should be expanded. There could be particular focus on areas of deprivation and high proportions of older people, who may benefit as much from hydrotherapy as from pharmacology. Not everyone can swim, so the sea is not necessarily an inviting prospect, but saltwater lidos on the beach, which are free to use and protect swimmers from the waves, are an alternative. The largest saltwater pool covers 4 acres in Walpole Bay, Kent, and varies in depth to cater for children and adults. It is unclear how much these pools cost to build, but upkeep can be minimal as the water is refreshed at high tide and the outlay can be recouped through the longer-term health of the local population.

Where this is not possible, the creation of more community groups like 'Chill' at Croyde, in Devon, could be supported, where people enter the sea with an instructor.[19] The first sea-bathing hospital opened in Margate in 1791, so this is not a new idea; however, it has gone out of fashion and over 200 sea-bathing lidos have been removed since their 1930s heyday.[20] Their reintroduction could offer NHS doctors an alternative to prescription drugs, while the pools are still accessible to those on the lowest incomes in deprived coastal communities.[21] This is particularly important for older people suffering with conditions like arthritis or swelling, where the sea salt can draw water out of the tissues. However, considering the number of older people who are unable to heat their homes or eat properly (many go to hospital malnourished), a holistic plan is required to support older people, and part of this should include safe access to the sea and perhaps less reliance on combinations of pills to treat ailments.

Horticulture

A focus on creating accessible green spaces is an opportunity for the anti-poverty and green agendas to work collaboratively together, while also giving the public the opportunity to grow their own food and destress at the same time. More allotments could be created on brownfield sites that are unsuitable for homes, or in the grounds of youth centres to educate and encourage young people to relax more naturally than by using addictive substances. Figures show that waiting times for some allotments can be up to ten years, with applications soaring since the pandemic began. In London, forty allotment sites have closed since 2013 and yet in some areas demand has risen by 500 per cent.[22] This trend continues nationwide, with around 100,000 people on allotment waiting lists and the average waiting time being two years and eight months.[23]

Viren Swami, professor of social psychology, is co-author of the report *Emotional Well-Being under Conditions of Lockdown*. His research found that people who spent more time outside during the pandemic were happier than those who remained mostly indoors.[24] According to the Royal Horticultural Society, its sector is worth £24 billion to the economy, and it only sees that increasing as firms in all sectors realise the importance of making their outdoor spaces greener as they move towards net zero. Horticulture is now a specialism in high demand and this is likely to continue long term.[25]

With small levels of funding, sites could be placed on the top of flat-roofed buildings, such as those used in eco-farms, where land-based fish farms feed organic, liquid fertiliser into hydroponic food systems, where crops are grown without soil.[26] As climate change continues to affect weather patterns, the UK's need for sustainable, domestic food production will expand, and if the cost of living continues to rise, access to these types of green spaces will be increasingly important.

Vandalism

The graffiti in our area is neither impressive nor artistic like the street art of Banksy. Tags litter the walls and yet the local authority's powers to remove them are limited to requesting the property owner remove them at their own cost. As a result, graffiti is less likely to be found in better-off neighbourhoods, where people have the time and money to remove tags from personal property. If the property is owned by a social housing association, it can stay there for years as it never becomes a priority and the residents' concerns can be easily ignored.

Yet, graffiti is one of the first things a visitor will notice when entering an area and use it to judge whether it is affluent or not, or if they are safe walking the streets. It is a passive-aggressive way of preventing areas from being attractive to tourists, investors and mobile workers. It can also compromise attempts to build more socially mixed neighbourhoods, as well as promote social cohesion at the town or city scale, by highlighting the gap between different types of neighbourhoods.[27]

Many people do not make use of their local open spaces because of a fear of anti-social behaviour or crime. This may range from a simple lack of respect, such as fly-tipping, litter, speeding, rowdiness or vandalism, to more serious crimes involving violence, theft, drugs and abuse.[28] Giving councils the power to clean graffiti off private property would be a very easy and visible way of showing that people are worth society's care, irrespective of their wealth. Local laws need to change to ensure everyone can live in an area that promotes respect for others and the environment.

Trust

Five years to eliminate poverty is a very short time compared with the scale of the job. However, there is also a need to understand that the public will only give politicians the benefit of doubt for a short period before cynicism and anger spread.

Politicians are not often afforded much trust or hope; the public are guarded, and often with good reason. Any government elected to office on the proposition of ending deprivation would need to act quickly and provide practical and visible solutions to ensure that the public's good will towards the policy was maintained across the five years.

A good example of why the public is careful with trusting politicians is our neighbourhood youth centre in East London. It is a large building with grounds that include a basketball court, climbing walls and a skate park, but the building is rarely open, the climbing walls are slimy with mould and the facilities become waterlogged when it rains. It does have a shelter covering its closed shutters, however, where young people can hang around and smoke dope.

Where facilities like this already exist and are primed for use, there must be a five-year funding pledge by government to ensure that when sites do open, they can stay open, whether it is a local swimming pool, library or youth centre. Stabilised funding is vital for building trust between the politicians and the public, but also for youth workers on the ground who often need time to build strong relationships with young people to keep them away from gangs and violence. In Darren McGarvey's *Poverty Safari*, he describes a similar situation in Glasgow:

> In youth clubs, young people play pool on wonky tables with cues that have no tips. When the table gives out, it won't be fixed or replaced for months ... Staff bring in their own property or purchase items like ... arts and crafts material and batteries with their own money to provide an acceptable level of service. Children turn up to take part in activities that have been advertised that youth workers either haven't been informed about or have no resources to provide ... There is a constant sense that nobody really knows what is going on ...[29]

There is a high demand for these services, but without committed funding the support becomes irregular and simply adds to the frustration and chaos of children's lives. It becomes a disincentive to get involved in positive pursuits, as the children then have to deal with the disappointment that comes from advertised services being cancelled without warning. It is demoralising, and not just for the children but also for the youth workers whose job insecurity constrains their ability to highlight and address the problems, so the issues go unsolved or ignored.[30]

Britain needs to open up again in order to facilitate social mobility. The situation of libraries provides a good indicator of how important any government believes social mobility to be. Funding for libraries has continued to decline since the 2010 austerity measures were introduced.[31] Over the subsequent nine years, almost 800 libraries closed across the country, and yet in 2019–20 over 165 million books were borrowed by over 7 million people.[32] It is not viable to suggest that these services are not wanted and have been taken over by digital media. Not everyone has a smartphone to download books and, in any case, a library provides more than just books. It affords the mental space to study quietly, to think and gain further education or advice, all of which are invaluable when trying to get yourself out of poverty.

This chapter has offered some methods that could be used as part of a poverty elimination agenda. It would require a wide-ranging strategy, but this is not impossible if worked through methodically and resourced properly. The plan must be largely formulated prior to taking office in Downing Street to ensure that no time is wasted once work begins. Everyone leading a government department, at either the national, devolved or local level, should know what is needed from them, and expectations need to be manageable to ensure the smooth running of the process. There is no real reason why eliminating poverty cannot happen. It just needs compassion, focus and a plan.

15

IMPACT OF SUCCESS

A well-ordered affluent society slows down ... An unequal, human economic world is unsustainable and so it will end; but some possible ends are much better than others.

Danny Dorling, Oxford University professor and author[1]

Esther Perel knows a lot. As a world-renowned psychotherapist and relationships expert, her online talks have garnered more than 30 million views and she offers an insightful and original voice on modern relationships.[2] When entrepreneur Richard Reed asked her what her most important piece of advice was, she offered this:

The quality of your life ultimately depends on the quality of your relationships. Not on your achievements, not on how smart you are, not on how rich you are, but on the quality of your relationships ... Ultimately at the end of your life, if people commend you, they will say what a wonderful human being you were ... it won't be the fact that you had a big bank account, it really won't. It will be about how you treated the people around you and how you made them feel.[3]

Eliminating poverty from Britain is not about making everyone millionaires. It is about ensuring people have enough of what they need (headspace and money) to make choices. The impact on our relationships is rarely discussed, yet teachers have known for decades that children with chaotic home lives need the stability of a good relationship with their teachers to begin to learn anything at all. In her TED Talk, educator Rita F. Pierson gave an extraordinary speech about the importance of relationships in children's lives and education:

> We know why kids drop out. We know why kids don't learn. It's either poverty, low attendance, negative peer influences. But one of the things that we never discuss or we rarely discuss is the value and importance of human connection. Relationships ...
>
> For years, I watched my mother ... buy peanut butter and crackers ... for kids that needed to eat, and a washcloth and some soap for the kids who didn't smell so good. See, it's hard to teach kids who stink!
>
> Can we stand to have more relationships? Absolutely. Will you like all your children? Of course not! And you know your toughest kids are never absent ... The tough ones show up for a reason ... It's the relationship.[4]

Pierson's speech always gives me shivers. Her talk shows the immense extra challenges that teachers face and the effort they make in order to educate children from a wide variety of backgrounds. Without poverty, though, many of these challenges would ebb away and schools could focus on broadening children's horizons instead of raising them up from the depths of deprivation, child abuse and low self-esteem. If we want better attainment at schools, ending poverty is the best place to start.

Darren McGarvey discussed the effect of these psychological stresses on his own childhood in his book *Poverty Safari*:

> Stressful social conditions have a psychological impact on everyone who is subject to them. Over time, they change the way people behave ... This strain can limit human capacity for empathy, tolerance and compassion and makes many people angry, agitated, resentful and frightened ...
>
> In terms of poverty, stress is one of the biggest variables in the equation. If we could significantly reduce stress levels across society, we could raise the quality of life for millions of people. Such is

the sheer scale of the task, the question that emerges is not so much 'How do we do it?' but rather, 'Who is responsible for doing it?'[5]

McGarvey argues that, as the government is unlikely to ever deal properly with poverty, it is left to individuals and communities to do it for themselves. While his point is understandable, and written from a pre-pandemic perspective, future governments can change the situation for millions of people, and make better choices on where to spend the national budget. How policies are conveyed to the voting public also matters, as innovative ideas need to be explained far enough in advance to make people feel comfortable about trying new things.

Rod Judkins is an artist and creative adviser for many companies and organisations around the world. His book *Make Brilliant Work* discusses how innovation is not something to be afraid of:

> Don't jump for the first obvious choice, consider the consequence of each move. [Stanley] Kubrick was a disciplined director because chess taught him strategy. Making a film is a battle ... and achieving the best outcome is a slippery and unpredictable business.
>
> One of the most common problems I deal with when working as a consultant for an organisation is the client settling for the first idea if it's OK. They're so relieved to solve the problem that they jump ahead and I have to encourage them to continue to see if there is a better, brilliant solution.[6]

It may seem strange to compare film making to public policy, but there are similarities. The complexities of deprivation mean that there will need to be multiple solutions, and some will work better than others, depending on the circumstances of the individual, community or district. This requires a flexible approach from government and the public, which isn't always appreciated. The desire for quick results over excellent ones, which may afford longer-lasting results, but are more expensive, should be properly considered. Short-term thinking in government rarely helps to produce long-term results of the type needed to end privation successfully. The media and public often have a short fuse when things go wrong. This is in large part because when the government makes mistakes, people's lives are directly affected and usually for the worse, so the plan needs to be understood and organised before a political party takes charge.

International Impact

It is impossible to know the full impact of removing deprivation from Britain, as the ripple effects are likely to have expected and unexpected consequences. The lessons learned would need to be monitored and understood over the years, and incorporated into the system to maintain progress.

Internationally, if Britain were to succeed, or even come close to succeeding, then the world would surely be watching. It would be a new situation for a Western, developed nation and the methods could be taken abroad to support other countries interested in doing the same thing. As every nation globally struggles with its own inequalities, it is likely that new ideas and methods of working would be of interest to others through the attraction of environmental stability and economic strength. This may be particularly marked in large European countries, such as France and Germany. Their populations may pressurise their governments to deal with their own poverty, if they see Britain succeed.

The European Parliament and Commission could equally come under pressure to provide more support to less developed parts of the EU and, in doing so, create further stability. In recent years, the European project has been under the spotlight for being overly bureaucratic and separate from the needs of many European citizens. The rise of far-right groups across Europe, in Hungary, Austria and Switzerland, has highlighted this in a concerning way, especially considering that Hitler and Mussolini were both elected. Democracy does not automatically protect a nation from extremist leaders. Brexit has also raised concerns that the EU is under threat. However, taking up the mantle to raise living standards for all people in Europe using more innovative methods may offer a new way of re-engaging with many European citizens and reducing the discontent upon which the far right feeds.

American deprivation also fuels its racial divide. The more conservative nature of its political system may prevent politicians from attempting the wide-ranging reforms that would be needed, and yet a poverty-free USA would be significantly more powerful than it is today.

Asylum-seekers

Refugees and migrants are on the move across the world, more now than at any other time in recent history. The combination of war, political instability, discrimination and environmental degradation has meant people are having to move more than they would otherwise choose to. Britain bears its share of responsibility after promising to bring stability to Iraq, Afghanistan and Libya, and yet none of these nations live in peace.

It is important that the UK softens its stance on immigration, particularly in light of the economic problems created by the departure of so many people after Brexit. The personal qualities that many migrants have – a desire to work hard, improve themselves, be brave and take risks – are ones that Britain should welcome with open arms. It is also well known that anti-immigrant attitudes reduce as poverty levels fall, so Britain's confidence both at home and abroad would grow and we could regain our reputation for stability and pragmatism, which is now so desperately needed around the world.

Energy Independence

On 24 February 2022, Russia invaded Ukraine. The NATO Secretary General, Jens Stoltenberg, spoke of a 'new reality' for European security in the long term.[7] One way that international instability affected Britain was through changes in oil and gas prices. The week of the invasion saw oil costs increase to $105 (£74) per barrel.

Seventy per cent of Russia's exports have been in the form of energy and minerals. China–Russia trade ties in natural oil and gas have become stronger in recent years and the two countries have signed a lucrative thirty-year contract. The gas agreement alone is worth $100 billion, so as Western sanctions against Russia mean that it must move away from supplying Europe, it has a ready buyer in China.[8] Weaning the international energy markets off Russian gas supplies has been an important way of promoting self-reliance and encouraging the expansion of green energy. As discussed in earlier chapters, the poverty elimination agenda and the green agenda must be complementary to one another, and operate in a way that benefits British manufacturers and the creation of new jobs. Given the international situation, this cannot come quickly enough.

Domestic Impacts

Some impacts will be more obvious than others, as more equal societies are well known to have less crime and fewer mental health problems. However, it is not just at the national level that the impact will be felt, but also locally as smaller communities discover what they are able to achieve when they no longer have to deal with the varying impact of poverty on their streets.

I put this idea to Fuzz Dixon at St Luke's church in the heart of the East End. The church provides a night shelter to the homeless and during the pandemic it ran a food bank for around 100 families in the area. Servicing the local community in this way takes up significant resources and time. I wondered, *If her church no longer needed to offer those services, what else could it do?* Her reply was diverse:

> We would deal with addiction, loneliness and early years support. Some parents don't have financial problems, but they do struggle with emotional loneliness. Parenting is hard and people need support, especially if they don't have any family nearby.
>
> If the parents haven't been parented properly themselves, then they often need training and support on how to parent their own children, so we would offer more parenting classes.

The problems that British society faces are varied and interwoven. Fuzz's church would clearly find other issues to deal with if it wasn't having to focus on poverty, but this also highlights how much extra we are missing from our society for as long as deprivation remains. If those are the options for one church in a small part of London, what would the impact be if multiplied across the country? The ripple effect could be immense, and local changes added together can create countrywide change and stability. Nowhere would this stability be more important than in Northern Ireland after the decades of violence that its population has endured. How would eliminating poverty affect peace in Northern Ireland? In his speech for the Nobel Peace Prize, the South African leader F.W. de Klerk spoke unequivocally about conflict prevention:

> There can be no real peace without constant effort, planning and hard work ... In our quest for peace we should constantly ask ourselves what we should do to create conditions in which peace can prosper ...
>
> Peace does not fare well where poverty and deprivation reign. It does not flourish where there is ignorance and a lack of education and information. Repression, injustice and exploitation are inimical with peace. Peace is gravely threatened by inter-group fear and envy, and by the unleashing of unrealistic expectations. Racial, class and religious intolerance and prejudice are its mortal enemies.[9]

The Northern Ireland peace is fragile and precious. Between the late 1960s and late 1990s, the Troubles killed more than 3,500 people, as the historically dominant Protestants and the Catholic minority fought against each other over whether to remain part of the United Kingdom or join the Republic of Ireland. While paramilitary groups still exist, they have mostly disarmed and to a large extent the violence has ceased. However, sectarian tensions endure, and the Troubles have left significant physical and mental scars on the population.

The Good Friday Agreement ended the fighting in 1998. However, official statistics show the impact on the population's mental health as more people committed suicide in Northern Ireland between 1998 and 2016 (4,400) than were killed during the thirty-year war.

Unhelpfully, the momentum towards stability was lost for three years after the 2016 election, which caused the collapse of the Northern Ireland Assembly and power-sharing executive.

On the twentieth anniversary of the 1998 Good Friday Agreement, the message from mental health organisations was clear:

> There can never be real peace in Northern Ireland until we have peaceful minds ... promised action on a regional trauma service, increased access to psychological therapies, recovery-focused provision, maternal mental health, and eating disorders has failed to materialise.[10]

Northern Ireland has significantly higher rates of mental health problems than the rest of the UK, with over a third of all GP appointments concerning mental health, and one of the highest prescription rates for anti-depressants in the world. Access to counselling is patchy and often limited.[11] In 2022, polling showed that the majority of adults (70 per cent) had experienced a mental health problem in the previous year, and estimates suggested that the cost to the area's economy was £3.4 billion each year.[12]

If peace in Northern Ireland is to last, then the population must receive the support it requires to deal with the after-effects of the Troubles, including help to stimulate the economy, eliminate poverty and prevent the mental health problems becoming intergenerational. The population has lived through serious pain and horror, and removing privation from this part of the country is vital to ensuring its future stability and prosperity. While the UK government seeks to support peace internationally, it must also ensure that peace is solidified in Northern Ireland at the same time. Dealing with destitution will do much to secure it.

The 2020 Global Social Mobility Index (prepared by the World Economic Forum) ranked the United Kingdom twenty-first out of eighty-two countries for social mobility. This is far behind many other European countries with similar-sized economies, such as Germany and France, ranked eleventh and twelfth respectively.[13] This shows quite how much work is needed to create a more equitable society. Five years is a tiny amount of time to do it in, and yet longer-term strategies often fail because of the fast turnover of governments and their priorities.

The former governor of the Bank of England, Mark Carney, spoke of his concerns on inequality for future generations in his BBC Reith Lecture during the 2020 pandemic:

> Covid is fundamentally unequal in its impact and it has exposed deep inequalities in our societies. The virus targets older populations, those with pre-existing conditions like obesity, hypertension and diabetes.
>
> In the UK, men in low-skilled jobs were found to be almost four times more likely to die from Covid-19 than professionals ... The economic impacts of containment measures also fall differently across populations. Lockdowns have decimated jobs in service, hospitality and entertainment industries. In the UK nearly half of the jobs that were at risk of permanent layoffs were those with wages of less than £10 an hour.
>
> The increases in unemployment affect the young, minority ethnic communities and women to a materially greater degree. Closure of primary and secondary schools will undermine equality of opportunity in the years ahead. Education under lockdown depends on parental guidance and access to a computer and good broadband, reinforcing the structural advantages of children coming from richer households.
>
> The cost of these inequities will mean greater income disparities and higher unemployment in the future. The young will pay a significant economic price and that's even before the possibility of higher taxes over their lifetimes to fund the current emergency. As the costs of preventative measures grow, so too does the imperative for a clear strategy that values life, opportunity, fairness and sustainability.[14]

I couldn't have put it better myself.

It is the responsibility of any government seeking to eliminate deprivation that it takes the issue seriously and with the appreciation that the public are not likely to afford it a second chance. The hope associated with voting for it is precious. Were a government to use the concept as a gimmick or an election tactic and then fail to produce any results, it would create such anger and cynicism that the opportunity might be lost for a generation or more. This would be a serious miscalculation with long-term consequences for the most vulnerable in our society. Care must be taken.

16

CONCLUSION

If we had more justice there would be less need of charity.
                    Henry Ford, American car manufacturer, 1934[1]

That was the twentieth century. This is the twenty-first ... It's time.

I wonder what it would feel like to be the first generation born in a Britain without poverty. I will never know. The 1980s were littered with social and economic strife, but as I look at the youngsters running out of primary school each afternoon, I have a keen sense that ending poverty will create lives of deep security and contentment. Children smile when they feel like that. They have no weight on their shoulders to hold them back. Parents smile too.

It has been written that children need a minimum of twelve hugs a day to grow up happy. They will often seek them out naturally when they have a stable home life. Watch a contented child play on the beach for a while and they will naturally go back to their loved one for a hug, to recharge before heading out to discover more. Children who are not sure how they will be received, pause and assess their parents' mood before going back or don't think of doing it at all.

This sense of security is bound up with a reliable routine and low levels of family stress. Children are born into an alien landscape unaware of the language, food, customs and dangers, so a child's routine offers safety points throughout the day. Poverty disrupts a parent's ability to provide that certainty, as British actor and director Kathy Burke knows:

I just remember as a kid, if we had money, it meant we had food. It meant we had heating ... but when there wasn't money, which was quite a lot of the time ... we did have to go to bed hungry and did have to go to bed cold.[2]

Children get used to poverty and that is a grotesque thought. Sadly, it remains the case that poverty is inextricably linked to where you are born, when you are born and to whom, and all of this is currently based on luck. Politicians and influencers often state that it is up to an individual to fulfil their own potential and that a person can do anything they want to, if they set their mind to it. This is an insulting fallacy for those born into poverty. The hurdles people must climb just to start on an equal footing with their more affluent peers means that this kind of utopian dream can be crushing when reality is revealed. Even for those who are moderately affluent, money and luck often go hand in hand.

In September 2022, the then Chancellor Kwasi Kwarteng announced a mini budget containing such extreme policies that it shook the financial markets and over 1,000 mortgage offers were removed from sale within a few days. Interest rates rose quickly, and it had serious consequences for people's housing and rental costs, all at a time when the cost of living was rising too. Those who fixed their mortgages earlier in the year saved hundreds of pounds per month in extra payments. For our household, it would have meant an extra £600 per month going to the bank, all for nothing. It was pure luck that we escaped. Not intelligence, not hard work. Luck.

This is a real example of why extreme policies and unstable revolutions that seek to end poverty are a bad idea. Stability and confidence matter, and having a government that is transparent about how it is going to pay for its policies is essential. A holistic strategy to deal with deprivation needs broad social acceptance, where everyone understands what will happen, when and why, to prevent the type of economic shock that happened in 2022.

The kind of piecemeal society where your background determines your health, opportunities and wealth cannot continue if we want our population to thrive, our economy to strengthen and our environment to be protected. We can choose how the next generation grows up and the type of country they enter into. Interestingly, much of that involves our mental health.

Relationships are often hard, and rejection is particularly difficult to take. Politicians often speak of their desire to support the institution of marriage and have often done so through a tax discount for married couples. Some MPs have gone further and blamed society's woes on single parents – as if life is that simple! Being a single parent is hard work and they hold the responsibility for their children close to their hearts. Some politicians lack the compassion needed to do their jobs, and so instead create easy headlines by making cannon-fodder of vulnerable people who are doing their best.

The blunt instrument of tax breaks bears little relation to the true help needed to make a relationship last. The two key needs of a marriage, beyond the foundations of love and respect, are good communication and financial stability. Michelle and Barack Obama did the world a great service by acknowledging that they had marriage counselling to stabilise their relationship long before entering the White House.[3] Maintaining long-term communication needs practice, self-awareness, humility and, often, help. It should be the expected norm that relationships will need support at some point.

The second key to a lasting relationship is financial stability. People argue over money, especially when it is in short supply. It degrades the mental health of every family member in the home and is often a precursor to domestic violence. Scientists Dr Julie Schwartz Gottman, Dr John Gottman and Bob Levenson studied relationships for decades. They worked with thousands of couples and measured their heart rates, blood speed, perspiration, body language and tone of voice as the pair spoke to each other over a contentious issue, such as owning a dog. Their research found that, for a couple to have a long-term future, they need to have five positive moments for every negative one, and they need to be physiologically calm when near each other (of course, after the early passions have tempered!).[4]

This research suggests that a country without poverty and without the fear of financial difficulty could be the best way to promote stable and happy relationships and lower the divorce rate.

Government policies need to support our emotional lives, as well as our physical ones, and an essential part of this is to have politicians in charge who do not believe that risky decisions are the best way to show leadership and strength. Humility and calm ability are not weaknesses, as the African American author Maya Angelou knew well: 'The quality of strength lined with tenderness is an unbeatable combination, as are intelligence and necessity when unblunted by formal education.'[5]

In his book *The Happiness Problem*, Sam Wren-Lewis writes about a new way of thinking about happiness. He highlights that populations continue to expect better from an uncertain world, but this is an unattainable aim. He suggests that we need to move away from the idea that, if we could only be in total control of our lives, such as having the perfect job, relationship or body and mind, then we would be happy. He sees the same desire for control at a national level, as governments focus on using economic growth and innovative technology as the only methods for curing society's problems. Wren-Lewis argues that this is too simplistic and can blind populations to the need for real social change. It is far easier to make simple headlines and adopt temporary solutions, but they often make things worse in the long run.[6]

Our consumerist society has been built on the foundation that having more is better. In the decades after the Second World War, when having more meant having the basics of our modern lives (like more than one set of clothes or hot running water), this did improve living conditions. However, as this mentality expanded and embedded itself in our economy and society, the psychological and environmental costs are now clear to see and our reliance on perpetual consumerism as a source of happiness is unsustainable. It affects our mental health and drives consumer debt. It generates shame for those who cannot afford to keep up with the latest trends, and generates snobbery and competition between groups. This is a recipe for neither a happy society nor strong mental health. To shift the dial away from this entrenched way of life may take time, or it could come quickly as the need for ending poverty becomes so blindingly obvious that our population welcomes it with open arms. We will only find out if we try.

August 2022

In a quiet public park in Somerset, the neatly kept flowerbeds and lawns lapped up the late afternoon sun as it painted its subjects in a peach light. It was an idyllic scene – one for the romance novels – and yet in reality the skies should not have been so warm at that time of year. It should have rained enough in the first six months to keep the lawns green, but instead they had yellowed, and the grass sat on dry, parched earth. The air should have been a show of nature's birds, vibrant and energetic, singing a chorus of songs, but between the canopy, there was only air. The ancient trees that edged the park formed a wind orchestra, the only sound available to accompany the wood pigeon's deep-cooing solo.

There were no dragonflies swooping overhead, flashing their elegant wings. No bees were humming. A barrier had been erected around a small patch of earth to keep passing humans out. The sign read 'Wild Flower Area' – a tiny, hope-filled effort to stem the loss of biodiversity. To an orderly mind, the park is a refined and beautiful space, but to a biologist, it is as unnatural as Ireland devoid of its emerald fields. Should the weather continue to be unpredictable, green summer leaves will dry out and fall earlier, and warm spring-like weather will begin in February, making precious little space for winter at all. The fruit-stones that need a deep frost to crack their shells may not germinate in some years and the cycle of new growth will be stunted.

I find the sound of soft rain comforting. It cleans the air, lowers the temperature and nurtures the hedgerows. It speaks of stability and that all is well with the world in a way that intense heat and clear, empty skies do not. However, there is hope and it can be found on the other side of the world. The global barometer – the Great Barrier Reef – is healing. Coral is regrowing where previously only white bleaching and empty, clear seas could be found. While it is unclear if this signals a return to the abundance of the past, or whether a new species that will dominate the reef, but it still brings some optimism to a bleak outlook.

The Knepp rewilding project has shown that, if you make space for nature, it will come. We cannot afford to lose it. Our mental and physical health relies on the natural world to maintain us. Even if we do end deprivation in monetary terms, there will be an emotional emptiness left if we have only concrete and technology to fall back on.

The care we take of nature will also have a direct effect on our food supplies. As extreme weather becomes increasingly common, our economy and food systems will become achingly fragile and cause unexpected price rises. The sooner we end poverty in Britain and achieve it in a way that is considerate to nature, the safer and stronger we will be in withstanding the shocks that are to come. Just as sea walls are built to cope with turbulent storms, so our society must be rebuilt to protect us from crises that are looming uncomfortably close on the horizon.

We will also need politicians who are committed to a full five years of effort. This is no small request. The intense workload and abuse that many of our leaders deal with can disincentivise good people from entering politics. On their podcast, Rory Stewart and Alastair Campbell highlighted the struggle that many politicians have with the pace of today's politics:

> Rory Stewart: 'It's a bandwidth problem ... Politicians end up not having any time to think ... One of the reasons they don't take on good people and good ideas is they're so stressed and overworked, that their brains have basically shut down.'

> Alastair Campbell: 'Tony Blair ... did make time to think and he did a lot of it on planes and he would literally turn the phones off for a few hours and he would think, and then he would write, and then he would send out notes.'[7]

It is concerning that people who make serious decisions for our country are not able to spend time properly considering the consequences of them. This may explain why there have been so many U-turns, policy failures and so much financial waste over the years. Having a clear strategy before entering government is vital, and while some people will stick to their manifesto pledges, there are many leaders who ignore their promises and make things up as they go along, often with disastrous consequences.

Parliament also does itself no favours by allowing time-wasters to slow down the House of Commons. In her book *Why We Get the Wrong Politicians*, Isabel Hardman discusses how this strategy is used to make life easier for the governing party:

> Loyal backbenchers who want a promotion and think that the best way of getting one is to be relentlessly positive about the executive, ask UPQs: Utterly Pointless Questions ... The pressure on MPs more often than not is not to be an excellent legislator, but to stay out of trouble ... Better to get attention by participating in meaningless parliamentary activities than plug away at the boring work of examining laws properly.[8]

Some politicians who work hard will no doubt feel quite stung at Hardman's words, as it is easy to lump everyone into the same camp. However, if they are honest, they will also recognise the truth behind her sentiment. Building consensus behind the scenes in Parliament is the best way to create change, but those who follow the party line and don't check what they are voting for can often get a shock when reality comes knocking on their door. Hardman continues:

> The most pernicious and inexcusable culture in the House of Commons is that of the yes-man ... they know that they are taking part in a culture of subservience on legislation, and they do little about it ... Often, parliamentarians only realise that a policy is a total mess once it's on the statute book and a desperate soul is sitting opposite them in a constituency surgery clutching one of those bags stuffed full of papers.[9]

A classic example of this is cuts to legal aid services, which have caused significant problems. In 2022, barristers voted overwhelmingly in favour of strike action, as many were being paid less than the minimum wage due to long, unsociable hours and a lack of staff.

A properly functioning Parliament would be essential to keeping the plan on track to end poverty in five years. With no time to waste, MPs might be invigorated and ensure that all of their time in Parliament is focused on doing the best for the most vulnerable, rather than their party. A 'coming together' would be refreshing for voters and stabilise the political system.

•••

This book has discussed the history of the undeserving poor and the wide-ranging impacts of deprivation on our society, our social relationships and the human body. Inequality is a morally and financially expensive situation that cannot continue; it is not an inevitable part of a developed economy. This book has shown that it can be dealt with through significant government focus, compassion and a detailed plan. The twin constraints of time and taxes have been addressed and options to fund the strategy have been suggested. The green agenda forms a vital part of ending deprivation, and both poverty elimination and green issues will benefit from a collaborative approach.

The ending of poverty in Britain cannot be the sole responsibility of any individual. Should a prime minister attempt it, there would be thousands of civil servants and professionals focused on the cause. The aim of writing this book has been to expand the debate about how we view it and discuss it, to consider the practicalities of eliminating it and the implications for the domestic population and those abroad.

The global financial crisis, the austerity years, the heated Brexit debate, the pandemic and the cost-of-living crisis have shifted Britons' discourse on inequality and called into question how we treat one another. It is generally understood that, for a political idea to become a reality, it must be financially viable, practical to implement and acceptable to most of the voting public. It is obvious that new concepts and innovations will be needed to pull the country out of its quagmire and enable it to thrive again.

This book has been written to leave readers with the space to think on. Given the immense scale and complexity of the problem, all the answers cannot lie within the pages of one book. On the contrary, this is a starting point, so here is a compilation of all the ideas that have been suggested and a few more. Please ruminate on them, debate them and put them to good use.

1. Focus – eliminating poverty must be a top priority and be funded appropriately.

2. A Minister for the Elimination of Poverty – a new senior Cabinet position.

3. Policies for a new Department for the Elimination of Poverty:
   - A free hotline to support those currently living on low incomes and the creation of personal plans to assist the public on what services there are to help in their area, what the government can do to help and how individuals can better support themselves. Staff need training in the benefit system and how to talk compassionately to those with mental and physical health needs.
   - A new Poverty Analysis Centre to understand which governmental and non-governmental systems create or maintain poverty. This could act as an area of expertise on analysing poverty in different parts of the country and determining which new policies are working and which are not. It should also publicise areas of best practice domestically and internationally.
   - Create a new national exchange system for children's second-hand clothes, shoes, toys and books, which is free to use and available to all.
   - Create a consultation system for the general public, charities, experts and research groups to help develop new public policies for local and central government before they are enacted.
   - Create new governmental strategies across all areas within the poverty elimination agenda to ensure they are working in conjunction with other departments' strategies to prevent the wasting of money and duplication of effort.
   - Combine the green agenda, the industrial strategy and efforts to tackle geographical inequality with the agenda on eliminating poverty.

4. Policies for a new Housing Department:

- Change current laws on non-UK taxpayers, non-British nationals and companies buying homes in the UK to reduce the number of properties being left empty for investment purposes and to ensure there is enough affordable housing available for the rest of the UK population. This should help to level up the current skew between housing supply and global demand for properties. It may also assist in the reduction of money laundering, which is rife in the UK housing market.
- Ensure that everyone who needs a bed or is living in furniture poverty has the basics that they need.
- Analyse and consider the use of rent controls to reduce the cost of living. A gradual implementation could be considered to see how many businesses would be affected and in what ways, and the knock-on effects on the housing market. Would it create a housing boom as more properties come on to the market? Would it reduce house prices and enable more people to buy their own homes? Could it create negative equity and unintended poverty or problems for current homeowners?
- Create a new type of social housing, involving studio flat complexes with a focus on saving money and financial education. This could act as an opportunity to start life again for middle-aged people, or just start, in the case of teenagers. Support officers could be permanently on site to provide help and training.

5. Policies for the Department for Work and Pensions:

- Raise the Carer's Allowance.
- Expand Child Benefit to include all children in families who need it.
- Reinstate Housing Benefit for all who need it.
- A universal benefits sanction amnesty, so everyone gets a fresh start at the beginning of the new parliament.

- Introduce StrengthsFinder questionnaires in job centres, so people know what they are good at, irrespective of the qualifications they may or may not have.
- Offer dyslexia tests, individual literacy and digital inclusion lessons at job centres and libraries.

6. Policies for the Justice Department:
   - Cease prison sentences for prostitutes and significantly expand the residential rehabilitation process, extending it to those with street homelessness and substance abuse issues. Provide magistrates with alternative options to prison.
   - Use innovative methods for reducing the cost of prisons while also increasing rehabilitation opportunities, such as using electricity-generating bikes and food gardens to reduce costs to the taxpayer and to become more environmentally friendly.
   - Make community orders more female-friendly (such as considering not placing women alone with a group of men) and make it easier for parents to support their children outside of school hours.
   - Implement dyslexia testing and brain scans for all inmates.

7. Procurement:
   - Change government procurement policies. Expand UK production of solar panels and wind farms, even if domestic production is more expensive. Move procurement policies away from 'cheapest is best' towards policies that will secure UK jobs, then EU jobs and then international jobs – if safeguarding checks have been carried out to prevent slave labour.
   - Encourage the UK clothing industry to focus on slow eco-fashions where staff are properly treated and paid.
   - Create a government website to highlight businesses that manufacture goods in the UK so that consumers can support British businesses more easily, reduce carbon emissions, reduce slavery and child labour, and boost British manufacturing.

- Central government needs to be more cynical about procuring services from companies that offer too much for too little. It should question: what corners are being cut? How are staff being paid and safeguarded?
- Expand the growth of British hemp and advertise its various uses to support the rural economy and enhance our manufacturing base.

8. The National Health Service:

- Should doctors prescribe sleep? Greater focus on sleep-based remedies in the NHS and care sector, especially on wards and in care homes.
- Recommendations from the Mental Health Foundation's report in 2018 on Northern Ireland's mental health crisis suggested the need for a mental health champion, greater investment in mental health support, a ten-year mental health strategy, and further research on the levels of mental health problems for children and young people.[10]

9. Local councils:

- Local authorities must have stable finances and be properly supported by central government.
- Local councils need to be more cynical about procuring services from companies that offer too much for too little and should not be pressurised by central government to do so. What corners are being cut? How are staff being paid and safeguarded?
- Should the home care system be brought in-house?

10. Non-governmental processes:

- Which non-governmental processes create or maintain poverty?
- What night-time shift work is genuinely necessary? Should businesses have to justify to their board or the government why sleep loss is necessary for the business to function? Are staff educated on the impact of lost sleep and compensated accordingly? How necessary are twenty-four-hour overnight

deliveries, if they require sleep loss for staff? Should those products carry an extra charge that is then passed on to the staff, rather than be offered for free as an incentive to buy more?

11. The green agenda:
- Shift to the Doughnut Economic model and prepare for a slowing, but thriving economy.
- Use new technologies such as hydroponics to improve food productivity and expand rewilding practices for unprofitable farms and disused land. Government incentives and grants could help here.
- Create Zero Carbon Transition plans and consider which sectors will be most affected by global warming and bio-diversity loss, including private jet travel and sea fishing.
- Create artificial dappled shade using recycled materials or solar panel 'trees' to prevent dustbowls and evaporation from rivers and reservoirs.
- Provide small grants for homes and businesses to use water butts to improve water storage, if bought from British manufacturers.
- Develop new styles and shapes of solar panels and wind turbines to ease installation on the sides of buildings. This would prevent the need for prohibitively expensive scaffolding and open up the opportunity for families to create their own electricity and protect themselves from future energy price rises.
- Buy land abroad to protect precious biodiverse landscapes from development. Create scientific research centres there and use them as foreign travel destinations for school child-ren from low-income families to expand their opportunities to learn and travel.
- Develop green towers for food production and create more biodiverse habitats in towns and cities to prevent urban heat islands. British manufacturers must be at the forefront of this.

- Expand the use of moss benches and use them to line major arteries through towns and cities to help clean the air of pollution.
- Ban the cutting down of mature trees.
- Remove barriers to hemp production and create a new industry and more jobs in rural areas.

12. **Child poverty. End Child Poverty called for the government to set out an ambitious and credible child poverty-reduction strategy.**[11] **This includes:**
    - Restoring the link between benefits (including housing support) and inflation, and then making up for the loss in the real value in children's benefits as a result of the forty-year freeze and previous sub-inflation increases in benefit rates.
    - Ending the two-child limit on child allowances in tax credits and Universal Credit – and reforming UC.
    - Reversing the cuts and investing in children's services such as mental health, education, childcare and social care.

13. **Crime and poverty:**
    - For traumatic brain injuries, there should be routine brain injury screening for prisoners and better training for staff.
    - Further research into how brain injuries affect reoffending and the development of effective neurological rehabilitation. (For further information, see the Disabilities Trust website.)[12]

ACKNOWLEDGEMENTS

This book has taken three years to write and it would not have been possible without a host of encouraging and supportive people along the way. My thanks to Moira Gibb for her knowledge and wisdom on housing and social care, Fuzz Dixon at St Luke's church in Millwall, Steve Glover at The British Hemp Company, Debbie Brixey, Marsha Powell at BelEve, Professor Danny Dorling at Oxford University and Rebecca Abrahams at St Luke's School, Tower Hamlets. Thanks to Jo De Vries, Laura Perehinec, Claire Hopkins and the whole team at Flint Books for being such wonderful people to work with. Thanks also to Karen Williams of Librotas for choosing my book to win the Page Turner Awards Mentorship Prize; having her help as a book mentor has been invaluable. I am eternally grateful to Elena for all the EMDR; without her, I would never have been able to focus on writing.

I would like to thank Rach, Shirin, Felicity, Mary, Sharon, Rebeka, Liz and Justin, Tina and Tim, Jane Reed, Graeme, the G6 and Michael for being such unswerving and supportive friends, and Rosie De Vekey and Daniel Smith for their advice and kindness as I navigated the publishing world. Thanks also to my parents for always discussing politics at the dinner table. It has made the whole subject much more accessible than it would otherwise have been. My unending thanks also go to Isobel Blythe for her unconventional world view and for pushing me to do things differently before sadly being taken from us.

Thanks to my darling daughter, who (while she didn't know it) provided the main impetus to start writing properly, and to my lovely husband Tim, who opened up the subject of economics to me and has been supportive and thoughtful throughout. And thanks to you, dear reader, for taking the time to read this book. It would all have been a bit pointless without you.

HR

APPENDIX 1

HOMELESSNESS

The Stop Mass Homelessness campaign has a five-point plan to address the long-term challenges of homelessness:

1. A Future Generations Act to end short-term thinking in government policy.
2. Improve support for financial literacy education.
3. Expand social housing and encourage innovative ways to increase housing stock.
4. Increase support for ethical property and letting firms.
5. Invest to create new green jobs.

Source: *Big Issue*, no. 1473, 2 August 2021, p.5. For more information, go to www.bigissue.com.

APPENDIX 2

LOCAL AUTHORITIES AND HOMELESSNESS

In its 2020 report on lessons learned from the pandemic, the Local Authority Association highlighted some serious issues that need to be dealt with:

- People with no recourse to public funds remain a dilemma and those without settled immigration status represent a significant proportion of those at risk of sleeping rough.
- The shortage of affordable housing is an inevitable blocker in finding move-on accommodation, in particular the need for more genuinely affordable one-bed accommodation in both the public and private rented sectors, given Housing Benefit and Universal Credit limits.
- It was clear that a one-off exercise was not adequate to maintain long-term reductions in rough sleeping in most areas.
- Despite enhanced levels of co-operation between services, it was nevertheless often difficult to get access to appropriate health services, especially mental health. This was a reflection of the lack of specialist services working in homelessness in many parts of the country and a continued wider lack of mental health resources relative to demand.

Source: Local Government Association, 'Lessons learnt from councils' response to rough sleeping during the COVID-19 pandemic', 19 November 2020, www.local.gov.uk/publications/lessons-learnt-councils-response-rough-sleeping-during-covid-19-pandemic.

APPENDIX 3

THE POVERTY PREMIUM

The table below shows examples of poverty premiums and what can be done to prevent them. This is not an exhaustive list.

Sector	Poverty premium	Possible solutions
Energy	More energy-efficient kitchen appliances are more expensive to buy, but cheaper to run in the long term.*	Zero-interest loans should be made available for basic white goods.
Shopping	'Buy two, get a third free.'	Many shops offer discounts on multiple purchases that inadvertently exclude people on low incomes. A buy one, get one free offer is accessible to everyone, but 'buy two, get a third free' excludes people on low incomes who cannot afford a second product, but would benefit greatly from it. Supermarkets and manufacturers could be encouraged to end the poverty premium on these products.

Insurance	The cost of car insurance is based on factors including postcode. If a person lives in an area with high levels of crime and deprivation, the cost of the car insurance will be higher than for those in more affluent, less crime-ridden areas.	The installation of gates on social housing developments can prevent car theft and reduce insurance premiums. More CCTV coverage and better lighting to be used across the UK to prevent car theft.
Finance	Loans and credit cards often charge higher interest rates to people on low incomes and with poor credit ratings.	Create a national system of exchange for children's clothes, shoes, toys and books to reduce families' need for credit (see Chapter 14). Expand linguistic literacy, financial literacy and digital literacy for those on low incomes. (This is already happening in some areas, but the support can be expanded.) Zero-interest loan schemes to provide a financial cushion for people unable to access existing forms of credit, but who can afford to repay small sums, offering a way to spread the cost of essential or emergency items.**

Finance	Mortgagors vs renters	In many cases across the UK, renters are paying higher amounts in rent than they would pay for a mortgage on the same or a larger property, but they remain unable to take out a mortgage. Banks could take the reliability of rent payments into account when deciding whether to offer first-time mortgages.

* No Interest Loan Scheme (NILS), fairbydesign.com/no-interest-loan-scheme/, November 2021.

** George Bowden, 'Greener kitchen goods could save thousands, *Which?* suggests', *BBC News*, 4 November 2021, www.bbc.co.uk/news/uk-59161949.

APPENDIX 4

JOSEPH ROWNTREE FOUNDATION DEFINITIONS OF ESSENTIALS AND BASICS

When we say people have cut back on the essentials, we mean they have done one or more of the following things, due to cost:

- Reduced spending on food for adults.
- Reduced spending on food for children.
- Changed the type of food their household buys.
- Heated their home less than they needed to/less often.
- Have not replaced clothing that is outgrown or worn.
- Skipped or cut down the size of meals.

When we say that they have cut back on the basics, it means they have done any of the above and/or any of the following, due to cost:

- Reduced spending on transport.
- Changed the way they cook (for example, used the oven less).
- Used appliances (for example, washing machine, dishwasher, microwave) less often.
- Reduced the number of showers or baths taken in their house.
- Have not replaced broken items.

- Stopped or reduced socialising with friends and family.
- Taken children out of nursery or childminder.
- Reduced spending on their child(ren)'s activities and hobbies.

The essentials are items that we need to keep ourselves warm and fed; the basics are items we need to get by with a very basic standard of living.

Source: Joseph Rowntree Foundation, *Poverty in Scotland 2022*, 3 October 2022.

APPENDIX 5

TRANSITION TO NET ZERO

Net zero: A just transition is necessary and is key for maintaining public support.

Joseph Rowntree Foundation

We need a just transition to net zero, one that does no harm to those on low incomes, while also combating social challenges. Such an approach in the UK must focus on three areas:

The fair distribution of transition costs
Adequate support must be in place to help lower income households to adopt new low-carbon technologies. The costs of transition (passed to households through taxes and levies) should be shared broadly.

The just transition of the workforce
Those employed in polluting industries, and the communities that rely heavily on these sectors, should be supported in the transition to net zero.

The equitable investment in climate resilience
Our approach must confront the fact that relatively more deprived neighbourhoods are the most exposed to the effects of climate change.

Source: Joseph Rowntree Foundation, 'Net zero: A just transition is necessary, and is key for maintaining public support', 2 November 2021, www.jrf.org.uk/blog/net-zero-just-transition-necessary-and-key-maintaining-public-support.

APPENDIX 6

HOW POVERTY IS MEASURED IN BRITAIN

There are different ways to measure poverty:

- **After housing costs** shows the income available to a household once rent, water rates, mortgage interest payments, buildings insurance payments, ground rent and service charges are paid. This enables a more accurate comparison of what households across the UK have available to spend on food, utilities, clothing and leisure, than looking at income alone, given the disparity of rents in different parts of the UK.
- **Before housing costs** takes no account of the fact that comparing incomes for households in different parts of the country, where housing costs vary, does not produce a like-for-like comparison of disposable incomes. As a result, 'before housing costs' figures greatly understate the impact of low incomes in areas with high housing costs, such as London.
- **Fuel poverty** is where the cost of fuel, including gas, electricity and petrol, usually exceeds 10 per cent of a household's income.
- **Absolute poverty** is a term used by the World Health Organization that refers to a daily income of below $2/ day. In the UK, the term 'absolute' can be misleading as it wrongly conjures up images of the destitution found in developing countries. Instead, the UK government uses a measure of relative poverty (see next).

- **Relative poverty** can be a more useful measure as it compares a household's income with the current incomes of other households within the UK. Rises in relative poverty show that more households are falling below the UK average household income and are not able to meet the financial costs of a basic standard of living. Households are considered to be living in relative poverty if their income is 60 per cent below the median UK household income for the year. The UK government calls this group 'Households Below Average Income' (HBAI). The Joseph Rowntree Foundation provides a Minimum Income Calculator for the public, to determine whether their earnings are enough for a decent standard of living, and to show what families with children require now to meet their material needs and participate in society.

Sources: Joseph Rowntree Foundation, *A Minimum Income Standard for the United Kingdom in 2020*, www.jrf.org.uk/report/minimum-income-standard-uk-2020. House of Commons Library, *Poverty in the UK: Statistics*, 31 March 2021, commonslibrary.parliament.uk/research-briefings/sn07096/.

CHILDREN AND FOOD INSECURITY

In the first three months of 2021, the Food Foundation found that households with children had higher levels of food insecurity than those without. An estimated 2.3 million children were living in households that had experienced food insecurity in the past six months. The situation was even worse in households with children receiving free school meals, where 41 per cent reported food insecurity in the past six months.

- 20 per cent of children aged 8–17 (over 1.5 million) reported some form of food insecurity (mild, moderate or severe).
- 5 per cent (410,000) said they were hungry but didn't eat because they didn't want to use up food in the house.
- 5 per cent (360,000) said they didn't eat because they didn't have enough food in the house.
- 6 per cent (500,000) said their parents didn't eat because of not having enough food to go around.
- 9 per cent (660,000) said they had to eat less and make food last longer because of lack of money.
- 5 per cent (370,000) said they sometimes didn't eat proper meals because of not having enough money to buy more food.
- 4 per cent (320,000) said they sometimes ate at friends' houses because they didn't have enough food in the house.

Source: Food Foundation, 'Food Foundation releases new report showing pandemic effect on food insecurity remains a crisis', March 2021, foodfoundation.org.uk/food-foundation-release-new-report-showing-pandemic-effect-on-food-insecurity-remains-a-crisis/.

NOTES

Chapter 1: Poverty and the Pandemic

1   Sean Coughlan, 'Hotel scheme "will cut rough sleeping after virus"', *BBC News*, 18 April 2020, www.bbc.co.uk/news/education-52332453.

2   Shelter, '1 in 4 people helped off the streets under the government's Everyone In scheme are no longer being accommodated', 27 August 2021, england.shelter.org.uk/media/press_release/1_in_4_people_helped_off_the_streets_under_the_governments_everyone_in_scheme_are_no_longer_being_accommodated.

3   Museum of Homelessness, Dying Homeless Project 2020, museumof-homelessness.org/2021/11/30/responses-to-official-figures-this-week/.

4   'More than half of homeless deaths are drug-related', *BBC News*, 30 November 2021, www.bbc.co.uk/news/uk-scotland-59476297.amp.

5   National Records of Scotland, *Homeless Deaths* 2020, 30 November 2021, www.nrscotland.gov.uk/statistics-and-data/statistics/statistics-by-theme/vital-events/deaths/homeless-deaths/2020.

6   Emily Maitlis, BBC *Newsnight*, 8 April 2020.

7   Professor Joseph Stiglitz, BBC *Newsnight*, 8 April 2020.

8   'Coronavirus: food bank shortage blamed on panic buying', *BBC News*, 13 March 2020, www.bbc.co.uk/news/amp/uk-england-london-51837892.

9   Jon Sopel, 'Coronavirus: Trump berates media at jaw-dropping briefing', *BBC News*, 14 April 2020, www.bbc.co.uk/news/world-us-canada-52276004; 'Coronavirus: how New Zealand relied on science and empathy', *BBC News*, 20 April 2020, www.bbc.co.uk/news/world-asia-52344299.

10 Health Foundation, 'The continuing impact of COVID-19 on health and inequalities: a year on from our COVID-19 impact inquiry', 24 August 2022, www.health.org.uk/publications/long-reads/the-continuing-impact-of-covid-19-on-health-and-inequalities.

11 Local Government Association, 'Health inequalities: deprivation and poverty and COVID-19', April 2021, www.local.gov.uk/health-inequalities-deprivation-and-poverty-and-covid-19.

12 NHS England, 'NHS Five Year Forward View: funding and efficiency', 2016–17, www.england.nhs.uk/five-year-forward-views/next-steps-on-the-nhs-five-year-forward-view/funding-and-efficiency/.

13 British Medical Association, 'Health at a price: reducing the impact of poverty', 25 March 2021, www.bma.org.uk/what-we-do/population-health/addressing-social-determinants-that-influence-health/health-at-a-price-reducing-the-impact-of-poverty.

14 Alison Bloomer, 'People living in poverty experience worse quality of NHS care', *British Journal of Family Medicine*, 24 January 2020, www.bjfm.co.uk/people-living-in-poverty-experience-worse-quality-of-nhs-care.

Chapter 2: Poverty and Physical Health

1 Matthew Walker, 'Sleep is your superpower', TED Talk, 3 June 2019.

2 Walker, 'Sleep is your superpower'.

3 Matthew Walker, *Why We Sleep: The New Science of Sleep and Dreams* (Allen Lane, 2017), p.151.

4 Buttle UK, 'Impact Report 2021–22', buttleuk.org/our-research/research-reports/impact-report-2021-22/.

5 Diabetes.co.uk, 'Shift work increases type 2 diabetes risk regardless of genetics, study says', 13 February 2018, www.diabetes.co.uk/news/2018/feb/shift-work-increases-type-2-diabetes-risk-regardless-of-genetics,-study-says-93985089.html.

6 C. Vetter, H.S. Dashti, et al., 'Night shift work, genetic risk and type 2 diabetes in the UK biobank', *Diabetes Care*, vol. 41, no. 4 (April 2018), pp.762–9, care.diabetesjournals.org/content/41/4/762.long.

7 C. Vetter, D. Fischer, J.L. Matera and T. Roenneberg, 'Aligning work and circadian time in shift workers improves sleep and reduces circadian disruption', *Current Biology*, vol. 25 (2015), pp.907–11.

8 Diabetes.co.uk, 'Cost of diabetes', 15 January 2019, www.diabetes.co.uk/cost-of-diabetes.html.

9 NHS, 'The health risks of gum disease', 31 August 2018, www.nhs.uk.

10 M. Bansal, M. Khatri and V.J. Taneja, 'Potential role of periodontal infection in respiratory diseases – a review', *Journal of Medicine and Life*, vol. 6, no. 3 (September 2013), pp.244–8. PMID: 24155782.

11 Harry Leslie Smith, *Don't Let My Past Be Your Future* (Constable, 2017), p.143.

12 Hugh Devlin, Tomos Williams, Jim Graham and Martin Ashley, 'The ADEPT study: a comparative study of dentists' ability to detect enamel-only proximal caries in bitewing radiographs with and without the use of AssistDent aritifical intelligence software', *British Dental Journal*, no. 231 (2021), pp.481–5, doi:10.1038/s41415-021-3526-6.

13 The definition of epigenetics is the study of changes in organisms caused by modification of gene expression rather than alteration of the genetic code itself. DNA methylation is an area of epigenetic study where some parts of the chromosome are tagged with small carbon and hydrogen molecules, often changing how genes function and affecting their expression.

14 Shawna Williams, 'As bees specialize, so does their DNA packaging',
    The Scientist, 11 September 2018, www.the-scientist.com/news-opinion/
    as-bees-specialize--so-does-their-dna-packaging-64779.

15 'Scientists discover how epigenetic information could be inherited',
    University of Cambridge, 25 January 2013, www.cam.ac.uk/research/news/
    scientists-discover-how-epigenetic-information-could-be-inherited.

16 Nicole L. Hair, et al., 'Association of child poverty, brain development,
    and academic achievement', *JAMA Pediatrics*, vol. 169, no. 9 (2015),
    pp.822–9, doi:10.1001/jamapediatrics.2015.1475; Kimberly G. Noble, et
    al., 'Family income, parental education and brain structure in children
    and adolescents', *Nature Neuroscience*, vol. 18, no. 5 (2015), pp.773–8,
    doi:10.1038/nn/3983.

17 University College London, 'Living in poverty can impact children's
    working memory through wear and tear on the brain and body',
    18 November 2020. Research used data from 4,525 children in the
    Avon Longitudinal Study of Parents and Children, www.ucl.ac.uk/ioe/
    news/2020/nov/living-poverty-can-impact-childrens-working-memory-
    through-wear-and-tear-brain-and-body; T. Kokosi, E. Flouri and
    E. Midouhas, 'The role of inflammation in the association between poverty
    and working memory in childhood', *Psychoneuroendocrinology*, vol. 123
    (January 2021), doi.org/10.1016/j.psyneuen.2020.105040.

18 Sharon Reynolds, 'Stress links poverty to inflammation and heart disease',
    National Institutes of Health, 9 July 2019. Based on research: A. Tawakol,
    et al., 'Stress-associated neurobiological pathway linking socioeconomic
    disparities to cardiovascular disease', *Journal of the American College
    of Cardiology*, vol. 73, no. 25 (July 2019), pp.3243–55, doi:10.1016/j.
    jacc.2019.04.042. PMID: 31248544.

19 Erika Hayasaki, 'How poverty affects the brain', *Newsweek*, 25 August 2016,
    www.newsweek.com/2016/09/02/how-poverty-affects-brain-493239.html.

20 Mary Helen Immordino-Yang, Linda Darling-Hammond and Christina R.
    Krone, 'Nurturing nature: how brain development is inherently social and
    emotional, and what this means for education', *Educational Psychologist*,
    vol. 54, no. 3 (2019), pp.185–204, doi:10.1080/00461520.2019.1633924,
    ISSN: 1532-6985.

21 K.G. Noble and M.A. Giebler, 'The neuroscience of socioeconomic
    inequality', *Current Opinion in Behavioural Sciences*, vol. 36 (2020), pp.23–8,
    doi:10.1016/j.cobeha.2020.05.007.

Chapter 3: Poverty and Mental Health

1   'Remarks by the First Lady at "Change Direction" mental health event',
    4 March 2015, White House Archives, obamawhitehouse.archives/gov/
    the-press-office/2015/03/04/remarks-first-lady-change-direction-mental-
    health-event.

2   EMDR Institute, 'What is EMDR – for laypeople' (paras 2, 3), www.emdr.
    com/what-is-emdr/. A full description of the theory, sequence of treatment
    and research can be found in F. Shapiro, *Eye Movement Desensitization and
    Reprocessing: Basic Principles, Protocols and Procedures*, 2nd edn (Guilford
    Press, 2001).

3   'Does EMDR work?', The Trauma Practice, traumapractice.co.uk/
    does-emdr-work/, viewed 14 September 2021.

4   F. Shapiro, 'The role of eye movement desensitization and reprocessing
    (EMDR) therapy in medicine: addressing the psychological and physical
    symptoms stemming from adverse life experiences', *Permanente Journal*,
    vol. 18, no. 1 (Winter 2014), pp.71–7, doi:10.7812/TPP/13-098.

5   'Latest Suicide Data (2021)', www.samaritans.org/about-samaritans/research-
    policy/suicide-facts-and-figures/latest-suicide-data/, viewed 10 July 2023.

6   Meleri Williams, 'Cost of living: woman chooses mental health therapy
    over heating', *BBC News*, 12 December 2022, www.bbc.co.uk/news/
    uk-wales-63903850.

7   Mental Health Foundation, 'Mental Health Statistics: Research Costs',
    2011, www.mentalhealth.org.uk.

8   Mental Health Foundation, 'Mental Health Statistics: Poverty', 2010, www.
    mentalhealth.org.uk.

9   Mental Health Foundation, 'Mental Health Statistics: Global and
    Nationwide Costs', 2013, www.mentalhealth.org.uk.

10 Money and Mental Health Policy Institute, 'Money and Mental Health:
    The Facts', 2019, www.moneyandmentalhealth.org.

11 Mental Health Foundation, 'Stress: are we coping?', May 2018, www.
    mentalhealth.org.uk. This report contained findings from a survey,
    commissioned by the Mental Health Foundation and undertaken by
    YouGov, that polled 4,169 adults in the UK in 2018.

12 Christians Against Poverty, 'On the Edge: Client Report', June 2022,
    p.9. Mental, Physical or emotional illnesses that caused debt problems:
    long-term illness 7 per cent, mental health 19 per cent, relationship
    breakdown 11 per cent, COVID 6 per cent, addiction 5 per cent,
    bereavement 3 per cent.

13 Gabor Maté, 'The Power of Addiction and the Addiction of Power', TED
    Talk, 9 October 2012.

14 Darren McGarvey, *Poverty Safari* (Luath Press, 2017), p.165.

15 McGarvey, *Poverty Safari*, p.175.

16 Mind Cymru, 'Too long to wait: specialist psychological therapies in
    Wales', 2021, available at: mind.org.uk.

17 Public Health Scotland, 'Child and Adolescent Mental Health Services
    (CAMHS) waiting times, quarter ending 30 September 2021', 7 December
    2021, www.publichealthscotland.scot/publications/child-and-adolescent-
    mental-health-services-camhs-waiting-times/child-and-adolescent-

mental-health-services-camhs-waiting-times-quarter-ending-30-september-2021/.

18 Commissioner for Children and Young People, Koulla Yiasouma, 'More than a number: a rights based review of child health waiting lists in Northern Ireland', 19 October 2021, www.niccy.org/wp-content/uploads/media/3976/more-than-a-number-child-health-waiting-lists-in-ni-final-19-october-2021.pdf.

19 Royal College of Psychiatrists, 'Two-fifths of patients waiting for mental health treatment forced to resort to emergency or crisis services', 6 October 2020, www.rcpsych.ac.uk/news-and-features/latest-news/detail/2020/10/06/two-fifths-of-patients-waiting-for-mental-health-treatment-forced-to-resort-to-emergency-or-crisis-services.

20 Denis Campbell, 'Strain on mental health care leaves 8m people without help, say NHS leaders', *The Guardian*, 29 August 2021, www.theguardian.com/society/2021/aug/29/strain-on-mental-health-care-leaves-8m-people-without-help-says-nhs-leaders.

21 Roxane Gay, 'My body is a cage of my own making', *The Guardian*, 1 July 2017, www.theguardian.com/books/2017/jul/01/roxane-gay-my-body-is-a-cage-of-my-own-making.

22 Reprinted by permission of HarperCollins Publishers Ltd © Bee Wilson (2020) *The Way We Eat Now: Strategies for Eating in a World of Change*, p.312.

23 Reprinted by permission of HarperCollins Publishers Ltd © Bee Wilson (2020) *The Way We Eat Now: Strategies for Eating in a World of Change*, pp.93, 96, 136.

24 Reprinted by permission of HarperCollins Publishers Ltd © Bee Wilson (2020) *The Way We Eat Now: Strategies for Eating in a World of Change*, p.133.

25 'New evidence links ultra-processed foods with a range of health risks', *British Medical Journal*, www.bmj.com/company/newsroom/new-evidence-links-ultra-processed-foods-with-a-range-of-health-risks/.

26 *What Are We Feeding Our Kids?* BBC documentary, 27 May 2021.

27 'BBC documentary featuring UCLH clinicians highlights harms of ultra-processed food', University College London Hospitals website, 25 May 2021, www.uclh.nhs.uk/news/bbc-documentary-featuring-uclh-clinicians-highlights-harms-ultra-processed-food.

28 Gabor Maté, *When the Body Says No: The Cost of Hidden Stress* (Vermilion, 2019), p.87.

29 Maté, *When the Body Says No*, p.16.

30 D.M. Kissen and H.G. Eysenck, 'Personality in male lung cancer patients', *Journal of Psychosomatic Research*, vol. 6 (1962), p.123; Maté, *When the Body Says No*, pp.85–6.

31 AgeUK, '1 in 10 (1.4m) aged 60+ have been eating less since the start of the pandemic', 12 March 2021, www.ageuk.org.uk/latest-press/articles/2021/1-in-10-1.4-million-aged-60-have-been-eating-less-since-the-start-of-the-pandemic/.

32 'Lecanemab confirmatory Phase 3 clarity AD study met primary endpoint, showing highly statistically significant reduction of clinical decline in large global clinical study of 1,795 participants with early Alzheimer's Disease', *Eisai Global*, 28 September 2022, www.eisai.com/news/2022/news202271.html.

33 Matthew Walker, *Why We Sleep: The New Science of Sleep and Dreams* (Allen Lane, 2017), pp.157–8.

Chapter 4: Poverty, Housing and Homelessness

1 Letter from Vincent van Gogh to Theo van Gogh, *c*.13 January 1883.

2 Rachel Maclean (2023), Lucy Frazer (2022–23), Marcus Jones (2022), Stuart Andrew (2022), Christopher Pincher (2019–20), Esther McVey (2018–19), Kit Malthouse (2018–19), Dominic Raab (2018), Alok Sharma (2017–18), Gavin Barwell (2016–17), Brandon Lewis (2014–16), Kris Hopkins (2013–14), Mark Prisk (2012–13), Grant Shapps (2010–12), John Healey (2009–10), Margaret Beckett (2008–09), Caroline Flint (2008).

3 Caitlin Wilkinson, 'Act now or homelessness is going to triple', *Big Issue*, no. 1473, 2 August 2021, p.7.

4 Wilkinson, 'Act now', p.7.

5 Local Government Association, 'Lessons learnt from councils' response to rough sleeping during the COVID-19 pandemic', 19 November 2020, www.local.gov.uk/publications/lessons-learnt-councils-response-rough-sleeping-during-covid-19-pandemic.

6 Local Government Association, 'Lessons learnt'.

7 P. Lynch, A. Homer, S. Ferguson and P. Sherlock, 'Covid leaves UK councils with £3bn financial black hole', *BBC News*, 9 July 2021, www.bbc.co.uk/news/uk-57720900.

8 Vicky Nevin, 'The problem: under-25s get less Universal Credit', Centrepoint, 5 June 2020, centrepoint.org.uk/about-us/blog/how-universal-credit-can-prevent-youth-homelessness/.

9 Mhairi Black speech on Budget Resolutions and Economic Situation, 14 July 2015, Hansard, Vol. 598, House of Commons.

10 'More than half of homeless deaths are drug-related', *BBC News*, 30 November 2021, www.bbc.co.uk/news/uk-scotland-59476297.amp.

11 Museum of Homelessness, Dying Homeless Project 2020.

12 'Deaths of homeless people in England and Wales: 2021 registrations: deaths by sex and age', Office for National Statistics, 23 November 2022, www.ons.gov.uk/peoplepopulationandcommunity/birthsdeathsandmarriages/deaths/bulletins/deathsofhomelesspeopleinenglandandwales/2021registrations.

13 Ed Miliband, *Go Big: How to Fix Our World* (The Bodley Head, 2021), chapter 3.

14 Miliband, *Go Big*, chapter 3.

15 Miliband, *Go Big*, chapter 2.

16 Alison Wallace, David Rhodes and Richard Webber, 'Overseas investors in London's new build housing market', Centre for Housing Policy, University of York, June 2017.

17 Campaign to End Loneliness, 'The facts on loneliness', www.campaign-toendloneliness.org/the-facts-on-loneliness/, viewed 14 January 2022.

18 'Housing Britain: moved miles away from home', BBC *Newsnight*, 6 August 2018.

19 Faiza Shaheen, director of the Centre for Labour and Social Studies, 'UK housing should be restricted to UK taxpayers', Viewsnight – Youtube video for BBC *Newsnight*, 10 May 2017, youtu.be/p1H_jxwg8ps.

20 Gareth Furby, 'Dangerous overcrowding in London homes', BBC *London News*, 26 July 2016, youtu.be/LMuzulhl1oo.

21 Lucie Heath, 'Rogue landlord ordered to pay back more than £700,000 earned from overcrowded housing', *Inside Housing*, 3 March 2021, www. insidehousing.co.uk/news/news/rogue-landlord-ordered-to-pay-back-more-than-700000-earned-from-overcrowded-housing-69828.

22 Paul Glynn, 'Year of the dog: film shows "lifeline" between homeless people and their dogs', *BBC News*, 9 January 2022, www.bbc.co.uk/news/entertainment-arts-59695141.

23 Royal Institution of Chartered Surveyors (RICS), 'Construction materials cost increases reach 40-year high', 19 November 2021, www.rics.org/uk/news-insight/latest-news/news-opinion/construction-materials-cost-increases-reach-40-year-high/.

24 'Why are these family homes standing empty?', *BBC News*, 30 November 2018, www.bbc.co.uk/news/av/uk-46402777.

25 Jeremy Howell, 'Launching new technology needs "perfect timing"', *BBC News*, 2 July 2018, www.bbc.co.uk/news/av/business-44602314.

26 Miles Brignall, 'Most buy-to-let lenders refuse loans when tenants are on benefits', *The Guardian*, 21 October 2018, www.theguardian.com/money/2018/oct/21/buy-to-let-90-percent-of-lenders-refuse-loans-to-benefit-claimants.

Chapter 5: Poverty, Crime and Prostitution

1 Maya Oppenheim, 'Cost of living crisis forcing more women into sex work and accepting dangerous clients', *The Independent*, 15 November 2022, www.independent.co.uk/news/uk/home-news/sex-work-cost-of-living-crisis-dangerous-clients-b2222507.html.

2 Anna Holligan, 'Tough times for Amsterdam sex business', *BBC News*, 19 January 2019, www.bbc.co.uk/news/world-europe-46919294.

3 Streetlight UK, 'Annual Report 2021', www.streetlight.uk.com/wp-content/uploads/2021/02/ANNUAL-REPORT-2021-MASTER.pdf.

4 Streetlight UK, 'Prostitution – The Facts', www.streetlight.uk.com/the-facts/.

5   The Chrysalis Project was a joint enterprise between Commonweal
    Housing, the homeless charity St Mungo's and Lambeth Council, www.
    homeless.org.uk/homeless-england/service/st-mungos-chrysalis-project.

6   Helen Johnson, 'Evaluation of the Amari Project: supporting women
    exiting prostitution and sexual exploitation', April 2019, www.solace-
    womensaid.org/get-informed/professional-resourcesamari-project-
    evaluation-report.

7   Prison Reform Trust, 'New report exposes system failure condemning
    6 out of 10 women leaving prison to homelessness', 14 October 2020.
    Commenting on Prison Reform Trust, London Prisons Mission and the
    Church of St Martin-in-the-Fields, 'Safe homes for women leaving prison',
    October 2020.

8   Prison Reform Trust, 'Safe homes for women leaving prison'.

9   Prison Reform Trust, 'Prison: the facts', *Bromley Briefings*, 14 June 2019,
    www.prisonreformtrust.org.uk.

10 Crown Prosecution Service, 'Brother of Manchester bomber jailed for
    55 years', 20 August 2020, www.cps.gov.uk/cps/news/brother-manchester-
    bomber-jailed-55-years.

11 HM Prison and Probation Service, 'Costs per place and costs per prisoner
    by individual prison', *Annual Report and Accounts 2019–20*, Ministry of
    Justice information release, 29 October 2020.

12 Institute for Government, 'Prisons' in *Performance Tracker*, 2019, www.
    instituteforgovernment.org.uk/publication/report/performance-
    tracker-2019.

13 Data as of 2019/20. HM Prison and Probation Service, 'Costs per place and
    costs per prisoner'.

14 Diane Taylor, 'Former prisoner sues Ministry of Justice over PTSD from
    rats', *The Guardian*, 29 January 2019, www.theguardian.com/society/2019/
    jan/29/former-prisoner-sues-ministry-of-justice-over-ptsd-from-rats;
    Lizzie Dearden, 'Prisoner found killing rats in "dirty and vermin-infested"
    Bedford prison, report finds', *The Independent*, 22 January 2019, www.
    independent.co.uk/news/uk/home-news/bedford-prison-hmp-rats-
    inspection-urgent-notification-suicides-violence-drugs-a8739421.html.

15 Peter Dawson, director of the Prison Reform Trust, 'PRT comment: safety
    in custody statistics', 30 January 2020, www.prisonreformtrust.org.uk/
    PressPolicy/News/vw/1/ItemID/795.

16 Lydia Polgreen, 'Rehabilitation comes to a prison and to its inmates',
    The New York Times, 18 July 2011, www.nytimes.com/2011/07/19/world/
    asia/19delhi.html.

17 'Inmates pedal for shorter sentences in a Brazilian prison', *BBC News*,
    13 July 2012, www.bbc.co.uk/news/av/world-latin-america-18832768.

18 Volatile incidents include: 'barricades/preventions of access: prisoners
    use a physical barrier to deny access to all or part of a prison; hostage
    incidents: prisoners hold people against their will; concerted indiscipline:

two or more prisoners refuse to comply with instructions/rules; incidents at height: any incidents taking place above or below ground level, including climbing over bars, on the roof or on netting'. Data from 2013–19. Institute for Government, 'Prisons', in *Performance Tracker*, 2019, www.instituteforgovernment.org.uk/publication/report/performance-tracker-2019.

19 House of Commons Library, 'UK prison population statistics', 3 July 2020, commonslibrary.parliament.uk/research-briefings/sn04334/.

20 K.K. Roessler, 'Exercise treatment for drug abuse: a Danish pilot study', *Scandinavian Journal of Public Health*, vol. 38, no. 6 (August 2010), pp.664–9, doi:10.1177/1403494810371249, PMID: 20529968.

21 Vikram Dodd, 'Tackle poverty and inequality to reduce crime, says police chief', *The Guardian*, 18 April 2021, www.theguardian.com/uk-news/2021/apr/18/tackle-poverty-and-inequality-to-reduce-says-police-chief.

22 McGarvey, *Poverty Safari*, pp.96–7.

23 Research carried out by the Disabilities Trust Foundation shows nearly half of male prisoners (47 per cent) have a history of traumatic brain injury (TBI): Disabilities Trust, 'Brain injury and offending', www.thedtgroup.org/foundation/brain-injury-and-offending.

24 Kim Gorgens, 'The surprising connection between brain injuries and crime', TED Talk, June 2018.

25 Disabilities Trust, 'Making the link: female offending and brain injury', research 2016–18, www.thedtgroup.org.

26 S. Sudarsanan, S. Chaudhary, A.A. Pawar, K. Srivastava, 'Psychiatric effects of traumatic brain injury', *Med J Armed Forces India*, vol. 63, no. 3 (2007), pp.259–63. doi:10.1016/S0377-1237(07)80150-X.

27 '300,000 children attend A&E in the UK with a head injury every year making traumatic brain injury the biggest cause of death and disability in children and young people', NHS statistics from Matrix Neurological, www.matrixneurological.org/information/local-statistics/.

28 'SEND crisis: despite increases, SEND funding faces a £2bn annual shortfall. This means inadequate provision, children educated in inappropriate settings, and over 1,000 children not receiving any education at all.' National Education Union, neu.org.uk/funding/send-crisis.

29 Daniel Amen, 'The most important lesson from 83,000 brain scans', TED Talk, 17 April 2014, tedsummaries.com.

30 In 2020, there were around 75,000 children in care in England, 14,500 in Scotland, 7,000 in Wales and 3,300 in Northern Ireland.

31 Dr Neil Harrison, Rees Centre, 'School exclusions are on the up – but training teachers in trauma could help', Department of Education blog, 20 June 2019, www.education.ox.ac.uk/school-exclusions-are-on-the-up-but-training-teachers-in-trauma-could-help-2/.

32 D.L. Bennett, D.K. Schluter, G. Melis, P. Bywaters, et al., 'Child poverty and children entering care in England, 2015–20: a longitudinal ecological study at the local area level', *The Lancet*, vol. 7, no. 6 (2022), e496–e503, doi:10.1016/S2468-2667(22)00065-2.

33 Patrick Butler, 'Delays to mental health treatment in England "putting more children in care"', *The Guardian*, 14 December 2022, www. theguardian.com/society/2022/dec/14/delays-to-mental-health-treatment-in-england-putting-more-children-in-care.

34 M.D. Albaugh, J. Ottino-Gonzalez, A. Sidwell, et al., 'Association of cannabis use during adolescence with neurodevelopment', *JAMA Psychiatry*, vol. 78, no. 9 (2021), pp.1031–40, doi:10.1001/jamapsychiatry.2021.1258.

35 Professor David Nutt, 'Drug testing and synthetic cannabis in prisons', *Drug Science*, 3 March 2021, www.drugscience.org.uk/drug-testing-prison-inmates-for-cannabis/.

36 'Random mandatory drugs testing (Traditional drugs)', Gov.uk Justice Data, data.justice.gov.uk/prisons/prison-reform/random-mandatory-drug-testing, viewed 10 July 2023. Spice is a psychoactive substance.

37 'Worrying increase in spice jail deaths highlights "crisis in prison system"', Middlesex University, 31 January 2023, www.mdx.ac.uk/news/2023/01/spice-prison-deaths. For full research paper see: K. Duke, H. Gleeson, S. MacGregor and B. Thom, 'The risk matrix: drug-related deaths in prisons in England and Wales, 2015–2020', *Journal of Community Psychology* (2023), pp.1–22.

38 D.C. Hergert, C. Robertson-Benta, V. Sicard, D. Schwotzer, et al., 'Use of medical cannabis to treat traumatic brain injury', *Journal of Neurotrauma*, vol. 38, no. 14 (2021), pp.1904–17, doi:10.1089/neu.2020.7148.

39 McGarvey, *Poverty Safari*, p.9.

40 Richard Wilkinson, 'The link between inequality and anxiety', TED Talk, 25 November 2021.

41 McGarvey, *Poverty Safari*, p.23.

42 Anthony Horowitz, *The House of Silk* (Little Brown & Company, 2011), p.52.

43 'Revealed: full links between poverty and violent crime in London', 15 July 2019, www.london.gov.uk/press-releases/mayoral/full-links-between-poverty-and-violent-crime. This statement was based on data from GLA Strategic Crime Analysis Team, *A Public Health Approach to Serious Youth Violence: Supporting Evidence*, July 2019, data.london.gov.uk/dataset/a-public-health-approach-to-serious-youth-violence.

44 House of Commons Library, '16–19 bursary scheme', 5 April 2017, www.commonslibrary.parliament.uk/research-briefings/sn06154.

45 Natalie Gil, 'Robbed of their futures: how austerity cuts hit young people hardest', *The Guardian*, 17 November 2014, www.theguardian.com/

education/2014/nov/17/robbed-of-their-futures-how-austerity-cuts-hit-young-people-hardest.

46 Jack Britton, Haroon Chowdry and Lorraine Dearden, 'The 16 to 19 bursary fund impact evaluation: interim report', Institute of Education and Institute for Fiscal Studies, revised June 2014.

47 National Audit Office, '16- to 18-year-old participation in education and training', 3 September 2014, www.nao.org.uk/report/16-to-18-year-old-participation-in-education-and-training/.

Chapter 6: Poverty and Barriers

1   Danny Dorling, 'The no-nonsense guide to equality', *New Internationalist* (2012), p.175.

2   Fair By Design, 'Ending the extra costs of being poor', www.fairbydesign. com, viewed November 2021.

3   'Extra costs for customers on prepayment meters to be scrapped in budget', *The Guardian*, 11 March 2023, www.theguardian.com/money/2023/mar/11/extra-costs-for-customers-on-prepayment-meters-to-be-scrapped-in-budget.

4   Email from Jane Elliott, 17 November 2022.

5   'ITV News investigation exposes racism in social housing sector', 9 November 2021, www.itv.com/news/2021-11-09/itv-news-investigation-exposes-racism-in-social-housing-sector.

6   Joseph Rowntree Foundation, 'Structural Racism in Housing', September 2021.

7   Joint Council for the Welfare of Immigrants, 'Windrush scandal explained', www.jcwi.org.uk/windrush-scandal-explained.

8   Mhairi Black, MP, House of Commons speech, 19 September 2022.

9   Felix Project, 'Impact Report', 2021.

10 The First Love Foundation's holistic model of support has been cited by the All-Party Parliamentary Group on Hunger and Poverty (2014) as the most effective in tackling poverty anywhere in the UK, www.firstlove-foundation.org.uk.

11 Kathy Burke, *Money Talks*, episode 2, Channel Four documentary, 5 July 2021.

12 Burke, *Money Talks*.

13 Burke, *Money Talks*.

14 Lord John Bird, House of Lords debate on poverty, 29 June 2016, Hansard, vol. 773.

Chapter 7: Poverty, Employment and Caring

1   Patrick Butler and Sarah Butler, 'Bonus blow for Greggs staff prompts call for benefit and tax rethink', *The Guardian*, 13 January 2020, www.theguardian.com/society/2020/jan/13/bonus-blow-for-greggs-staff-prompts-call-for-benefit-and-tax-rethink.

2   Joseph Rowntree Foundation, 'UK Poverty 2022: The Essential Guide to Understanding Poverty in the UK', www.jrf.org.uk/report/uk-poverty-2022.

3 'The Clifton StrengthsFinder assessment helps identify the areas where you have the greatest potential for building strength. It measures recurring patterns of thought, feeling and behaviour. Knowing this information is a starting point, which then helps individuals leverage their talents and turn them into sustainable strengths.' www.leadershipvisionconsulting.com/what-is-the-clifton-strengthsfinder/.

4 Richard Reed, *If I Could Tell You Just One Thing: Encounters with Remarkable People and Their Most Valuable Advice* (Canongate, 2016), p.325.

5 Joseph Rowntree Foundation, 'Poverty in Scotland 2022', 3 October 2022, www.jrf.org.uk/report/poverty-scotland-2022.

6 'Parliament: Tory MPs to refuse unconscious bias training', *BBC News*, 24 September 2020, www.bbc.co.uk/news/uk-politics-54282685.amp.

7 'Carer's Allowance: how it works', www.gov.uk/carers-allowance, viewed 26 June 2023.

8 Aoife Kiely, 'A fresh START: reducing symptoms of depression and anxiety in carers', Alzheimer's Society, 12 September 2019, www.alzheimers.org.uk/Care-and-cure-magazine/autumn-19/fresh-start-reducing-symptoms-depression-and-anxiety-carers.

9 Yuval Noah Harari, *21 Lessons for the 21st Century* (Penguin Random House, 2018), p.37.

10 Joseph Rowntree Foundation, 'Poverty in Scotland 2022'.

11 Giacomo Vagni, Richard Breen, 'Earnings and income penalties for motherhood: estimates for British women using the individual synthetic control method', *European Sociological Review*, vol. 37, no. 5 (October 2021), pp.834–48, doi:10.1093/esr/jcab014.

12 Christine Lagarde, head of the International Monetary Fund, 'Ten years after Lehman: lessons learned and challenges ahead', IMF Blog, 5 September 2018, www.imf.org/en/Blogs/Articles/2018/09/05/blog-ten-years-after-lehman-lessons-learned-and-challenges-ahead.

13 Lagarde, 'Ten years after Lehman'.

14 J.K. Rowling, *Very Good Lives* (Sphere, 2008), p.29.

15 Sophie McBain, 'Why Britain's childcare system is on the brink of collapse', *New Statesman*, 22 September 2020, www.newstatesman.com/uncategorized/2020/09/why-britains-childcare-system-brink-collapse.

16 Bureau of Investigative Journalism, 'Revealed: thousands of care jobs pay below living wage despite promises', www.thebureauinvestigates.com/stories/2021-07-13/revealed-thousands-of-home-care-jobs-pay-below-living-wage-despite-promises.

17 Bureau of Investigative Journalism, 'Revealed: thousands of care jobs pay below living wage'.

Chapter 8: Poverty and Education

1 'Remarks by the First Lady at the "Let Girls Learn" event celebrating International Women's Day', White House, Office of the First Lady, 8 March

2016, obamawhitehouse.archives.gov/the-press-office/2016/03/08/remarks-first-lady-let-girls-learn-event-celebrating-international.

2   Harry Leslie Smith, *Don't Let My Past Be Your Future* (Constable, 2017), p. 176.

3   Louise Tickle, 'Food, clothes, a mattress and three funerals: what teachers buy for children', *The Guardian*, 1 May 2018, www.theguardian.com/education/2018/may/01/teachers-buy-children-food-clothes-mattress-funerals-child-poverty.

4   '"Period Poverty" sanitary products "improve school attendance"', *BBC News*, 28 November 2018, www.bbc.co.uk/news/av/uk-england-hampshire-46361899.

5   Tickle, 'Food, clothes, a mattress and three funerals'.

6   Child Poverty Action Group, Scotland, 'The Cost of School Day Toolkit', 2021, cpag.org.uk/scotland/CoSD/toolkit.

7   Northern Ireland Commissioner for Children and Young People (NICCY), 'A "free" education? The cost of education in Northern Ireland', August 2017.

8   NICCY, 'Statement on children's rights in Northern Ireland 3, main report,' November 2022.

9   NICCY, 'Response to the expert panel on educational underachievement', 16 October 2020.

10   NICCY, 'Response to the expert panel on educational underachievement'.

11   Interview with Rebecca Abrahams, 22 February 2022.

12   Nurture groups are based on attachment theory, first proposed by J. Bowlby, *Attachment and Loss*, Vol. 1: *Attachment* (Hogarth Press and Institute of Psycho-Analysis, 1969).

13   S. Sloan, K. Winter, P. Connolly and A. Gildea, 'The effectiveness of nurture groups in improving outcomes for young children with social, emotional and behavioural difficulties in primary schools: an evaluation of nurture group provision in Northern Ireland', *Children and Youth Services Review*, vol. 108 (January 2020), 104619, doi:10.1016/j.childyouth.2019.104619.

14   Department for Education, 'Statutory guidance: cost of school uniforms', 19 November 2021, www.gov.uk/government/publications/cost-of-school-uniforms/cost-of-school-uniforms.

Chapter 9: The Green Agenda

1   Kate Raworth, 'A healthy economy should be designed to thrive, not grow', TED Talk, 14 May 2018.

2   COP26 topics were: Action on Climate and Sustainable Development Goals, Adaptation and Resilience, Capacity-Building, Climate Finance, Climate Technology, Education and Youth, Gender, Global Stocktake, Innovation, Land Use, Local Communities and Indigenous People's Platform, Market and Non-Market Mechanisms, Mitigation, Pre-2020 Ambition and Implementation, Science: unfccc.int/topics.

3 'What is action for climate empowerment?', unfccc.int/topics/education-youth/the-big-picture/what-is-action-for-climate-empowerment.

4 George Orwell, 'Some thoughts on the common toad', *Tribune*, 12 April 1946.

5 Danny Dorling, *Slowdown: The End of the Great Acceleration – and Why It's a Good Thing* (Yale University Press, updated edn, 2021), pp.318–19.

6 Dorling, *Slowdown*, p.295.

7 Dorling, *Slowdown*, p.323.

8 Dorling, *Slowdown*, p.312.

9 Dorling, *Slowdown*, pp.329–31.

10 Raworth, 'A healthy economy should be designed to thrive, not grow'.

11 Kate Raworth, 'How to live within the Doughnut', TED Talk, 10 December 2021.

12 Raworth, 'A healthy economy should be designed to thrive, not grow'.

13 Pedro Gomes, *Friday Is the New Saturday: How a Four-Day Working Week Will Save the Economy* (Flint, 2022), chapter 7.

14 Gomes, *Friday Is the New Saturday*, chapter 7.

15 House of Lords Library, 'Negligence in the NHS: liability costs', 29 November 2021, lordslibrary.parliament.uk/negligence-in-the-nhs-liability-costs/.

16 T. Draycott, C. Yau, B. Leigh, E. Liberati, et al., 'Clinical negligence costs: taking action to safeguard NHS sustainability', *British Medical Journal* (2 March 2020), p.368, doi:10.1136/bmj.m552.

17 Gomes, *Friday Is the New Saturday*, chapter 7.

18 Kate Raworth, Doughnut Economics Action Lab, 'Turning Doughnut Economics from a radical idea into transformative action', www.doughnuteconomics.org.

19 'Time is running out'. Prince William introduces the first-ever Earthshot Awards on BBC One, 17 October 2021.

20 Prince William introduces the first-ever Earthshot Awards on BBC One.

21 Darren Baxter, 'Net zero: a just transition is necessary, and is key for maintaining public support', Joseph Rowntree Foundation, 2 November 2021, www.jrf.org.uk/blog/net-zero-just-transition-necessary-and-key-maintaining-public-support.

22 Mary Robinson with Caitriona Palmer, *Climate Justice: A Man-Made Problem with a Feminist Solution* (Bloomsbury, 2018), p.122.

23 'COP26: what's the climate impact of private jets?' BBC *Reality Check*, 4 November 2021, www.bbc.co.uk/news/59135899.

24 Kai Tabacek, 'Private jet flights in the UK soar to new heights – analysis', 30 March 2023, www.greenpeace.org.uk/news/private-jet-flights-in-the-uk-soar-to-new-heights-analysis/.

25 Estimated rural populations as of 2020–21: Wales 634,000, England 9.7 million, Scotland 1.56 million, Northern Ireland 670,000.

26 Statistics for 2020 from Public Health Wales.

27 Summary statistics for Wales, by region: 2020. Statistical first release by the Welsh government (data 2013–18), 20 May 2020.

28 N. Serpetti, A.R. Baudron, M.T. Burrows, B.L. Payne, et al., 'Impact of ocean warming on sustainable fisheries management informs the ecosystem approach to fisheries', *Scientific Reports*, vol. 7 (2017), 13438, doi:10.1038/s41598-017-13220-7. Also published in Nature, www.nature.com/articles/s41598-017-13220-7.

29 'The maximum body size fish can reach is determined by the supply and demand of limiting resources like oxygen. Warmer water typically contains less oxygen but also increases metabolic rates and therefore demand for oxygen. Fish in warming waters may sooner reach the size where they can no longer acquire the oxygen needed for maintaining metabolic demands, thereby limiting adult body size.' Idongesit E. Ikpewe, Alan R. Baudron, Aurore Ponchon and Paul G. Fernandes, 'Bigger juveniles and smaller adults: changes in fish size correlate with warming seas', *Journal of Applied Ecology* (2020), doi:10.1111/1365-2664.13807.

30 House of Commons, 'UK fisheries statistics', Briefing Paper no. 2788, 23 November 2020.

31 Deborah Zabarenko, 'One-third of world fish catch used for animal feed', *Reuters*, 29 October 2008, reuters.com/article/us-fish-food-idUSTRE49SOXH20081029.

32 Oceana, 'All but two of Scotland's offshore marine "protected" areas are paper parks', 5 August 2021, europe.oceana.org/en/press-center/press-releases/all-two-scotlands-offshore-marine-protected-areas-are-paper-parks.

33 Matt Reynolds, 'The race to stop fish becoming the next factory farming nightmare', *Wired*, 22 September 2021, www.wired.co.uk/article/future-of-food-fish.

34 House of Commons, 'UK fisheries statistics'.

35 Porthmeor Studios and Cellars, *The St Ives Pilchard Seine Fishery in 1850*, Borlase Smart John Wells Trust, www.bsjwtrust.co.uk/wp/wp-content/uploads/Pichard-Fishery.pdf.

36 David Attenborough, *Extinction: The Facts*, BBC One, 13 September 2020.

37 Mary Robinson, 'Why climate change is a threat to human rights', TED Talk, 14 October 2015.

38 Dorling, *Slowdown*, p.295.

39 *Life at 50°C: Using Ice to Battle India's Heat*, BBC documentary, first shown 5 October 2021.

40 Becky Dale and Nassos Stylianou, 'Climate change: world now sees twice as many days over 50C', *BBC News*, 13 September 2021, www.bbc.co.uk/news/science-environment-58494641.

41 Damian Carrington, 'Reflecting sunlight into space has terrifying consequences, say scientists: but "geoengineers" say urgent nature of climate change means research must continue into controversial

technology to combat rising temperatures', *The Guardian*, 26 November 2014, www.theguardian.com/environment/2014/nov/26/geoengineering-could-offer-solution-last-resort-climate-change.

42 Holly Jean Buck, *After Geoengineering: Climate Tragedy, Repair, and Restoration* (Verso, 2019), p.46.

43 'Your COP26 questions answered: carbon capture', video by Dan Fox for *Nature*, 10 November 2021, youtu.be/FEVRKcAdZCA.

44 'Air pollution: coroner calls for law change after Ella Adoo-Kissi-Debrah's death', *BBC News*, 21 April 2021, www.bbc.co.uk/news/uk-england-london-56801794.amp.

45 British Lung Foundation, 'How does air pollution affect children's lungs?' (2021), www.blf.org.uk/support-for-you/risks-to-childrens-lungs/air-pollution.

46 In July 2018, the Air Quality Expert Group (AQEG) produced a report, *Impacts of Vegetation on Urban Air Pollution*.

47 Mayor of London, 'Using green infrastructure to protect people from air pollution', April 2019. This guide was produced in consultation with the Birmingham Institute of Forest Research (University of Birmingham), the Global Centre for Clean Air Research (University of Surrey) and Transport for London, www.london.gov.uk/sites/default/files/green_infrastructure_air_pollution_may_19.pdf.

48 Cross River Partnership, 'Waltham Forest CityTrees: improving air quality through biotechnology and urban greening', October 2020, crossriver-parnership.org/wp-content/uploads/2020/10/Waltham-Forest-CityTrees-Healthy-Streets-Everyday-Case-Study.pdf. The CityTree is made by Green City Solutions. For more information, see greencitysolutions.de/en/products/citytree/.

49 Marina Spironetti, 'Why Milan is covering its skyscrapers in plants', *BBC Travel*, 9 October 2017, www.bbc.com/travel/article/20170925-why-milan-is-covering-its-skyscrapers-in-plants.

50 Eunice Lo and Dann Mitchell, 'Guest post: How "urban heat islands" will intensify heatwaves in UK cities', 1 October 2020, www.carbonbrief.org/guest-post-how-urban-heat-islands-will-intensify-heatwaves-in-uk-cities.

51 Isabella Tree, *Wilding: The Return of Nature to a British Farm* (Picador, 2018), p.24.

52 Tree, *Wilding*, p.23.

53 Claire Marshall, 'Strictest targets pledged to tackle England sewage discharges', *BBC News*, 26 August 2022, www.bbc.co.uk/news/science-environment-62687856.amp.

54 Henry Ford, *Ford News*, July 1935, p.125, www.thehenryford.org/collections-and-research/digital-resources/popular-topics/henry-ford-quotes/.

55 'Industrial hemp licensing: factsheet', www.gov.uk/government/publications/industrial-hemp-licensing-guidance/industrial-

hemp-licensing-factsheet#what-is-the-light-touch-regime, viewed
November 2022.

56 Foreign Agricultural Service, US Department of Agriculture, with Global
Agricultural Information Network (GAIN), 'An overview of the Dutch
hemp market', 18 May 2020.

57 British Hemp Company, 'Why we love hemp', britishhempco.com/pages/
why-hemp', viewed 24 November 2022.

58 Foreign Agricultural Service, US Department of Agriculture, with GAIN,
'An overview of the Dutch hemp market', 18 May 2020.

59 British Hemp Company, 'Why we love hemp'.

Chapter 10: Finance

1 D. Gunnell, J. Donovan et al., 'The 2008 global financial crisis: effects
on mental health and suicide' (2015) Policy Bristol, University of Bristol,
www.bristol.ac.uk/policybristol/policy-briefings/financial-crisis/.

2 Frederico Mor, 'Bank rescues of 2007–09: outcomes and cost', House
of Commons Library, 8 October 2018, commonslibrary.parliament.uk/
research-briefings/sn05748/.

3 'HS2: what is the route, when will it be finished and what will it cost?' *BBC
News*, updated 18 November 2021, www.bbc.co.uk/news/uk-16473296.amp.

4 'In 2008, UK gross domestic product (GDP) fell to −4.2% and after the
2020 pandemic it fell to −9.7%.' 'Gross domestic product: year on year
growth', Office for National Statistics, 11 November 2021, www.ons.gov.uk/
economy/grossdomesticproductgdp/timeseries/ihyp/pn2.

5 House of Commons Library, 'The budget deficit: a short guide', 21 May
2021, commonslibrary.parliament.uk/research-briefings/sn06167/.

6 'UK government debt and deficit: March 2022', Office for National
Statistics, 29 July 2022.

7 'UK taxpayers forecast to make £32.1 billion loss on RBS privatisation',
Reuters, 11 March 2020, reuters.com/article/uk-britain-budget-rbs-
idUKKBN20Y260.

8 Jack Goodman, 'Why are there still so many nuclear weapons? Reality
Check takes a look', 26 September 2021, www.bbc.co.uk/news/av/
world-49755995.

9 House of Commons Library, 'Reducing the UK's aid spending in 2021',
5 November 2021, commonslibrary.parliament.uk/research-briefings/
cbp-9224/.

10 'The queen's funeral, United Nations, and fracking', *The Rest Is Politics*
podcast, 21 September 2022.

11 'Official Statistics – United Kingdom Food Security Report 2021: Theme 2:
UK food supply sources', 22 December 2021, www.gov.uk.

12 'Sahel: tree planting', UK Parliament, question for Department for
International Development tabled on 22 February 2018, questions-
statements.parliament.uk/written-questions/detail/2018-02-22/129105.

13 For more information on Official Development Assistance, see www.gov. uk/government/collections/official-development-assistance-oda--2.

14 OECD, 'Untied aid – OECD', www.oecd.org/dac/financing-sustainable-development/development-finance-standards/untied-aid.htm, viewed 1 October 2021.

15 Maria Abi-Habib, 'How China got Sri Lanka to cough up a port', *New York Times*, 25 June 2018, www.nytimes.com/2018/06/25/world/asia/china-sri-lanka-port.html.

16 For more about Give Directly, see www.givedirectly.org/about/, viewed 21 September 2022.

17 For more information, see Financial Conduct Authority, 'Climate change and sustainable finance', 22 April 2021, www.fca.org.uk/firms/climate-change-sustainable-finance.

18 Jonathan Josephs, 'Climate change: shipping industry calls for new global carbon tax', *BBC News*, 21 April 2021, www.bbc.com/news/business-56835352.

19 Jonathan Josephs, 'Maersk: consumers can foot shipping's climate change bill', *BBC News*, 19 February 2021, www.bbc.co.uk/news/business-56126559.

20 'What impact do ships have on human and marine life?' *Hydrosphere*, 2 September 2020, hydrosphere.co.uk/how-do-ships-impact-human-and-marine-life/.

21 Bill McGraw, 'The incredible, recent, global rise in the stranding of marine mammals', *Sevenseas Media* (January 2021), no. 68, sevenseasmedia.org/the-incredible-recent-global-rise-in-the-stranding-of-marine-mammals/. Philip Hoare, 'The increase in beached whales may be due to military sonar exercises, say experts', *The Guardian*, 24 August 2020, www.theguardian.com/environment/2020/aug/24/beached-whale-increase-may-be-due-to-military-sonar-exercises-say-experts.

22 'What impact do ships have on human and marine life?' *Hydrosphere*, hydrosphere.co.uk/how-do-ships-impact-human-and-marine-life/.

23 'Wind propulsion solutions', International Windship Association, 25 November 2021, www.wind-ship.org/en/category/wind-propulsion-solutions/.

24 Christiaan De Beukelaer, 'Sail cargo: charting a new path for emission-free shipping?' *UNCTAD Transport and Trade Facilitation Newsletter*, no. 88 (Fourth Quarter 2020), article 65, unctad.org/news/sail-cargo-charting-new-path-emission-free-shipping.

Chapter 11: Procurement

1 News conference, 12 August 1986. Ronald Reagan Presidential Foundation and Institute, Reagan quotes and speeches, www.reaganfoundation.org.

2 'Tory MP Hogg to repay "moat cost"', *BBC News*, 14 May 2009, news/bbc. co.uk/1/hi/uk_politics/8051027.stm.

3   'Carillion collapse exposed flaws in UK government policy: lawmakers', *Reuters*, 9 July 2018, reuters.com/article/us-carillion-collapse-idUSKBN1JZ1H7.

4   Labour Party, 'Dossier of waste in the Ministry of Defence 2010–2021', January 2022.

5   House of Commons Public Accounts Committee, '"Unimaginable" cost of Test & Trace failed to deliver central promise of averting another lockdown', 10 March 2021, committees.parliament.uk/committee/127/public-accounts-committee/news/150988/unimaginable-cost-of-test-trace-failed-to-deliver-central-promise-of-averting-another-lockdown/.

6   House of Commons Public Accounts Committee, *COVID-19: Test, Track and Trace (Part 1)*, 10 March 2021.

7   Comptroller and Auditor General, National Audit Office, 'Investigation: the Department for Transport's funding of the Garden Bridge', 11 October 2016, www.nao.org.uk/wp-content/uploads/2016/10/Investigation-the-Department-for-Transports-funding-of-the-Garden-Bridge.pdf.

8   James O'Brien, LBC Radio, 23 September 2022.

9   Cabinet Office and Lord Agnew, 'Procurement teams must consider wider benefits of public spending', 3 June 2021, www.gov.uk/government/news/procurement-teams-must-consider-wider-benefits-of-public-spending.

Chapter 12: Eliminating Poverty from Britain

1   The End Child Poverty campaign states that 'Households are living in poverty if their household income (adjusted to account for household size) is less than 60% of the median. All poverty rates are calculated on an after-housing costs basis.' J. Stone and D. Hirsch, 'Local indicators of child poverty, 2017/18', Loughborough University Centre for Research in Social Policy, May 2019, www.endchildpoverty.org.uk.

2   'On 18 March 1999, the British government pledged to be the first to end child poverty in a generation. By 2010, there were 1.1 million fewer children in poverty. We proved once and for all that child poverty is policy-responsive, that it can be cut, and we were half way to showing it could be eliminated ... Since 2012, child poverty has risen by 500,000 and projections show we can expect a further one million children in poverty by 2021.' 'It was 20 years ago today', blog by Alison Garnham, chief executive, Child Poverty Action Group, 18 March 2019, www.cpag.org.uk.

3   Centre for Homelessness Impact, mission statement, www.homelessnessimpact.org/mission-and-impact.

4   Between 2021 and 2022, the number of households in England in fuel poverty grew from 4.93 million to 7.39 million. The highest levels of fuel poverty were found in single-parent households and those living in the private rented sector, as social housing tends to be more energy efficient. Department for Energy Security and Net Zero, 'Annual Fuel Poverty

Statistics in England 2023 (2022 data)', 28 February 2023, pp.1, 18, 36, 39, assets.publishing.service.gov.uk/government/uploads/system/uploads/attachment_data/file/1139133/annual-fuel-poverty-statistics-lilee-report-2023-2022-data.pdf.

5   In Wales, estimates in spring 2022 suggested that 614,000 (45 per cent) of households were struggling with their energy bills. Welsh Government, 'Fuel Poverty modelled estimates for Wales (headline results): as at October 2021', 13 April 2022, www.gov.wales/fuel-poverty-modelled-estimates-wales-headline-results-october-2021-html#95651.

6   Question to the Scottish Parliament from Miles Briggs MSP, 24 February 2023. Question Reference: S6W-14736, www.parliament.scot/chamber-and-committees/questions-and-answers/question?ref=S6W-14736.

7   A. Keung and J. Bradshaw, 'Who are the fuel poor?', University of York, Social Policy Research Unit, 21 March 2023, cpag.org.uk/sites/default/files/files/policypost/Who_are_the_fuel_poor_revised.pdf. Figures on Northern Ireland are inconclusive as the lack of a devolved government at Stormont prevents full measurements from being collated. There is no clear government data for Northern Ireland beyond 2016, which found that 21.5 per cent of households were in fuel poverty. House of Commons Library, 'Local area data: Fuel Poverty', 19 June 2023, commonslibrary.parliament.uk/local-area-data-fuel-poverty/

8   P. Alston, 'Visit to the United Kingdom of Great Britain and Northern Ireland: report of the Special Rapporteur on extreme poverty and human rights', 23 April 2019, A/HRC/41/39/Add.1, digitallibrary.un.org.

9   S. Kennedy, 'Child Poverty Act 2010: a short guide', House of Commons Library, 4 July 2014, commonslibrary.parliament.uk/research-briefings/sn05585/.

10 Child poverty facts and figures from Child Poverty Action Group, based on statistics from Department for Work and Pensions, 'Households below average income: for financial years ending 1995 to 2020', 25 March 2021, www.gov.uk/government/statistics/households-below-average-income-for-financial-years-ending-1995-to-2020/households-below-average-income-an-analysis-of-the-income-distribution-fye-1995-to-fye-2020.

11 F. Munro, 'Public sector finances, UK: March 2021', Office for National Statistics, 23 April 2021, www.ons.gov.uk.

Chapter 13: Poverty and Compassion

1   Martin Luther King, Jr. Copyright @ The Nobel Foundation 1964.

2   Elizabeth Bruenig, 'The undeserving poor: a very tiny history', 7 January 2018, medium.com/@ebruenig/the-undeserving-poor-a-very-tiny-history-96c3b9141e13.

3   Benjamin Disraeli, *Sybil, or The Two Nations* (1845), www.bbc.co.uk/history/british/victorians/bsurface_01.shtml.

4 The Grenfell Tower fire occurred on 14 June 2017 and caused seventy-two deaths and seventy-four hospitalisations. The police investigation and public inquiry are ongoing, www.grenfelltowerinquiry.org.uk.

5 Margaret Thatcher interview, *Catholic Herald*, 5 December 1978, www.margaretthatcher.org/document/103793.

6 Financial Conduct Authority, 'Wonga to pay redress for unfair debt collection practices', 25 June 2014, www.fca.org.uk/news/press-releases/wonga-pay-redress-unfair-debt-collection-practices.

7 Boris Johnson, 'The poor are being robbed in Labour's class war', *The Telegraph*, 8 December 2005, www.telegraph.co.uk/comment/personalview/3621585/The-poor-are-being-robbed-in-Labours-class-war.html.

8 Trussell Trust, *State of Hunger Report*, November 2019, p.33, www.stateofhunger.org.

9 G. Tyler, 'What do the latest food bank statistics tell us?' House of Commons Library, 21 January 2020.

10 Harry Leslie Smith, *Don't Let My Past Be Your Future* (Constable, 2017), p.48.

11 'In ten constituencies across Britain, over half of children are trapped in poverty: Poplar & Limehouse, Bethnal Green & Bow, East Ham, Birmingham–Hodge Hill, Blackburn, Islington South & Finsbury, Manchester–Gorton, Blackley & Broughton, Bradford West, West Ham', www.endchildpoverty.org.uk.

12 Loughborough University, 'Child poverty growing fastest in the UK's most deprived areas', 15 May 2019, www.lboro.ac.uk/media-centre/press-releases/2019/may/child-poverty-growing-fasted-in-deprived-areas/.

13 '14% of UK families with children have experienced food insecurity in the past 6 months', Food Foundation, September 2020, foodfoundation.org.uk/new-food-foundation-data-sept-2020/. Further information: '14% of adults living with children reported experiencing moderate or severe food insecurity in the last six months. Four million people including 2.3 million children live in these households. This compares to pre-Covid-19 levels of 11.5% amongst households with children.'

14 Public Health England, 'England's poorest areas are fast food hotspots', 29 June 2018, www.gov.uk/government/news/englands-poorest-areas-are-fast-food-hotspots.

15 House of Commons debate on free school meals, 21 October 2020, Hansard, vol. 682, hansard.parliament.uk/commons/2020-10-21/debates.

16 On 21 October 2020, Conservative MPs voted against plans to extend free school meals over holidays. The outcome was 322 against to 261 for.

17 'Rashford "proud" after government U-turn on free school meals at Christmas', *ITV News*, 8 November 2020, www.itv.com/news/2020-11-07/rashford-proud-after-government-u-turn-on-free-school-meals-at-christmas.

18 Richard Reed, *If I Could Tell You Just One Thing: Encounters with Remarkable People and Their Most Valuable Advice* (Canongate, 2016), p.144.
19 'Poverty in the UK: a guide to the facts and figures', 27 September 2019, fullfact.org/economy/poverty-uk-guide-facts-and-figures/.
20 www.compassioninpolitics.com.
21 Benjamin Disraeli, *Sybil, or The Two Nations* (1845), p.69.

Chapter 14: The Plan

1   Frances Wright, 'Of free enquiry considered as a means for obtaining just knowledge', Course of Popular Lectures – Lecture 2, 8 October 1829, openlibrary.org/works/OL2518405W/Course_of_popular_lectures_as_delivered_by_Frances_Wright_.
2   R. Hasdell, 'What we know about universal basic income: a cross-synthesis of reviews', Basic Income Lab (2020), basicincome.stanford.edu.
3   David Deans, 'Welsh universal basic income pilot could focus on care leavers', *BBC News*, 17 May 2021, www.bbc.com/news/uk-wales-politics-57142970. Child poverty levels research was carried out by Loughborough University for the UK End Child Poverty Coalition, 'Dramatic rise in child poverty in the last five years', 19 May 2021, www.lboro.ac.uk/media-centre/press-releases/2021/may/dramatic-rise-in-child-poverty/.
4   Welsh Government, 'Welsh Index of Multiple Deprivation (WIMD) 2019: Results Report', 2019.
5   Robyn Sundlee, 'Alaska's universal basic income problem', *Vox*, 5 September 2019, www.vox.com/future-perfect/2019/9/5/20849020/alaska-permanent-fund-universal-basic-income.
6   A. Painter and C. Thoung, *Creative Citizen, Creative State: The Principled and Pragmatic Case for a Universal Basic Income* (London: Royal Society of Arts, Manufacturers and Commerce, 2015), www.thersa.org.uk/basic-income.
7   McGarvey, *Poverty Safari*, pp.129 and 105.
8   Edelman Trust Barometer Launch 2019 with Rt Hon. Tony Blair and Ed Williams, CEO of Edelman UK & Ireland, 29 January 2019, Royal Institute of Great Britain, Albemarle Street, London.
9   Social Mobility Commission, 'Monitoring social mobility, 2013–2020: is the government delivering on our recommendations?', June 2020, www.gov.uk/official-documents.
10 Halifax UK, 'Costly kids: almost a fifth of average salary spent on raising a child', press release, 20 December 2017. Costs adjusted for inflation between 2017 and 2022.
11 'Attenborough: "Curb excess capitalism" to save nature', *BBC News*, 7 October 2020, www.bbc.co.uk/news/science-environment-54268038.
12 Environmental Audit Committee, 'Fixing fashion: clothing consumption and sustainability', 19 February 2019, publications.parliament.uk/pa/cm201719/cmselect/cmenvaud/1952/full-report.html.

13 'Prato: the Italian town turning rags into new clothes', *BBC News*, 16 December 2020, www.bbc.co.uk/news/av/world-europe-55267992.

14 'Fast fashion: the dumping ground for unwanted clothes', *BBC News*, 8 October 2021, www.bbc.co.uk/news/av/world-africa-58836618.

15 Yuval Noah Harari, *21 Lessons for the 21st Century* (Penguin Random House, 2018), pp.20, 29 and 35.

16 Harari, *21 Lessons for the 21st Century*, p.21.

17 'Disabled fashion: "There are so many clothes that I can't wear"', *BBC News*, 2 September 2020, www.bbc.co.uk/news/av/uk-wales-53989567.

18 Childline is a free, private and confidential service where children under 19 can talk to a Childline counsellor about anything. The organisation has a presence online (www.childline.org.uk) and over the phone (0800 1111), any time and any day. Their phone number is free to call and doesn't show up on the phone bill.

19 John Henderson, 'Sea swimming is "amazing" for mental health and menopause', *BBC News*, 24 August 2020, www.bbc.co.uk/news/av/uk-england-devon-53851253.

20 Rosee Woodland, 'Britain's best lidos and seaside pools', *Countryfile Magazine*, 13 April 2021, www.countryfile.com/go-outdoors/get-active/britains-seaside-lido-revival-history-of-the-lido-and-best-places-to-swim/.

21 A. Nivethitha Mooventhan, 'Scientific evidence-based effects of hydrotherapy on various systems of the body', *North American Journal of Medical Sciences*, vol. 6, no. 5 (May 2014), pp.199–209, doi:10.4103/1947-2714.132935.

22 Lily Waddell and Jonathan Prynn, 'So much for the Good Life ... waiting list for London's allotments "out of control"', *Evening Standard*, 20 October 2021, www.standard.co.uk/news/london/london-allotment-waiting-list-out-of-control-b961468.html.

23 MyJobQuote, 'Longest waiting lists for an allotment in the UK', 8 October 2021, www.myjobquote.co.uk/blog/longest-waiting-lists-for-an-allotment-in-the-uk.

24 S. Stieger, D. Lewetz and V. Swami, 'Emotional well-being under conditions of lockdown: an experience sampling study in Austria during the COVID-19 pandemic', *Journal of Happiness Studies*, vol. 22 (2021), pp.2703–20.

25 Katherine Latham, 'How more of us are leaving screens behind to work outdoors', *BBC News*, 4 November 2021, www.bbc.co.uk/news/business-59132672.

26 Square Mile Farm is a hydroponic rooftop farm in Paddington, London: www.squaremilefarms.com.

27 Joseph Rowntree Foundation, 'Street cleanliness in deprived and better-off neighbourhoods', November 2009, www.jrf.org.uk.

28 Forest Research, 'Crime and vandalism – challenges and practical considerations', www.forestresearch.gov.uk/tools-and-resources/fthr/urban-regeneration-and-greenspace-partnership/greenspace-in-practice/practical-considerations-and-challenges-to-greenspace/crime-and-vandalism-challenges-and-practical-considerations/, 31 January 2022.

29 McGarvey, *Poverty Safari*, pp.134–5.

30 McGarvey, *Poverty Safari*, pp.134–5.

31 Chartered Institute of Public Finance and Accountancy, 'Spend on British libraries drops by nearly £20m', 4 December 2020, www.cipfa.org/about-cipfa-press-office/latest-press-releases/spend-on-british-libraries-drops-by-nearly-20m.

32 Alison Flood, 'Britain has closed almost 800 libraries since 2010, figures show', *The Guardian*, 5 December 2019, www.theguardian.com/books/2019/dec/06/britain-has-closed-amost-800-libraries-since-2010-figures-show.

Chapter 15: Impact of Success

1 Danny Dorling, *Slowdown: The End of the Great Acceleration – and Why It's a Good Thing* (Yale University Press, updated edn, 2021), pp.316, 43.

2 Esther Perel, 'Personal Profile', TED, www.ted.com/speakers/esther_perel.

3 Richard Reed, *If I Could Tell You Just One Thing: Encounters with Remarkable People and Their Most Valuable Advice* (Canongate, 2016), p.27.

4 Rita F. Pierson, 'Every kid needs a champion', TED Talk, May 2013.

5 McGarvey, *Poverty Safari*, pp.138, 176.

6 Rod Judkins, *Make Brilliant Work* (Pan Macmillan, 2022), p.185.

7 NATO Secretary General, speech and press briefing, 24 February 2022.

8 Mariko Oi, 'Why China matters in the Ukraine conflict', *BBC News*, www.bbc.co.uk/news/av/world-asia-china-60500307.

9 F.W. de Klerk. Copyright @ The Nobel Foundation 1993.

10 Mental Health Foundation with Together For You, 'Mental health in Northern Ireland', 20 February 2018, www.amh.org.uk/wp-content/uploads/2018/02/Briefing-Mental-Health-Crisis-in-Northern-Ireland.pdf.

11 NESTA, 'Northern Ireland's mental health emergency', December 2019, www.nesta.org.uk/feature/social-movements-health/northern-irelands-mental-health-emergency/.

12 Mental Health Foundation, 'Northern Ireland Manifesto 2022', 8 April 2022, www.mentalhealth.org.uk/explore-mental-health/publications/mental-health-foundation-northern-ireland-manifesto-2022.

13 Germany ranked eleventh and France ranked twelfth in the 'Global Social Mobility Index 2020: why economies benefit from fixing inequality', 19 January 2020, www.weforum.org/reports/global-social-mobility-index-2020-why-economies-benefit-from-fixing-inequality.

14 Mark Carney, 'How we get what we value: from Covid crisis to renaissance', BBC Reith Lectures, 2020.

Chapter 16: Conclusion

1   Meigs Frost interview, *New Orleans Times Picayune*, 22 July 1934, www.thehenryford.org/collections-and-research/digital-resources/popular-topics/henry-ford-quotes/.

2   Kathy Burke, *Money Talks*, episode 2, Channel Four documentary, 5 July 2021.

3   Michelle Obama interview with Oprah Winfrey, '2020 Vision: Your Life in Focus Tour', 8 February 2020.

4   Dr John Gottman, 'The science of love', TED Talk, 7 October 2018. For more information, visit the Gottman Institute at www.gottman.com.

5   Maya Angelou, *I Know Why the Caged Bird Sings* (Random House, 1969), p.235.

6   Sam Wren-Lewis, *The Happiness Problem: Expecting Better in an Uncertain World* (Bristol University Press, 2019), youtu.be/wgLMpCouaxo.

7   *The Rest is Politics*, *Question Time* podcast, 29 September 2022.

8   Isabel Hardman, *Why We Get the Wrong Politicians* (Atlantic Books, 2018), pp.111, 119.

9   Hardman, *Why We Get the Wrong Politicians*, pp.228–9.

10 Mental Health Foundation, 'Mental health in Northern Ireland', 20 February 2018, www.mentalhealth.org.uk.

11 End Child Poverty, www.endchildpoverty.org.uk.

12 Disabilities Trust, 'Making the link: female offending and brain injury', www.thedtgroup.org. In the first study of its kind, the Disabilities Trust provided a dedicated service to support the identification and rehabilitation of female offenders with a history of brain injury, in HMP/YOI Drake Hall.

INDEX

.